ECONOMICS OF PUBLIC POLICY:
The
Micro View

3rd Edition

ECONOMICS OF PUBLIC POLICY: The Micro View

3rd Edition

John C. Goodman
University of Dallas
Irving, Texas

Edwin G. Dolan
George Mason University
Fairfax, Virginia

West Publishing Company

St. Paul   New York   Los Angeles   San Francisco

Library of Congress Cataloging in Publication Data

Goodman, John C.
    Economics of public policy.

    1. Policy sciences--Economic aspects.   2. Economic
policy. I. Dolan, Edwin G.   II. Title.
H97.G665   1985   361.6'1   84–17209
ISBN 0–314–85238–7

1st Reprint—1985

Contents

Preface to the Third Edition

We have all met people who tell us that economics was the most boring subject they took in college. "Economics?" they react, "that's a course in definitions, graphs and dull theoretical abstractions." For many of them, that is the way it was. But not today.

Economic theory *is* abstract. And that is the way it should be. All of those abstract concepts you are about to encounter make up the meat and potatoes of any course in economics. They have to be mastered in order to think logically about the world around us. They are as important to economics as the rules of the English language are to speaking and writing, as the rules of mathematics are to adding and subtracting.

In the past, a typical course in economics was confined to the learning trinity: instructor, textbook, and student. The text book presented the abstract principles. The student struggled to learn them. The instructor stood in the middle. His job was to help shift the principles off the pages of the text and into the student's head.

So far, so good. But an important ingredient was often missing—the *relationship of economic theory to the real world.* This did not happen by design. At the end of important lectures, most instructors would try to squeeze in some practical applications of the principles being discussed. Textbooks would do the same thing at the end of important chapters. But this practice often did more harm than good.

Discussions of real-world events were necessarily brief. After all, the class had to move on. There were more definitions, graphs, and theoretical abstractions to master. So time in the classroom and space in the textbook permitted only scant references to the relationship of economics to the outside world. Even then, students were all too often left to wonder if they were getting only the "economic side" of the question.

Today things are different. Trial and error have convinced us that a fourth cornerstone must be added to the learning of economics. That's where this book comes in.

Its primary purpose is to help students understand how economic theory applies to the real world. It does this by showing how some of our most important (and often controversial) public policies reflect economic principles in action.

The book is organized to complement practically all major textbooks in use today. As the textbook presents a key economic concept, this book shows what that concept means when applied to an important public issue or policy. The concepts discussed here arise in the same order as they arise in most introductory courses in microeconomics.

We have not simply presented the "economic side" of public policies, however. Each chapter furnishes the historical and institutional background of the policies analyzed. We look briefly at where our current policies came from, and how they differ from policies adopted in the past.

Why do we have the policies we have, rather than some other policies? Each chapter addresses this question too. We look at a number of the political forces at work and some of the reasons why some interest groups are more successful than others.

Naturally, different people have different values. Ethical views about what policies we ought to have vary a lot from person to person—even among professional economists. In the first chapter we look at some of the most popular standards used to evaluate public policies. In each suc-ceeding chapter we show what these standards mean when applied to specific policies.

This book, then, not only shows how economics relates to the real world. It also shows how economics relates to other disciplines as well—history, sociology, political science, and even ethics.

In preparing the third edition of this book, we were struck by the truth of the old saying, "The more things change, the more they stay the same." In the world of public policy economics, things do change but the same issues continue to arise in new forms. We have responded to change in three ways.

First, there are issues that, while not really new, have achieved a new level of prominence. An example is equal pay for work of comparable worth—the women's issue of the 1980s, as it has been called. Specialized books on personnel management and compensation policy have discussed this issue for years, but it has only recently become an issue on the national political stage. We have added an entirely new chapter on comparable worth.

Second, there are issues that provide new illustrations of old principles. The ethical and economic problems raised by technically possible but extremely expensive organ transplants are an example. We lead off our chapter on rationing of medical care with an organ transplant example. Similarly, our chapter on the environment now highlights the problem of acid rain. Again, familiar principles are applied to new headlines.

Third, there are changes in policies themselves. These are the basis for the greatest number of changes in this edition. Accordingly, we discuss the Reagan administration's unsuccessful PIK experiment in our farm policy chapter; we discuss policy changes introduced by FTC Chairman James Miller in our consumer fraud chapter; we discuss the effects of impending deregulation in our natural gas chapter; and we discuss the controversy over the Simpson-Mazzoli immigration reform bill in our chapter on supply and demand divided by the Rio Grande. Every chapter is thoroughly updated to take recent policy changes into account.

We are grateful for all the help we have received in preparing this and previous editions. Our own students and colleagues at the University of Dallas and George Mason University have been especially helpful. Users of the book at colleges and universities across the country have passed along their suggestions, many of which we have used. Finally, we want to thank the very able staff at West Publishing Company for bringing out such an attractively designed and produced book.

ECONOMICS OF PUBLIC POLICY: The Micro View

3rd Edition

1

Thinking about Public Issues and Policies

Every day we hear about public issues. Some of these issues are called crises: we hear there is an energy crisis, a teenage unemployment crisis, or an environmental crisis. Others are problems that could become crises: we hear about the worsening problems of illegal aliens, of Social Security, and of the volunteer army. Other issues are simply constant irritations: food prices rise or postal delivery seems to get worse.

So what should we do? Should we keep the volunteer army? Should we raise the minimum wage? Do we need more consumer protection? Should we deregulate the price of natural gas? The list of possible solutions is even longer than the list of issues, and the longer both lists get, the more people turn to economists for help. But what kind of help can economists give?

Economists can, of course, suggest policies and offer opinions. They can say, "Keep the volunteer army" or "I personally don't think we should raise minimum wages." Offering opinions like these is as much the right of economists as it is the right of other citizens, but it is not really economists' professional specialty. Their real specialty is providing a certain *way of thinking* about public issues and policies.

That is where this book comes in. We haven't written it just to give you our opinions—we could have done that in a newspaper editorial. Instead, we have written it to help you understand the economic way of thinking by showing that way of thinking in action, applied to some of the major issues of contemporary public policy.

Tracing the economic effects of public policy

Learning what questions to ask is a large part of understanding the way economists think about issues and policies. Probably the most important question, and often the most difficult to answer, is What are the effects of a certain policy? This question is difficult to answer because public policies usually have a whole network of indirect effects in addition to their direct effects. These indirect effects are often unexpected and unintended, and they are often partly or wholly hidden from view. The first step in analyzing a public issue, then, must be to trace the direct and indirect effects of the policies that are being used or suggested to deal with that issue.

When economists set out to trace the economic effects of public policies, they use certain well-established tools of their trade. Learning how to use these tools is an important part of every introductory economics course. As you read through this book, you will be introduced to practical applications of these tools one by one. First, we will examine such concepts as scarcity, opportunity cost, and the production-possibility frontier. Next, we will show how supply and demand analysis can be put to work. From there, we will explore theories of consumer choice, monopoly and competition, factor markets, and more. Taken together, these tools constitute what we call *positive economics*—the scientific study of economic institutions, policies, and actions.

Evaluating economic policy

After we have examined the effects of a policy, we are in a position to ask a second important question: Is the policy *good* or *bad?* Should we institute the policy, or, if it is already in force, should we keep it? Should we instead reject the policy, or should we abolish it if it is now in force?

Whether a policy is good or bad is not a question of positive economics. The evaluation of public policies is often called *normative economics*, but this term is misleading in an important sense. What we call "normative economics" is not really a branch of economics at all: it would be more accurately described as the application of ethics or philosophy to economic issues. The economist's special tools of the trade, so useful in tracing the effects of a policy, cannot tell us whether that policy is good or bad.

But this fact does not mean that we have to grapple with these questions bare-handed. To determine whether a policy is good or bad, we need not rely on whims, hunches, or reflexes. Instead, we can use clearly defined normative standards. It is true, as we will see, that not everyone agrees on which normative standards are valid or on which ethical principles are more important than others. Yet such disagreements are no excuse for failure to think and express ourselves clearly in the realm of normative economics.

We wish to keep all of this in mind whenever we evaluate economic policies in this book. It is not our aim, however, to ask you, the reader, to agree with our own ethical viewpoint. Instead, we will look at the issues from the point of view of three different kinds of normative standards: efficiency, equality, and liberty. We will describe these briefly here, and their meaning will become clearer as they are applied in a number of cases throughout the book.

Efficiency

Our first standard is one that occupies a prominent place in the thinking of many economists: the standard of economic efficiency. In the most general sense, the word *efficiency* means the property of producing or acting with a minimum of expense, waste, and effort. Whether you are repairing a car, baking a cake, or producing something for someone else, there are usually a number of ways to perform the task. The efficient way is the one that minimizes the time, effort, and money required. The concept of efficiency also applies to the choice of how to spend your income. Efficiency in this case means buying those items that give you the most satisfaction or happiness, given your limited budget.

Efficiency also applies to choices about the courses you take in college, the way you spend your leisure time, and the choice of a career. In fact, just about every choice you make can be judged by the standard of efficiency. In each case, the efficient choice is the one that results in the largest benefit given the cost or the one that results in the smallest cost given the benefit we seek.

Most of us, then, have some idea of what efficiency means when applied to our personal lives. We may even have some idea of what it means for a business firm to be efficient. But economists go beyond this: they not only apply the concept of efficiency to individuals and to business firms—they also ask about the efficiency of markets and even of entire economic systems.

That's where economic theory comes in. In many ways the study of economics *is* the study of efficiency, so the more you learn about economics, the more you will learn about efficiency. As a starting point, however, we will simply note that notions of *cost* and *benefit* can be applied to the economic system as a whole. In a general sense, an efficient economy is one that maximizes the value of its resources or one that minimizes the costs of producing the goods and services consumed.

The concept of efficiency can also be applied to public policy. For example, one of our most important public policies is the policy of enforcing contracts. If a person fails to keep a promise agreed to in a contract, courts of law stand ready to enforce the contract or to award damages to the injured party. Imagine what would happen if there were no contract law or no system of enforcement. You would spend an enormous amount of time and energy investigating the character and reputation of people with whom you wanted to make agreements. Most sellers would insist on cash, rather than credit, purchases. There would be a lot less lending, a lot fewer long-term agreements. And a great many goods and services we now enjoy would not be produced at all. So, at least in principle, the policy of contract enforcement makes our economy much more efficient than it would be otherwise.

Almost every public policy involves a cost. Whether we are paving a road, building a bridge, constructing a dam, or even enforcing contracts, the benefits do not come free. By the standard of efficiency, a policy or a change in policy is judged to be good if the benefits exceed the costs. It is judged to be bad if the costs exceed the benefits. But *the standard of efficiency does not require that the people who benefit be the same people who bear the costs.* Typically, some individuals will be better off because of a policy; others will be worse off. Efficiency only requires that we look at the *sum* of the benefits and the *sum* of the costs.

In comparing the costs and benefits of a policy to see if it is efficient, economists often find it useful to ask this question: Can the people who like a policy potentially *compensate* the people who do not like it and still be better off than they would have been without the policy? If compensation is possible, the benefits of the policy are said to be greater than the costs of the policy.

Consider, for example, a policy of prohibiting all smoking in restaurants. Let's say that Ed, a typical nonsmoker, would be willing to pay $10 more than the cost of his meal to enjoy his food in a smoke-free environment. John, a typical smoker, would be willing to pay up to $8 for the pleasure of enhancing the taste of fine food and drink with that of fine tobacco. Given these preferences, Ed could pay John $9 in return for a promise not to smoke during dinner and both would be better off than if John smoked. If Ed and John were really typical of smokers and non-smokers, a nonsmoking policy for restaurants would be efficient in the sense that it contains the potential for making everyone better off. Most economists do not insist that compensation payments actually be made. A policy is declared efficient as long as it generates a "fund" of benefits potentially large enough to cover, or more than cover, all costs.

Of course, many of our public policies are not very efficient. As we will see, a lot of government policies raise costs for producers, reduce benefits for consumers, and create other forms of waste. In fact, if we were only concerned with efficiency, we should be prepared to make some pretty radical changes in the way we do things.

But efficiency isn't the only standard that people care about. Let's look briefly at two other criteria.

Equality

Our second standard focuses on the distribution of income and wealth. By this standard, a policy that causes income and wealth to be more equally divided would be judged to be a good policy, even if by our first standard it were judged to be inefficient. For example, whenever we tax the rich and distribute the proceeds to the poor, administrative costs are incurred. The dollar value of the burden on taxpayers exceeds the dollar value of benefits received at the other end. Nonetheless, such transfers are judged to be good because they promote equality.

On the other hand, it might be very efficient to spend tax dollars to build a particular bridge or dam. But suppose the project would mainly benefit the wealthy and leave most of the poor worse off than before. The project would then be a bad one by the standard of equality.

Just as they have discovered ways of measuring costs and benefits, economists have also developed ways of measuring the degree of inequality. This allows them, in principle, to say whether a policy creates more equality even if it affects millions of different people in different ways. There are some sticky problems, however. Suppose one family has two children. Another has no children. In order to achieve equality, should the first family have twice the income of the second? Or suppose that one person works 80 hours a week while another works only 40. Does equality mean that both workers should receive the same monetary income? Or should the extra leisure time enjoyed by the second worker count as a form of income in kind?

These questions are not trivial. What to do about the value of leisure time and the problem of comparing people in different generations is very important in some issues, such as Social Security. In fact, in Chapter 15 we will see that according to one set of answers Social Security appears to create more equality; according to another set of answers, the system appears to create more inequality.

Our analysis of illegal aliens in Chapter 13 reveals another problem. Does the standard of equality apply only to U.S. citizens, or do illegal aliens count too? Our discussion will demonstrate that the flow of illegal aliens probably creates more inequality among our own citizens, but if the citizens of other countries are included, the flow of aliens undoubtedly leads to more overall equality of income and wealth.

When they think about creating more equality, most people are typically thinking about raising the incomes of those in poverty. And, true enough, most policies that help the poor tend to create more equality and most policies that hurt the poor tend to create more inequality. But not always. Consider a policy that takes a little bit of income from the poor, a lot of income from the rich, and transfers all of this income to middle-class citizens. Such a policy could actually increase overall equality while harming those at the bottom of the income ladder.

What all of this means is that while we can often talk about equality in a rigorous way, the concept is not quite so simple as it first might seem.

Liberty

Our third standard—that of liberty—comes from a long tradition in Western political thought. This standard is based on a view of liberty that was formally developed in England by John Locke and that later influenced many of our founding fathers, including Thomas Jefferson. In its strictest form, the standard holds that each individual has a right to act in accordance with private choice, free from force, threat, or coercion by others.

Most of us are familiar with such fundamental civil liberties as freedom of speech, freedom of the press, and freedom of religion. But economic liberties are included here too: the right to own property, the right to produce goods and services, and the right to engage in voluntary exchange with others. As applied to the evaluation of public policy, this standard says that any policy is bad if it violates the individual's civil and economic liberties. For example, forcing the rich to give to the poor would violate this standard even though it might result in more equality. On the other hand, a policy of enforcing contracts is judged to be good by the standard of liberty because it protects property rights and facilitates voluntary exchange.

So what about taxes and government-provided goods like streets and highways? Some advocates of liberty take the extreme position that all taxes are coercive and that all goods and services (even the police and courts!) should be provided through the private marketplace. This is not the traditional view, however, nor is it the interpretation we will be concerned with here.

For our purposes we will consider government taxes and spending policies to be consistent with the standard of liberty so long as, on balance, each individual is left no worse off than before. That means that it is all right for government to impose a tax on a person so long as the tax creates benefits for that person that are greater than or equal to the value of the taxes collected. Thus, taxing the citizens of Idaho to build a dam in Idaho might be consistent with the standard of liberty. But taxing the citizens of New York to build a dam in Idaho would be inconsistent with that standard. Unlike the standard of efficiency, therefore, the standard of liberty, at minimum, requires that *those who bear the costs of a policy be the same people who receive the benefits.*

These three are not the only standards that can be used to evaluate public policy. Many other standards exist. In fact, the list of all possible standards is probably infinite. We have selected these three for three reasons. First, all three of these standards are frequently used in debates over public issues. Second, each of these three standards has fairly clear-cut implications, and each can be used to judge a wide variety of policies. Third, all three standards require some knowledge of economics. In each case, we need to discover the economic effects of a policy before we can say whether it promotes efficiency or equality, or whether it is consistent with the standard of liberty.

We suspect many of our readers will not fully agree or disagree with any one of the standards we have discussed. That creates no problem when a policy is judged to be good by all three standards. Enforcement of contracts, for example, promotes economic efficiency, is consistent with the standard of liberty, and probably contributes to a little more equality as well. Surprising as it may seem, a lot of other policies and policy changes are also consistent with all three standards.

But many policies are not. That's where *value trade-offs* come in. For example, most economists believe that achieving complete equality of income for all citizens would have disastrous effects for economic efficiency. If each person were guaranteed an equal share of the income pie, regardless of contribution, there should be very little incentive for the individual to produce much. As a result, few people favor total equality of income. On the other hand, staying strictly with the efficiency standard might lead to widely different incomes for different individuals, and very few people are indifferent to extreme inequality. Most people prefer something in between. They are willing to trade off some efficiency for more equality. The exact trade-off, of course, can differ a lot from one person to another.

Similarly, most of us do not particularly like the idea of government restrictions on our behavior. We may even dislike the idea of restricting the behavior of others. But suppose that by giving some people a little less liberty we could have more efficiency or more equality. Many people would be willing to make such a trade-off.

You may want to consider other standards not discussed here. In fact, we encourage you to develop your own value trade-offs and apply them to the issues as you read this book. But, to be honest with yourself, don't decide which policies you like and then search for a way to defend them. First decide what fundamental values you accept, and then see what these imply about public policy. You may be surprised.

Explaining public policy

In addition to tracing the effects of public policies and evaluating those policies, this book will tackle a third job: the job of trying to explain why we have the particular policies we do have. For example, in a later chapter we will argue that our current policy on pricing electric power causes waste and inefficiency, gives few benefits to the economically disadvantaged, and violates the rights of consumers and potential competitors. Evaluation raises a question: If the policy is so bad, why don't we change it?

Answering questions like this is the job of a relatively young branch of economics called *public-choice theory*. Public-choice theory analyzes policy choices made through our political system, using the same kinds of tools economists routinely use to analyze the private choices made in the marketplace. For example, an important principle of public-choice theory is that all political actions and decisions—and the bits of information on which those actions and decisions are based—are *costly*. This principle helps explain why some public policies are not in the best interest of the majority of voters even though our system of government is democratic.

It is well known that small special-interest groups can often get favors from the government at the expense of the general taxpayer. The explanation of why such favors are granted is often that it is much less costly for a small special-interest group to organize and promote its interests than it is for a large group, such as taxpayers in general, to organize and defend itself.

As it progresses, this book will closely examine some of these costs and will introduce a number of other applications of public-choice theory. Now let's look at some selected policies one by one, trace their consequences, evaluate them, and attempt to explain their origins.

Questions for thought and discussion

1. Which of the three standards of evaluation discussed in this chapter seems the most reasonable to you? Is your choice a matter of emotional preference or can you defend it logically?

2. Can you think of any ethical standard for evaluating public policy that would require no knowledge of economics?

3. Three other standards are not discussed in this book:
   a. A policy is good if it benefits society as a whole;
   b. A policy is good if a majority of people prefer it;
   c. A policy is good if it forces people to do what they ought to.

   Can you discover any problems with these standards? (Can their terms be rigorously defined? Can logical implications for public policy be derived from them?)

Selected references

At the conclusion of each chapter additional readings on the issue or issues discussed will be listed. Most are written for the nonspecialist; the suggested readings differ considerably in level of difficulty, however. Hence, some additional comments are warranted.

The concept of economic efficiency as it is normally used to evaluate public policy is lucidly presented by Mishan—some knowledge of basic economics is required, however. Rawls favors a certain type of equality and believes that public policy should be designed to maximize the well-being of the least well-off citizens. The relationship of equality, efficiency, and liberty is discussed; but his book, while important, is not easy reading. Some knowledge of basic ethical philosophy is suggested. Nozick argues for liberty but discusses its relationship to equality and efficiency as well. Most writers do not fully accept any of these three standards, and they search for some kind of trade-off. Friedman's work primarily focuses on the trade-off between liberty and efficiency; Okun focuses instead on the trade-off between efficiency and equality. Again, some knowledge of basic economics is helpful in reading both books.

Friedman, Milton. *Capitalism and Freedom.* Chicago: University of Chicago Press, 1962.

Mishan, E. J. *Economics for Social Decisions: Elements of Cost-Benefit Analysis.* New York: Praeger Publishers, 1973.

Nozick, Robert. *Anarchy, State, and Utopia.* New York: Basic Books, 1974.

Okun, Arthur. *Equality and Efficiency.* Washington, D.C.: Brookings Institution, 1975.

Rawls, John. *A Theory of Justice.* Cambridge, Mass.: Belknap Press of Harvard University Press, 1971.

2

Bring Back the Draft?

Measured in terms of the resistance it has generated, perhaps no government policy has had a greater history of controversy than the military draft.

During the War of 1812, Massachusetts and Connecticut came close to seceding from the Union over the draft issue. When a draft measure nearly became law in 1814, the two state legislatures committed their full resources to protecting their citizens from conscription by the federal government.

When the first national draft was finally initiated during the Civil War, it touched off violence and bloodshed. Antidraft mobs fought pitched battles with police and the militia and controlled the streets of New York for three days in 1863. As many as twelve hundred people are believed to have died. Property damage reached the then enormous figure of $5 million. To cope with this massive resistance, President Lincoln—the great libertarian—ordered suspension of the writ of *habeas corpus*. Over the objections of a powerless Supreme Court, more than thirteen thousand people were arrested, tried by military tribunals, and imprisoned—all without right of appeal. Many of them were executed by firing squads. Ironically, only 2 percent of the Union Army during this period were draftees.

Considering this background, resistance to the draft during the Vietnam War seems as American as apple pie. Tens of thousands protested in the streets, went abroad, or went to jail. Some remain in exile to this day.

As American involvement in the war ended, Congress heaved a collective sigh of relief and ended the draft. For a while it looked as if the draft would become a dead issue, fading gradually from public attention and from the pages of books on pressing economic issues. However, young men are still required to register with local draft boards. This policy has kept the issue alive.

Why is the military draft, opposed by some so passionately and so long, so persistently attractive to others? Let's put our economic way of thinking to work and see what kind of an answer we can come up with.

Tracing the economic effects of the draft

The issue of cost is central to the debate over the draft versus a volunteer army, so we'll begin there. To an economist, the cost of doing anything is measured in terms of the value of other opportunities that must be foregone in order to do that thing. The cost of buying a steak for dinner is measured in terms of passing up the opportunity to spend the same money on chicken, fish, a movie, or a haircut. The cost of studying for an economics exam is the loss of the opportunity to spend the time sleeping or studying chemistry. Similarly, but on a larger scale, the cost of maintaining an army is properly measured by the opportunities given up to put the same labor and capital to work producing other valuable goods and services. Economists refer to costs expressed in terms of foregone opportunities as *opportunity costs*.

A simple diagram will help make the concept of opportunity cost more vivid. In Figure 2–1 the level of military preparedness is measured along the horizontal axis, and the quantity of all other goods and services produced by the economy is shown on the vertical axis. Between the two axes we have drawn a curve showing the possible packages of military preparedness and other goods among which we may choose. This curve is called a *production-possibility frontier*. As a nation we can move back and forth along the frontier, opting for a little more of this at the cost of a little less of that. With the limited resources available, however, we cannot move outside the frontier. In a world of scarcity the frontier represents the hard fact that a limit exists beyond which we cannot have more of one thing without giving up the opportunity to have something else.

Suppose that in the past we have chosen the combination of military preparedness and other goods represented by point *A* in Figure 2–1. We now decide to increase our military preparedness by shifting one person from civilian production to a job in the army. This moves us down and to the right along the production-possibility frontier to, say, point *B*. The distance we have moved to the right measures our gain in military preparedness, while the distance we have moved down measures the

FIGURE 2-1   Production-Possibility

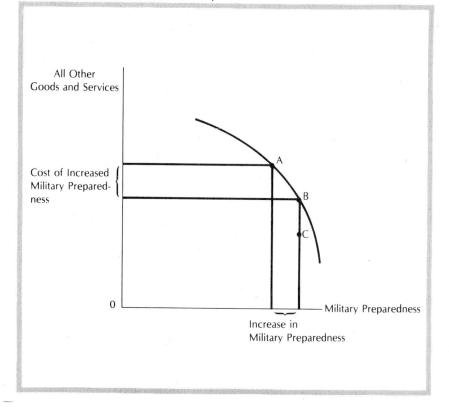

opportunity cost of this gain in terms of sacrifice of other goods and services.

So far we have not put any numbers on the axes. How can we place a dollar value on the cost of moving one person from a civilian to a military job? As a starting point, we could use that person's civilian wage or salary. In a market economy, workers in the private sector are usually paid according to what they produce. No employer can make a profit by paying a worker $10,000 a year unless the worker adds at least that much to the firm's output. At the same time, competition among employers assures that such a worker will not have to settle for a job that pays much less than $10,000. So $10,000 a year would be an adequate guess at the opportunity cost of moving a $10,000-a-year worker from a civilian to a military job.

To get a more refined estimate of opportunity cost, other factors would have to be considered. First, the civilian job might give the worker a little more (or a little less) valuable on-the-job training than does the military job. In addition, life in the army might be a little more (or a little less) hazardous, boring, or unpleasant than civilian life. Since the category "other goods and services" includes such intangibles as on-the-job training, security, and peace of mind, we must adjust the original figure of $10,000 to take these into account.

All things considered, most economists would say that the best estimate of the opportunity cost of shifting a person from a civilian to a military job is the minimum amount that person would have to be paid to take the military job voluntarily. If it would take a $12,000 inducement to shift our $10,000 civilian worker to the military voluntarily, then the opportunity cost of making the shift is that $12,000.

It is important to understand that the same opportunity cost must be borne regardless of whether people are shifted from civilian to military life by the draft or by a payment large enough to induce them to volunteer. The primary effect of using draftees rather than volunteers is not to *reduce* the cost of military preparedness, but simply to *shift* the cost. If our hero were offered $12,000 a year, and enlisted voluntarily, he would end up no worse off than in civilian life. In this case, the entire burden of the increase in military preparedness falls on the general taxpayer. If the same person is drafted and paid only $8,000 a year, the burden on the general taxpayer is reduced, but the draftee bears an implicit annual tax of $4,000. This implicit tax is equal to the difference between the pay of a draftee and the pay of a volunteer. The total burden is the same in both cases; the draft simply shifts that burden.

What we have said is at least true as a first approximation. Further examination of the matter suggests that the draft may actually increase the burden of military preparedness at the same time it shifts it. Why the increase? Draftees tend to reenlist less often than volunteers; this in turn tends to lower productivity and raise training costs. Morale tends to be lower in an army of draftees. Military commanders, thinking of draftees as "cheap" manpower, may use them wastefully, disregarding their personal skills or the possibility of substituting hardware for personnel. Finally, a draft induces many civilians to undertake costly draft-avoidance measures, such as choosing a draft-exempt but otherwise unattractive career, retaining expensive legal counsel, or even spending years in jail or exile.

Many of these costs are intangible and hard to measure. Nonetheless, there has been at least one attempt to estimate them. A presidential commission established near the end of the Vietnam War concluded that for each $1.00 of implicit tax collected from draftees, a burden of approximately $2.50 was placed on the general public. That suggests that the implicit tax of the draft is far more expensive to levy than the explicit taxes used to finance a volunteer army.

An evaluation

This analysis of the economic effects of conscription gives us a basis on which to evaluate proposals to abandon the volunteer army and reestablish a draft. Some critics condemn the volunteer army as unfair and excessively costly. How do their arguments stand up against the standards for policy evaluation that we outlined in Chapter 1?

Let's begin with efficiency. Generally, achieving a goal efficiently means achieving it at minimum cost. This means minimizing the sacrifice required to achieve the goal. It is true that the budgetary cost of a drafted army is lower than the budgetary cost of a volunteer army: with a drafted army the government pays less. But the budgetary cost is not the only cost: when *all* of the costs are considered, evidence strongly suggests that the volunteer approach is the less costly one.

This idea can be illustrated by returning again to Figure 2–1. If the higher level of military preparedness is achieved efficiently (the volunteer approach), we will be at point *B*. On the other hand, if a draft is used, we will end up at a point like point *C*. Note that point *C* is *inside* the production-possibility frontier; this reflects the fact that a draft requires more sacrifice of other goods and services than necessary.

Some think the current volunteer army is inefficient because the quality or productivity of volunteers is lower than it ought to be. The quality of military recruits, however, can be directly related to military pay. Between 1972 and 1979, manufacturing wages rose 77 percent. Consumer prices also rose 77 percent. But military pay only rose 51 percent. In fact, in the spring of 1981, the salary of an E-2 enlisted man was little more than the minimum wage. As the buying power of military pay fell, the quality of recruits dropped. At one point only 60 percent of recruits even had high school diplomas.

Then, in the 1980s, inflation slowed down, military pay was raised, and two recessions made civilian jobs hard to find. In response, the quality of recruits rose again, and the efficiency of the armed forces improved.

Let's turn now to another standard of evaluation. How should we judge the draft as compared with a volunteer army in terms of how each affects the most disadvantaged members of the community? This standard of evaluation has figured prominently in the debate and deserves careful attention.

Curiously enough, both the draft (during the Vietnam era) and the volunteer army (at present) have been attacked as being unfair to the poor—and to poor blacks in particular. Youths from poverty-level backgrounds, including many blacks, have been heavily overrepresented in the lowest military ranks under both systems. This has been among the factors leading Senator Edward Kennedy and others to favor a truly universal national service that would draw forces proportionately from all segments of the community because no one at all would be exempt.

Before accepting this solution to the problem, however, we need to understand more clearly the nature of the problem itself. The overrepresentation of poor and black youth in the military actually has very different implications under a volunteer system than under a draft.

Under the draft each conscript bears the burden of a large implicit tax; having shouldered this burden the draftee then performs defense services for all citizens. If most draftees are drawn from lower-income groups, then the draft acts as a mechanism for transferring income and wealth from the poor to everyone else, including the middle class and the rich.

Under a volunteer army things are quite different. Volunteers are fully compensated for defense services they render. If a person feels that the compensation is inadequate, he or she simply need not volunteer. We can expect that some volunteers will be paid the bare minimum necessary to compensate them for giving up civilian life. But for a person whose civilian opportunities are meager, joining the army might lead to a significant boost in income. The lower the volunteer's civilian income, the greater the net benefit of joining the army. If the poor are overrepresented in a volunteer army, the volunteer army is probably working to transfer income and wealth from the general taxpayer to the poor.

We come now to our third standard of evaluation. How do the draft and volunteer army rate in terms of protecting the rights and liberties of individual citizens? Answers to this question vary according to one's conception of just what rights and liberties are important to protect. Let's consider three possibilities.

First, there is a strongly ingrained American tradition that freedom of conscience and religion are among the most important of all individual rights. A draft that did not respect religious belief would be opposed even by many who favored a draft on other grounds. By treating conscientious objectors according to special rules, our Selective Service System has at least partially recognized the force of this argument.

Second, some oppose the draft on much broader grounds than simple freedom of conscience: many Americans honor a tradition of self-defense under which each person has a right to defend his own person and property and has no right to impose that responsibility on others. In Revolutionary War times, self-defense meant keeping a rifle beside your plough; in modern times, it means either volunteering for military service yourself or accepting the responsibility of paying someone else to provide defense services for you. A tax-supported volunteer army is thus reasonably consistent with the self-defense tradition; the draft is not.

Finally, we ought to take note of an almost opposite tradition that imposes a duty on young men to defend their community and that grants a right to all others so to be defended. This tradition is much older than the self-defense tradition—older, in fact, than Western civilization itself. Even in the twentieth century, there have been those who believe it to be not simply expedient but just and proper that young men bear a disproportionate share of the defense burden through the draft. President Dwight D. Eisenhower, for example, favored universal national service as much on moral grounds as he did for the value of services it produced. "If the program accomplished nothing more," he wrote, "than to produce cleanliness and decent grooming, it might be worth the price tag."

So why the draft?

Let's take a moment to summarize our analysis and evaluation of the draft. The draft, we found, does not cut the cost of military preparedness. If anything, it increases the cost and discourages efficient resource use. As it has worked in the past, the draft has transferred income from the poor to the rich, while our present volunteer army transfers income from the rich to the poor. And many people consider the draft offensive to individual rights and liberties. Why, then, is the idea of a draft always being revived?

To answer this question we turn to economics of public choice, a branch of economics that tries to explain why individuals acting within the framework of our political institutions collectively choose one policy rather than another. In the present case, the theory of public choice suggests not just one, but several possible explanations of the political popularity of the draft.

The first possible explanation is best understood in terms of a hypothetically perfect direct democracy. Suppose that, instead of our complex system of representation and delegation of authority, all political questions were put directly to the voters, to be decided by simple majority. A theorem of public choice economics holds that, in such a system, policies that provide benefits equally to all voters while concentrating their costs disproportionately on a minority of voters can be approved, even if their total costs outweigh their total benefits. Why? Because voters do not weigh the total costs against the total benefits; they weigh only their personal share of the costs against their personal share of the benefits. Individual benefits may at least slightly outweigh individual costs for a majority, even though for a minority costs overwhelmingly outweigh benefits.

It is clear how this theorem applies to the draft. Draftees are a minority. In fact, until the voting age was lowered they were a disenfranchised minority. How convenient for everyone else to ask them to foot a disproportionate part of the bill for military preparedness!

Of course, our political system is not a perfect direct democracy. In a representative system, special-interest groups often wield political power that is out of proportion to the numerical voting strength of those groups. In particular, groups that are compact, that regularly communicate with each other through their daily activities, and that share easily identified common interests tend to be proportionately more politically powerful than groups that are large, scattered, and diffuse. Potential draftees normally have not constituted an effective pressure group—although when the draft began to threaten college students during the Vietnam War, they at least briefly became one. On the other side, certain prodraft groups have long enjoyed significant political influence. Among these are:

- Professional military officers. Although the draft does not cut the opportunity cost of military preparedness, it does significantly cut the budgetary cost. That leaves more dollars in the budget for sophisticated hardware, weapons research, and military retirement benefits.

- Defense industries. When people are drafted during a conflict, civilian labor supply is reduced and wages increase. If defense jobs carry draft exemptions, however, defense industries are insulated from this upward pressure on costs, resulting in more profits for arms makers.

- The agricultural establishment. Like defense jobs, farm jobs have always carried deferments. By enhancing the supply of farm workers, the draft subsidizes farm labor costs. Until the draft was discontinued in 1971, the law even contained a provision that farm deferments would continue even when there were agricultural surpluses.

So far, our discussion of the public-choice economics of the draft has assumed that voters and pressure-group members are rational and well-informed—but information and rational thought have opportunity costs of their own. Recognizing this suggests another possible explanation of the political popularity of the draft: when voters balance the individual costs and benefits of some policy measure, they pay more attention to explicit taxes than they do to implict taxes. Compared with a volunteer army, the draft involves a shift from explicit to implicit taxes. Some voters apparently misperceive this shift as an actual reduction in the opportunity cost of military preparedness, and they then support the draft as an apparently economical way of raising an army.

For the time being, the political balance favors a volunteer army. Nonetheless, the national debate on the issues continues. If proposals for universal national service were ever to win out, conscription might be instituted on a wider scale than ever before. We can only hope that before any sweeping programs are instituted they are subjected to careful and informed consideration.

Questions for thought and discussion

1. During the Civil War, people who were drafted could hire a substitute to take their place. Some thought this provision of the law was horribly unfair; others contended that it only made visible the inequities inherent in any system of conscription. What do you think?

2. Compare, on the one hand, a system that drafted limited numbers of young people—mostly poor or black—with a system that drafted everyone. Which system do you think would place the greater burden on blacks and on the poor? Does it matter whether you calculate the burden in absolute or in relative terms?

3. During the Vietnam War, some people thought it was not enough just to permit conscientious objection to military service. These people also wanted to legalize conscientious objection to the payment of war-supporting taxes. Evaluate this proposal using various standards of normative economics.

4. We have suggested as a theorem of public choice economics that in a perfect direct democracy, policies that provide benefits equally to all voters while concentrating their costs disproportionately on a minority can be approved—even if their total costs outweigh their total benefits. A corollary of this theorem is that in such a system, proposals that impose tax costs equally on all citizens, but that exclude a minority from the enjoyment of resulting benefits, can also be approved, even if total costs outweigh total benefits. Can you think of an example that fits this corollary? Can you think of other corollaries?

5. Aside from military service, almost the only other example of conscription in the United States is compulsory jury duty. Sketch possible cases for and against compulsory jury duty and compare them with the cases for and against the draft as they were outlined in this chapter. Alternatively, consider conscription of firemen, policemen, bricklayers, or aircraft designers. (Some countries have experimented with all of these.)

6. Suppose, in order to improve the quality and broaden the socioeconomic background of recruits, we doubled military pay. At that pay level, more people might volunteer than the military could take. How would you choose who got to serve? By education? I.Q. tests? Racial quotas? To get the kind of middle class, racially balanced army many people want, many poor black volunteers would have to be turned down. How would such a policy rate in terms of equality? In terms of efficiency?

Selected references

Binkin, Martin, and Mark J. Eitelberg, *Blacks and the Military*. Washington, D.C.: Brookings Institution, 1982.

Leach, Jack F. *Conscription in the United States: Historical Background*. Rutland, Vt.: Charles E. Tuttle Publishing Company, 1952.

Miller, James C., ed. *Why the Draft?* Baltimore, Md.: Penguin Books, 1968.

The Report of the President's Commission on an All Volunteer Armed Force. New York: Macmillan, 1970.

3

Organ Transplants and Other Problems of Rationing Medical Care

Because of scarcity, only limited quantities of any good or service can be produced. This is as true for health care services as for any others. Consider the case of organ transplants. Through the end of 1983, just 417 liver transplants had been performed in the United States. The number of candidates for this complex operation—which can cost $140,000 or more—is estimated at two thousand to five thousand per year. Potential demand for heart transplants is even greater, and doctors are beginning to transplant lungs, pancreases, and intestines.[1]

What happens to the patients who need transplants but do not get them or do not get them in time? Many of them die. Take the case of five-year-old Donje McNair. Donje did not have insurance that would pay for the operation. By the time the state of Illinois agreed to pay for his transplant, he was too ill to undergo surgery. Without a new liver, he died.

Unmet needs for medical care give rise to public demands that the government "do something" about the problem. In this chapter, we will look at one of the best-known responses to public demands to eliminate scarcity in medical care: the British National Health Service (NHS).

---

1. David Wessel, "Transplants Increase, and So Do Disputes over Who Pays," *Wall Street Journal,* 12 April 1984.

The British National Health Service

The NHS was established in 1948. According to the original plan, it was to provide every British citizen with the most modern, up-to-date medical care available. This care was also to be "free" to the patient at the time of treatment. This was to insure that no one would be denied care because of an inability to pay for it. The basic goal of the program was clearly spelled out in the *Beveridge Report*, the early blueprint for the British welfare state. The report promised that the NHS would provide "full preventive and curative treatment of every kind for every citizen without exceptions."

Would such a program be enormously expensive? The founding fathers of the NHS did not think so. Aneurin Bevan, the first Minister of Health under the NHS, actually thought the total cost of medical care would go down as a result of the plan. Bevan believed that if medical problems were treated in their early stages, they would be prevented from developing into more serious and more expensive-to-treat problems later on. He thought that when patients were charged prices for medical care, many medical problems went untreated because people were unable or unwilling to pay those prices. Under the NHS, however, medical care was to be made available on the basis of *need*, rather than on the basis of ability or willingness to pay for it. Patients would be encouraged to seek medical treatment when the need for treatment first arose rather than when the problems became more serious. In this way, he argued, the total cost of medical care would be reduced in the long run.

The arguments seemed persuasive at the time. The goal seemed noble. But almost thirty years after the NHS was started, a British Minister of Health declared that the term "medical need" was "meaningless" and that "there is virtually no limit to the amount of medical care an individual is capable of absorbing." A few years later, a British health economist stated, "We could easily spend the entire GNP of Britain on the health service— and still want more."

Similar statements could be made about medical care in every other country in the world. To see why, we need to take a closer look at the market for medical care.

Taking a closer look at modern medicine

The founding fathers of the NHS apparently made three mistakes, which are still made by many participants in debates on health-care policies today: (1) they believed that there was a limited amount of illness; (2) they believed that there were limited and only moderately expensive methods of treating illness; and, as a consequence of these beliefs, (3) they believed that scarcity could actually be eliminated in the field of medical care. In the

1940s, these beliefs did not seem unreasonable. But with the advance of medical science, things have changed radically. Today, health economists know that each of these beliefs is wrong.

Take illness, for example. Not long ago, many doctors, and almost all lay people, thought that it was sensible to think of people as being either healthy or ill. Today, most health experts realize that illness is a matter of degree, and that virtually everyone is, to some degree, "ill." This realization dawned gradually, with development of new and better techniques for diagnosing illness.

Modern medical technology not only improves our ability to *cure* illness, it also improves our ability to *find* it. And the better our ability to diagnose, the more illness we find. As medical technology becomes more sophisticated, we will undoubtedly find even more illness. There is no reason to believe we will ever reach a point when we will cease discovering new and different kinds of illness.

Consider the following theory about illness. Unless we die from an accident, homicide, or some other violent death, each of us will die because something inside us malfunctions. Some day, something inside our bodies will stop working. Many researchers believe that the seeds of our demise are germinating inside us right now.

If this theory is correct, in a sense we are all "ill." We carry inside of us the potential cause of our death. For example, about ten thousand people die each year from alcohol-related deaths. Scientists now believe that the tendency to become an alcoholic is caused by a chemical imbalance in the body. There is even evidence that the tendency to commit suicide is related to the amount of a certain chemical in the body. These chemical imbalances may be thought of as "illnesses" which may some day be curable.

Current medical technology does not give us the ability to detect the early seeds of heart attacks, strokes, and most forms of cancer. That is, we do not really know why these conditions occur although we have some ability to treat them once they do occur. Some day we may discover that by giving a drug to children, we may prevent the onset of cancer, stroke, and heart disease for the rest of their lives. But when that happens, these children will ultimately die of other conditions, and we will begin searching for the seeds of those conditions.

Even if we do not fully accept this theory, there is another sense in which all of us are ill—we age. Some medical researchers actually regard aging as a form of illness. And right now research is being done to find a chemical cure for the disease of aging.

Some other unconventional notions of illness are also in use these days. New and exotic research is being conducted to discover ways of altering the DNA makeup of our genes. The prospective results of this research are impressive. Scientists expect to be able to prevent genetic defects in children and even to alter their susceptibility to disease.

Is aging really an illness? Is a genetic defect or a genetic susceptibility to a disease an illness? One thing is for certain: medical science is rapidly expanding the horizons of what is possible in order to improve our health. It is precisely because these horizons are so broad and so all-encompassing that the former Minister of Health in Britain was able to declare the term "medical need" meaningless. He might have gone on to say that if we steadfastly insist on using the term, we are forced to admit that the "need" for medical care is limitless.

If the extent of illness is virtually unlimited, the potential cost of treating illness is even more so. The NHS was started in the days before many modern medical techniques were discovered. Its founders knew nothing of microsurgery, open-heart surgery, hip replacements, liver transplants, and dozens of other medical techniques—all of which could easily bankrupt the NHS, and perhaps Britain as well, if used to their full potential.

Doctors today can replace elbows, knees, and hips with artificial joints. They can reattach the nerves of a severed hand or finger with microsurgery. They can replace heart valves and entire organs with artificial ones. Artificial hearts and artificial eyes and ears appear well within our scientific capabilities.

As an example of the enormous potential for spending money on treatment, consider CAT scanners and magnetic resonance (MR) scanners. With them, doctors can "see" into the body and detect brain tumors, the presence of heart disease, damage from a heart attack, and a great many other conditions that could previously be analyzed only with surgery.

As they are currently used, these scanners are mainly reserved for patients who are thought to be seriously ill. But they also have enormous potential in preventive medicine. A scanner can detect lung cancer in its early states—long before it can be detected by conventional x-ray. It can also detect many other life-threatening conditions in their early stages. As a result, people who show no apparent symptoms of disease can still benefit from the scanner in the same way they can benefit from a general checkup.

The trouble with scanners is that they are expensive. If every American got an annual scan as part of a general checkup, we would increase our nation's total medical bill by 50 percent! And that would be the result of making full use of just *one* diagnostic technique.

The example of scanners helps explain why many health economists believe that if we fully used all known medical techniques, the cost would exceed our entire gross national product. No nation, however, is going to spend all or even most of its income on medical care. What that means is that scarcity cannot be eliminated in the field of medical care. It also means that only a fraction of medical needs can be met. Many needs, perhaps even most, must go unmet. In other words, medical care must be rationed.

──────── Medical "need" versus medical "demand"

Most non-economists, including most doctors and most politicians, tend to think about the market for medical care in terms of the need for medical care. Like the founders of the NHS, they see the problem of medical rationing as the problem of getting medical care to those who need it most. This is not the way economists think about the market for medical care, however. Economists think in terms of *demand* rather than in terms of *need*.

For each individual, the quantity demanded of a good or service is the quantity the individual is willing and able to purchase. *Demand* is different from *need* precisely because people do not necessarily demand what they need. But demand is also different from *want*. People might want something but be unwilling or unable to pay the price necessary to obtain that thing.

One of the reasons it is so common for non-economists to think in terms of need rather than demand is that a great many people tend to view medical care primarily in terms of the critical alternative between life and death. An image quickly comes to mind of an unconscious victim being rushed to the emergency room of a hospital for life-saving treatment. In what sense can this patient be said to "demand" medical care? The most we can say in this case is that if the patient receives emergency care he may live. If he does not receive it, he may die. For this reason, it seems quite proper in this case to focus on the patient's "need" for medical care, rather than on the demand for it.

There are many other headline-grabbing instances in which medical care represents the difference between life and death. Donje McNair's case was a clear example. Because he did not get a transplant, he died; if he had received the transplant, he would have had a chance to live. In such cases, patients' "demand" for medical care seems largely irrelevant. If we ask what is the most they would be willing to pay for medical treatment, we are in effect asking what is the most they would be willing to pay for life! Many of them would probably be willing to trade their entire personal wealth, if necessary, in return for the treatment.

The problem with these examples is that they are so misleading. It is true that immediate medical treatment may mean the difference between life and death for some patients. But such cases are actually quite rare in comparison to the broad range of medical services given to the population as a whole. In any one year, fewer than 13 percent of patients suffer from life-threatening conditions. Moreover, most of these patients do not require emergency care, or even immediate hospitalization.

The vast majority of medical services, then, cannot be thought of as life-saving for the patient. These services cover almost all physician visits and diagnostic tests, the great majority of surgical procedures, and well over 90 percent of trips to hospital emergency rooms. For each of these services, what patients desire is an improvement in their health, an increase in the odds of survival, or perhaps an assurance that they do not have a particular illness. The quantity demanded of these medical services depends very much upon the prices which are charged. Numerous economic studies have verified that the demand for these services obeys the law of demand: the lower the price, the higher the quantity demanded.

Tracing the economic effects of rationing medical care

In keeping with the economic approach to medical care, we have represented a hypothetical market for physicians' services in Figure 3-1. We have made the demand curve relatively steep to reflect the fact that the quantity demanded of physicians' services changes only moderately in response to price changes. The supply curve in Figure 3-1 is completely vertical. This represents the fact that a limited number of physicians have only so much time to spend with their patients, and that in the short run, total time spent with patients cannot be changed very much in response to price changes.

Figure 3–1 shows that at a price of zero, the number of visits patients would like to make to see physicians would be the quantity Q_b. The quantity available, however, is the lower quantity Q_a. At a price of zero, patients will not be able to make as many visits to physicians as they would like to make. There will be a shortage equal to $Q_b - Q_a$ visits per day. How can we decide which patients will be able to visit a physician and which ones will not? One way of making this decision is through the price system.

The price system is one system of rationing. Viewed from the demand side, variable price is a method of determining who will be able to consume a good or service, and in what quantity. In our diagram, the price must rise to $21service, and in what quantity. In our diagram, the price must rise to $21.00 per visit in order to achieve an equilibrium. At the price of $21.00, all who wish to visit a physician may do so, and they may make as many visits as they would like to make.

The price system is not considered by all to be a fair system, but it does have certain advantages. In the face of a limited supply of physicians, consumers are encouraged to compare the value they place on a physician visit with the price they must pay for it. Consumers will tend to restrict their visits to those visits which are worth at least $21.00 to them. Thus, the physicians' time tends to be allocated to its highest valued uses— something important for economic efficiency.

Allowing the price to rise until an equilibrium is reached is not the only method of rationing. In Britain, as we said, patients are not charged for treatment. Instead, patients are seen mainly on a first come, first served basis. Since the number of visits demanded at a zero price exceeds the number of visits physicians can supply, many patients who would like to

FIGURE 3–1   Daily Market for Physicians' Services

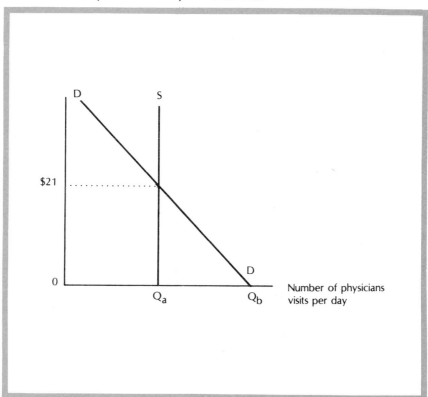

see a physician will not be able to do so. Those who actually get to see a doctor will be those who get there first and who are willing to wait the longest. Rationing in this way is sometimes called "rationing by waiting," and with good reason. In Britain, patients wait and wait and wait.

To see a general practitioner (family doctor), for example, patients may wait up to a week for an appointment. Once in the doctor's office, they may wait up to three or four hours before being examined. Patients who are referred to specialists face even longer waits: several weeks for an appointment and long hours spent in the specialist's waiting room. Once it is determined that a patient has a serious problem which requires hospitalization, the waiting really begins. At any given time, hundreds of thousands of people are waiting to get into British hospitals. Many of these people have been waiting for operations for years.

One alternative to waiting is not to see a doctor at all. Another alternative is to go to Britain's small, but thriving, private market for medical care. In the private market, there is very little waiting, but patients must pay the market price for the treatment they receive. Private sector medical care in Britain is in a position similar to private education in the United States. All must pay taxes to support the state system, whether or not they use its services.

What determines how long a person is willing to wait rather than turn to one of these alternatives? Two things: the value that the person places on the medical service being offered, and the opportunity cost of waiting. In general, the more valuable a service is, the longer people will be willing to wait in order to receive the service for "free" from the NHS. For example, the services of a specialist are usually more valuable than the services of a general practitioner. A surgical operation is usually more valuable than a routine examination. So within the NHS, people are willing to wait longer to see specialists than they are willing to wait to see general practitioners. They are willing to wait longer for operations than they are willing to wait for routine examinations.

An important thing to remember is that waiting always has an opportunity cost. One way in which patients bear this cost is through the use of their time. Time spent waiting in a doctor's office is time that might have been spent doing other things. Some patients miss work, which often means a loss of salary. Other patients give up valuable leisure time.

Patients who choose to wait for care from the NHS forego the opportunity to receive immediate care in the private sector. The choice to wait rather than to receive immediate care may mean living with the uncertainty of an undiagnosed disease. It may mean living in pain. It may mean risking the patient's life. Patients waiting for gall bladder surgery, orthopedic surgery, and many other types of operations may wait for several years in constant pain. Although the experience is not common, the British press and medical journals contain examples of patients dying because they were not promptly admitted to NHS hospitals.

People choose to wait, then, as long as the costs of waiting are less than or equal to the value they place on the service they seek. Within the NHS, prices cannot rise above zero. But waiting costs can rise. And they tend to rise until they are roughly equal to the value of the service being rationed. In Figure 3–1, for example, the market value of a physician's visit is about $21.00. That means that, on the average, people will have to bear about $21.00 worth of waiting costs in order to be able to see a physician. Those who are unwilling to bear $21.00 worth of waiting costs will have to turn to other options.

What we have said so far about rationing by waiting is true as a first approximation. Actually, things are a bit more complicated. To understand more fully the consequences of rationing by waiting in medical care, we must take a look at some indirect effects of this type of rationing.

_____ **Some indirect
effects of rationing by waiting**

During the 1970s Americans experienced a number of severe episodes of rationing by waiting in the market for gasoline. Each of these episodes occurred when government price controls held the price of gasoline below its free market level. The result was a gasoline shortage, and, in general, gasoline was made available on the basis of first come, first served. Long lines formed at gas pumps. What does gasoline have to do with the market for medical care? A great deal. The way British doctors have responded to non-price rationing of medical care turns out to be very similar to the response of service stations to non-price rationing of gasoline in the United States.

1. Less time per patient

During the gasoline crises in the U.S., many service stations put a restriction on the amount of gasoline each customer could buy. On the theory that as many cars as possible should be serviced, many attendants refused to give motorists more than one-half or one-third of a tankful. British doctors have responded in a similar way. In order to see as many patients as possible, British doctors have substantially reduced the amount of time they spend with each patient.

Whereas doctors in the U.S. spend about fifteen minutes, on the average, with each patient, British doctors spend less than five minutes. In other words, the British patient gets the medical equivalent of about one-third of a tankful. Moreover, as in the U.S., doctors in Britain occasionally see patients with serious problems, requiring thirty minutes or more of the doctor's time. This means that a lot less than five minutes is spent with most of the other patients. In fact, the majority of patients in Britain probably spend only about one or two minutes with their doctor on a typical visit.

It might seem that patients would strongly object to being short-changed on the time they are able to spend with their doctors. In fact, most patients tend to prefer this type of adjustment. By spending less time with each patient, a doctor is able to see a greater number of patients each day. Many patients are willing to give up the ability to spend more time with their doctor in return for the increased probability that they will be able to have at least some of the physician's time. Their attitude is similar to the attitude of many U.S. motorists who approved of the practice of limiting gasoline sales to each customer in order to increase the probability that all customers would get at least some gasoline.

In addition, when doctors reduce the time spent with each patient, something else happens—waiting costs are lowered. In Figure 3–1, for example, $21.00 might be the equilibrium price of fifteen minutes of the physician's time. But if physicians spend only about five minutes with each patient, the value of a physician visit will be lower. The market price of five minutes of time with a physician might be about $7.00. This means that patients will have to bear only $7.00 of waiting costs in order to see a physician. From the patients' point of view, then, there is a tradeoff between time spent with the physician and the cost of waiting. Many are willing to give up more time with the physician in return for lower waiting costs.

2. Fewer services per patient

Another response of service station attendants to non-price rationing of gasoline was to eliminate a great many services that customers had come to expect under price rationing. With long lines of cars waiting at the gasoline pumps, most attendants neglected to clean windshields, to check the air pressure in tires, to check oil levels, batteries, and water levels in radiators. Instead, they just stuck to pumping gas.

In a similar way, the British doctor has eliminated a vast array of services that most American patients expect from their doctors as a matter of course. As we noted above, the British doctor simply does not have the time to provide "full service" to all of his patients, even if he were inclined to do so. The result is that most British patients miss out on the medical equivalent of having their batteries, oil level, and tire pressure checked.

One of the ironies of this indirect effect is that the services which British doctors tend to skimp on are the very services which were near and dear to the heart of Aneurin Bevan—preventive medical services. The general checkup, for example, is virtually unknown within the NHS. In order to get one, a patient has to turn to Britain's private medical sector. Only 8 percent of all eligible women in Britain get an annual PAP smear, a test which is necessary in order to detect cervical cancer in its early stages. (The U.S. rate is six times that high.) In addition, the vaccination rates for childhood diseases are currently at such a low level that the British government has expressed public alarm over the situation.

It is important to remember that this indirect effect does not occur because Britain has too few doctors. Actually, Britain has more general practitioners per capita than the U.S. has. The effect occurs because of the rationing problem we have been discussing. British patients, on the average, make about four times as many visits to their general practitioners as American patients do. If American patients suddenly quadrupled the number of physician visits they make each year, American doctors would not be able to offer more than the minimum services British doctors now provide.

3. Discrimination

One of the problems that occurred during the gasoline shortages in the U.S. was the frequent charge that service stations discriminated among customers, giving some more gasoline than others. One type of discrimination that was fairly common, for example, was for service stations to favor those motorists who had been traditional customers.

Within the British NHS, discrimination is also alleged to exist. Doctors, it is charged, favor some patients over others. In particular, the claim is made that doctors spend more time with and deliver more services to those patients who have educational and social backgrounds similar to their own. A number of studies, for example, have shown that doctors spend from 32 to 39 percent more time per visit with patients from the families of professional workers than they spend with patients from the families of manual laborers.

Another type of discrimination that apparently occurs is politically based. Several years ago a member of the British Parliament, speaking before a group of students, announced that he had the political influence to get any patient into an NHS hospital immediately. A student, challenging this claim, told the speaker that his father had been waiting for an operation for three years. The member of Parliament accepted the challenge. Within two days, the student's father was admitted into an NHS hospital for his operation. (Political influence plays a role in rationing health care in the United States too, by the way. For example, President Reagan used a radio speech in July 1983 to appeal for public help in finding livers for three children. A White House aide is regularly assigned to field calls for organs, money, and emergency air transportation.)[2]

4. Black markets and illegal agreements

The practice of jumping to the head of the line in Britain is called "queue jumping." Most queue jumping within the NHS is not done by intervention of members of Parliament, however. It is more likely to come about because of friendly (and illegal) arrangements between doctors and patients.

Suppose a patient prefers not to wait for three days for an appointment and one or two additional hours in a waiting room. An alternative is to offer the doctor an illicit payment for prompt service. Both the doctors and the patients stand to gain. Doctors gain because they get additional income that they would otherwise not have. Patients gain because they get prompt (and probably better) service which is worth the price they pay.

An arrangement such as this is described as a *black market*. Black markets exist within the NHS for a wide range of services. But no one knows to what extent they exist. Precisely because such transactions are illegal, parties to the arrangement have strong incentives not to tell British authorities what they have done.

---

2. Ibid.

——————————————— **Rationing and economic efficiency**

Most economists believe that rationing by waiting is a very inefficient form of rationing. The reason is that a basic requirement of economic efficiency is that goods and services be produced at minimum cost. The fundamental cost of a medical care system is the opportunity cost of the real resources used in that system. These real resources include human resources such as doctors, nurses, and physician's assistants, and nonhuman resources such as hospitals, ambulances, and diagnostic equipment. When medical care is rationed by prices, market prices tend to reflect the opportunity cost of these resources. That means that the prices that consumers pay tend to be equal to the social costs of the goods and services they are buying.

In the British NHS, however, consumers face some additional burdens. British patients not only pay taxes to fund the cost of the real resources used in their medical care system, but they also face the costs of waiting in order to obtain medical services. These waiting costs, as we have seen, can be quite high. Moreover, these waiting costs are avoidable. By simply charging prices to patients for the services they use, the British could eliminate a lot of the waiting costs that patients currently face.

A second requirement of economic efficiency is that for any given cost, resources should be used in a way that maximizes their social value. The training of physicians, for example, uses real resources. Once this cost has been borne, efficiency requires that we use physicians' time in such a way that we maximize its value. In the market, this tends to happen naturally. Physicians tend to provide those services for which their patients are most willing to pay. Within the NHS, however, physicians appear to devote far too much of their time to trivial and inconsequential services— the types of services that can be rendered in one or two minutes of their time. This, as we have seen, is a result of the system of rationing by waiting. Were British patients paying market prices for physician visits, they would probably demand, and receive, the types of services most American patients get from their doctors.

Does this mean that nonprice rationing is always inefficient? Not necessarily. Sometimes nonprice rationing may be preferred to price rationing by consumers. For example, there are a number of medical plans in the U.S. which charge patients a fixed annual fee and then ration medical care among patients by means other than price. Patients in these plans face higher waiting costs than patients elsewhere, but they receive other benefits (such as a lower annual medical bill) in return. An example of such a plan is a health maintenance organization (HMO).

The difference between these medical plans and the NHS is that these plans successfully compete in the market. The NHS does not. Rationing within the NHS is not only *nonprice* rationing, it is also *nonmarket* rationing. The NHS does not compete in the market for funds. It gets its funding through taxes. Although British patients are free to leave the NHS, they get no refund on their taxes if they choose to do so.

Many of the inefficiencies we observe within the NHS, then, are not due solely to nonprice rationing. They are probably due more to the fact that the way medical care is rationed in Britain is determined by politics rather than by the market. Political considerations also account for many other features of the NHS.

The politics of medicine

As we noted earlier, one of the original objectives of the founders of the NHS was to ration medical care on the basis of need. Medical care, they claimed, should be given to those who need it most. As it has turned out, however, the British system seems to operate on the reverse of that principle. Those with the most serious medical needs appear to have the greatest difficulty in acquiring treatment. Within the NHS, it is far easier to get treatment for a minor medical condition than it is to obtain treatment for a serious condition. Most patients, for example, can obtain a prescription for sleeping pills in a matter of days. But literally thousands of patients suffering from kidney failure, heart disease and many forms of cancer face long and risky waiting periods before they receive treatment. And, large numbers of these patients never receive the treatment most doctors think they should have.

Why is it that the actual operation of the NHS is so different from the goals of its founders? The basic reason is politics. Medical resources within the NHS are ultimately allocated by politicians. And, in allocating these resources, politicians are very sensitive to the political costs and political benefits of the decisions they make.

An unfortunate fact about medical care is that treatment of patients with acute conditions can be very expensive. Moreover, money spent in this way affects only a small percentage of the population in any one year. By contrast, if that same money is spent on the treatment of minor medical conditions, the effects will be spread out over a large percentage of the population. Given the choice of either spending money on a few people or spending that same money on a large number of people, politicians respond to political incentives. They spend the money where the votes are.

The results of these choices are startling. Many American doctors believe that the treatment of seriously ill patients in Britain is almost inhumane. By contrast, the treatment given to patients with minor medical problems sometimes seems almost lavish by American standards. The British ambulance service is a good example. Each year there are about twenty-two million ambulance rides in Britain. That is about one ambulance trip for every two people in the country. The vast majority of these journeys, about 93 percent, are for non-emergency purposes. The British ambulance service has been described as a "free taxi service" for the many who use it. But for those few patients who have a serious medical emergency, such as a heart attack or a stroke, things look bleak. British ambulances have very little of the equipment most American ambulances have to deal with these problems.

Another example is the treatment of elderly, handicapped, and chronically ill patients. Each year home nurses and health visitors make about eight million visits to the homes of these patients. That is about one visit for every two households in Britain. The scope of this activity extends well beyond comparable services in the U.S. But if these British patients develop serious medical problems, their plight is very different. The NHS has very few CAT scanners, pacemakers, dialysis machines, and other forms of modern medical technology. What equipment there is usually is reserved for the treatment of productive members of the population of working age.

Why don't British voters tell their representatives to change these priorities? The main reason appears to be a problem of knowledge. Like most Americans, British citizens, on the average, know very little about complex medical technology. Yet they are well acquainted with free ambulance rides and free home visits. Were the NHS to cut back spending on ambulance rides and home visits, there would be a large public outcry. But very few people understand the implications of the decision not to buy a CAT scanner. As a result, there is very little political pressure to spend money on expensive medical technology.

In fact, lack of knowledge seems to be the best explanation of why the entire NHS has continued in its present form. Public opinion polls show that most British voters greatly underestimate the amount of taxes they actually pay to support the NHS. About 60 percent of voters, for example, believe that they pay only one-twentieth of the amount they actually pay in taxes to finance the health service. Given this perception, small wonder that the NHS is one of the most politically popular programs in Britain.

An evaluation

Nonprice rationing of medical care is not necessarily an inefficient form of rationing. This is especially true if the scheme which employs nonprice rationing is able to compete successfully in the free market. The British NHS and many similar schemes in other countries, however, have not been established by competition in the market. Consumers are forced to pay taxes to support such schemes whether or not they use the services. These schemes, then, not only adopt a policy of *nonprice* rationing, they also adopt a policy of *nonmarket* rationing. On balance the evidence suggests that such schemes are a lot less efficient than rationing through the market. Nonmarket rationing tends to result in large and unnecessary waiting costs for patients, in lower quality of service than would otherwise exist, and in a different mix of services than would otherwise exist. Medical services are not produced at minimum cost, nor are medical resources allocated to their highest valued use.

How does a medical care system like the NHS rank in terms of the standard of equality? Until recently many economists believed that a system of nonmarket rationing would benefit low-income patients relative to high-income patients. The reason was that low-income patients put a lower value on their time. A patient who works for $3.00 an hour, for example, only sacrifices $3.00 of income in return for an hour of waiting. The opportunity cost of waiting in a doctor's office for this person will be much lower than for a person who earns $50.00 an hour. As a result, the argument went, low-income patients will be willing to wait longer and will receive more medical services than high-income patients.

The argument sounds plausible, but the evidence suggests that things are very different in practice. While high-income patients have a high opportunity cost of time, they also seem to be more adept at working their way through the NHS bureaucracy. As a consequence, high-income patients in Britain tend to get more and better medical care than low-income patients receive. A government-sponsored study, released in 1979, concluded that there was no evidence of an increase in equality of access to medical care after thirty years of operation of the NHS. In fact, some evidence shows more inequality in medical care today than there would have been had the NHS never existed.

Take the case of elderly patients. The elderly tend to have lower incomes and greater health needs than the younger population. For this reason, elderly patients are thought to be natural beneficiaries of government-directed "free" medical care schemes. Yet evidence collected by the Center for Health Policy Studies at the University of Dallas indicates that the elderly are the worst victims of such schemes. The apparent reason for this fact is that under nonmarket rationing, doctors are more frequently faced with tough decisions about which patients will receive treatment and which ones will not. In these situations, there is a tendency to choose younger patients over older ones.

Most people believe that society should provide some medical care to those who cannot afford to purchase it on their own. On balance, however, it appears that low-income and elderly patients do better under programs specifically designed to meet their needs than they do under comprehensive, nationwide programs which include the entire population.

Programs of nonmarket rationing also fare poorly under our third standard of evaluation: the standard of liberty. It is not necessarily inconsistent with the standard of liberty for a government to sell services, including medical services, in the market. What is inconsistent with the standard of liberty is the practice of forcing people to pay for such programs whether or not they wish to use the government's medical services. Advocates of the standard of liberty believe that individuals should be free to choose how they will spend their own medical dollars. Thus, they are firm advocates of rationing medical care through the free market.

Comprehensive programs of government-provided medical care, then, seem inconsistent with our three standards of evaluation. This does not mean that such programs cannot be justified in some other way. As we enter the decade of the 1980s, the U.S. is the only developed country that does not have some form of national health insurance. The choice we face is one of continuing special programs for the poor (Medicaid) and the elderly (Medicare), while allowing other citizens to remain in the market, or adopting a single national health insurance plan for everyone. In making this choice we are in the enviable position of being able to learn much from the experiences that other countries have had. One thing is certain: advances in medical technology, such as the ability to transplant organs, will keep the issue in the public eye.

Questions for thought and discussion

1. In order to meet the cost of unexpected, large medical bills, most people have some form of medical insurance. A typical policy works this way. patients (or their employers) pay a monthly premium for the insurance policy. When the patient receives treatment, the insurance company pays about 80 or 90 percent of the medical bill.
   a. Using your knowledge of economics, explain how health insurance policies might lead to "overconsumption" of medical care.
   b. Can you think of any techniques that insurance companies might use to prevent "overconsumption" from occurring?

2. A health maintenance organization (HMO) is a medical plan that charges customers a fixed fee at the beginning of the year and agrees to provide them with all of the medical care they require during the year. There are no additional charges to patients, regardless of the amount of medical services they consume. There are many HMOs in operation in the U.S.
   a. What kinds of rationing problems do you think HMOs experience?
   b. Do you see any differences between an HMO and the British NHS?
   c. Do you think that the way HMO doctors practice medicine is more like the medical practice of other American doctors or more like the practice of doctors in the NHS?

3. Here are some alternative policies for distributing tickets to sporting events:
   a. Charge market-clearing prices.
   b. Charge a set of prices that maximizes income to the box office.
   c. Give tickets away free by means of a lottery.

What do you see as the advantages and disadvantages of each of these three schemes?

4. Many apartments in New York City are subject to rent controls. This means there is a maximum rental price that can be charged to tenants. (Most new buildings are exempt from the law.) Here are some features of New York City housing:
   a. There is a housing shortage.
   b. There is substantial deterioration of many buildings.
   c. Many buildings are abandoned by their owners.
   d. Most of the tenants in rent-controlled apartments are middle class. Very few poor people and very few rich people are living in them. Using your knowledge of economics, show how each of these features may be indirectly related to rent controls.

5. Jerome Kraut, a Chicago pediatrician who cared for Donje McNair, says that "little sick kids should get whatever's necessary, no matter what it costs. . . . If they would make one less MX missile, Donje McNair could have had a liver transplant."
   a. In a world of scarcity, would it be possible to provide medical care for children "no matter what it costs"? Should we try to do so? Why or why not?
   b. Given the pressure of scarcity, should "little sick kids" get a bigger slice of the available health-care pie than big sick adults? Than elderly patients? Why or why not?
   c. Do you agree that it would be worth giving up one MX missile to get a liver transplant for a child who needs it? What other items that the government spends money on would be worth giving up to buy more liver transplants?

Selected references

Goodman, John C. *National Health Insurance in Great Britain: Lessons for the U.S.A.* Dallas, Texas: Fisher Institute, 1980.

Goodman, John C. *The Regulation of Medical Care: Is the Price Too High?* San Francisco: CATO Institute, 1980.

Jacobs, Philip. *The Economics of Health and Medical Care: An Introduction.* Baltimore: University Park Press, 1980.

Lindsay, Cotton M. *National Health Issues, the British Experience.* Santa Monica, California: Roche Laboratories, 1980.

Meyer, Jack A. *Market Reforms in Health Care.* Washington, D.C.: American Enterprise Institute, 1983.

4

Product Safety

It is said that Congress never does anything unless there is a crisis—at least that seems to be the case in the area of consumer protection. Our most important laws protecting consumer safety were passed on the crest of widespread public alarm.

At about the turn of the century, Upton Sinclair electrified the nation with his novel *The Jungle.* The book was an exposé of conditions in Chicago's meat-packing plants and was given major credit for the passage of the Meat Inspection Act and the Pure Food and Drug Act of 1906. The Pure Food and Drug Act in turn established the Food and Drug Administration (FDA).

Decades later—in the 1950s—a European drug called thalidomide was sold as a sleeping pill. When pregnant women took it, the drug produced a horrible side effect—hundreds of malformed babies were born. The then-new medium of television allowed millions of viewers actually to see the damage. Congress quickly responded by beefing up the FDA's authority to control the entry of new drugs onto the market.

The next shock came in 1965. Ralph Nader's best-seller *Unsafe At Any Speed* was a muckraking attack on the Corvair, a popular General Motors car. Nader argued that the car's flawed design made it a death trap for unsuspecting drivers. His book, like Sinclair's, is given credit for subsequent federal legislation. In this case, Congress established the National Highway and Traffic Safety Administration (NHTSA) and set the stage for a number of auto safety regulations.

More recently, stories of children sleeping in flammable pajamas and of children getting lead poisoning by eating the paint on the walls near their cribs have brought still more legislation. Congress formed the Consumer Product Safety Commission (CPSC), an agency that now has authority over ten thousand consumer products. Like the FDA and the NHTSA, it has the power to ban from the market products that are found to seriously endanger the health and well-being of product users. It also can order changes in the design and physical characteristics of the products we buy.

Surely, we think, agencies such as these perform a valuable public service. After all, who is opposed to product safety? Yet a lot of people have vigorously opposed the actions of the regulators of safety. Upton Sinclair himself, for example, was strongly opposed to the Meat Inspection Act—he saw the 1906 act as primarily benefiting the large meat-packers at the expense of smaller companies and the consuming public.

Ralph Nader, by contrast, has been fairly happy with the legislation he inspired. But criticism similar to Sinclair's has been leveled at auto safety regulations from other quarters. The FDA has also come under attack. And President Reagan's director of the Office of Management and Budget has been critical of the CPSC.

What's the controversy all about? Before we look at the particulars of the debate, let's look at some economic theory.

Safety and consumer choice

When we purchase a car, a pair of skis, a lawnmower, or even a stepladder, we want to be sure the product is safe. Right? Of course. Yet in a sense, our actions belie our words. The problem is that the terms *safe* and *unsafe* are a lot like the terms *hot* and *cold*. They only come in degrees. No matter how much safety we have, we can usually have more of it. No matter how little safety we have, we can usually have less of it.

Other things being equal, most of us would prefer more safety. But additional safety is rarely free—it normally costs something in terms of time, effort, and money. In most markets a spectrum of products exists, with some being safer than others. But if we insist on driving only the safest car, skiing on only the safest skis, and consuming only the safest of every other product we buy, then we had better have a pretty deep pocket.

Most of us, however, would not always buy the safest of everything even if our budgets allowed it. How, then, do we make choices about safety? Economists tend to focus on the trade-offs that we face as consumers. Generally speaking, in order to "consume" more safety we have to reduce our consumption of other goods and services. Alternatively, by reducing the level of safety we enjoy we are often able to consume more of everything else.

That is why economists often speak of a demand curve for safety in much the same way that they speak of a demand curve for other goods. They reason that the lower the "price" of safety, the more safety people will consume; the higher the price, the less they will consume. The principle is that rational consumers will tend to allocate their budgets so as to maximize the satisfaction they derive from those budgets. This means that consumers will divide up their expenditures so that a dollar's worth of safety will yield the same satisfaction—at the margin—as a dollar's worth of any other good or service. Or, if it won't yield exactly the same, it will be as nearly equal as possible.

Economic theory also predicts that people will allocate their time and their energy in much the same way as they allocate their monetary income. For example, people will budget their time so that a minute devoted to safety will, at the margin, do them just as much good as a minute devoted to anything else. As a result, consumers are seen as constantly comparing the benefits of additional safety to the costs of that safety in terms of time, money, and effort. When the costs and benefits change, the level of safety consumed will also change.

Do people really act as theory predicts that they will? Although we can't open up people's heads and implant a mind-probe, we do have some pretty good external evidence that is consistent with the theory. We often find circumstances where we believe that the costs or the benefits of safety have changed substantially, and when we look closely we find that consumer actions have changed as well.

Take the case of seat belt use in automobiles. For many drivers, seat belt use involves a cost—the cost is the sacrifice of convenience and comfort required to buckle up and to wear them. Against this cost there is a benefit: in most cases seat belts reduce injury that results from accidents. Economic theory, therefore, predicts that drivers will use seat belts more often when the benefits are high relative to the cost. Seat belt use should be more frequent when the risk of accident is high and when the severity of injury is likely to be great.

Federal studies tend to confirm this prediction. It turns out that drivers use seat belts more often for highway driving than for city driving—on the highway the severity of injury from an accident is likely to be greater. Drivers also use seat belts more often in rush hour traffic, when the risk of accident is greater. Furthermore, the data show that, on the average, drivers of small cars wear seat belts more than drivers of larger cars. This is consistent with the fact that smaller cars give less protection in accidents. That makes the value of seat belt use greater for the drivers of small cars.

There is also evidence that cost-benefit calculations affect driving performance. The more carefully and the more cautiously we drive, the greater the effort we must make, and often, the longer it takes us to get where we are going. We expect people to weigh these costs against corresponding benefits. For this reason, we expect to see more cautious driving in bad weather conditions when the risks of accident are higher. We also expect to see owners of small cars drive more cautiously than owners of large cars. These predictions, once again, seem consistent with the facts. A recent study by Professor P. L. Yu of the University of Texas surveyed traffic accidents in Texas. Yu found that cars weighing less than 3,000 pounds accounted for a little less than 20 percent of automobile registrations. Yet the drivers of these cars were involved in only 13 percent of the accidents and only 16 percent of the injuries. By contrast, cars weighing from 4,000 to 5,000 pounds made up 31 percent of the registrations; but they were involved in 57 percent of the accidents and 51 percent of the injuries. Other studies have reported comparable results for North Carolina and Canada.[1]

Evidence also suggests that consumers take safety into account in the purchase of consumer products. Some products are safer than others; there is also often a lot of variation in the level of safety attached to different products in the same product line. In each case, consumers are making choices about the amount of safety they want to buy. Very few of us, as we noted, invariably buy the safest products available. Our actions show that the increased safety is simply not always worth the additional cost.

If decisions about safety are left to the market, the level of safety will be determined by supply and demand. Producers must decide how much safety to supply with their products. Typically, the more safety features that are added, the more costly the product will be, so the producer must decide whether buyers will be willing to pay the higher prices that additional safety features demand. This, of course, means that some safety features may not be produced. In the 1950s, for example, Ford Motor Company added certain safety options to its cars such as seat belts and padded dashboards. But when Ford discovered there was little demand for these options, it quickly abandoned them. General Motors followed suit with a brief experiment with optional airbags in the 1970s.

Today many of these decisions are not left to the market. Seat belts, padded dashboards, rubber bumpers, window defrosters, and many other items are required by federal law. Federal laws also affect the standards met on many other product lines. What difference do these regulations make? Let's take a look.

───────── Tracing the effects of safety regulations

When safety regulators order that a product be taken off the market or that characteristics of products that remain on the market be changed, there is

---

1. Economists do not contend that statistics such as these *prove* that economic theory is valid; many other explanations of the evidence are also possible. Instead, economists treat such evidence as *consistent* with economic theory. So long as it is consistent, they feel justified in continuing to use the theory to explain and predict human behavior. We will consider some additional examples of this technique later in this chapter.

one obvious direct effect: the products available to the consumer are safer than they would have been. But there are also some important indirect effects that are often hidden from view. They may also be highly complex and difficult to measure.

One indirect effect, for example, is that the prices of safety-regulated products will normally be higher than they otherwise would have been. Some estimates of the costs of automobile safety legislation have been made by Murray Weidenbaum and Robert DeFina of the Center for the Study of American Business at Washington University in St. Louis. The two economists reported that safety regulations enacted between 1968 and 1978 have added at least $450 to the price of a new car. Of course, some of these safety features might have been added in response to changing consumer demand even without regulation. But many of them probably would not have been added—or at least not to all cars. Moreover, the price of safety is expected to rise. Air bags, which will not be installed without regulation, will add from $800 to $1,200 to the price of a car, if regulations requiring airbags ever go into effect. And each time a bag is inflated the owner may have to pay twice that amount to have it replaced.

Higher prices, of course, lead to still other indirect effects. Other things being equal, as the price of a regulated product rises, fewer purchases will be made. Some consumers will turn to substitute products, which may be less safe than the regulated product. As a result, safety regulations can have the wholly unintended effect of reducing the overall level of safety.

In the face of higher prices for new cars, for example, potential buyers are encouraged to seek out alternatives. They may continue driving the cars they have. They may purchase used cars. Or they may turn to less expensive forms of transportation such as motorcycles, mopeds, or even bicycles. These are the kinds of indirect effects that are likely to decrease the level of safety. Alternatively, some consumers may turn to public transportation such as subways or buses. To the extent they do so, the overall level of transportation safety is likely to increase.

We do not know all the kinds of product substitutions people make in the face of higher automobile prices. The point is simply that these indirect effects need to be considered in evaluating the net effects of safety regulations. The same principle applies to products other than cars. Take the case of ladders. Safety regulations being considered by the CPSC would add from 10 to 15 percent to ladder prices. But if consumers buy fewer ladders they may use substitutes like tables and chairs when they need to climb up to change a light bulb. And CPSC figures show more accidents involving tables and chairs than ladders.

In tracing the indirect effects of safety regulation, we must often distinguish between product *design* and product *use*. We argued in the case of automobiles that driving behavior is likely to be affected by the kind of cars people drive. Other things being equal, people are likely to drive faster and take more risks if they believe their cars are safer.

Conversely, drivers of less safe automobiles tend to drive more cautiously. These considerations led economist Sam Peltzman to investigate the effects of automobile safety legislation on traffic accidents and highway deaths.

Peltzman reasoned that many of the safety features required by law were unwanted by consumers—the consumers would have preferred a little less safety equipment in return for a cheaper price. Of course, because of regulation they had to buy safer cars if they bought new cars at all. But since people knew their cars were safer, Peltzman argued, they had a reduced incentive to take safety precautions in driving.

Actually, Peltzman himself expected this indirect effect to be small. But the statistics he gathered shocked him. They seemed to show that the additional safety required by regulation was almost completely offset by more reckless driving!

In particular, Peltzman found that more than a proportional share of accidents occurred in cars that had the new safety equipment than in those that did not have it. He also found that, after adjusting for other factors, the new safety standards had no overall effect on the highway death rate. In fact, the only major result of safety regulation was a change in the way people died. The death rate went down for the occupants of automobiles, but it went up, by an offsetting amount, for pedestrians, bicyclists, and motorcyclists! Could it be that people thought their cars were so safe that they didn't bother to look where they were going?

Not all economists accepted Peltzman's interpretation of the data, but virtually everyone who looked at the study agreed that it raised an extremely important issue in the debate over safety regulation. Most safety regulations focus on product design; Peltzman focused on product *use*. And it turns out that for most consumer products, product use is a far more important cause of accident and injury than product design. In fact, the CPSC estimates that two-thirds of all injuries related to consumer products are caused by misuse of those products. If people are going to be so stupid as to pick up their lawnmowers and use them to trim hedges, no conceivable product design change can save them from injury!

If the CPSC tries to change the nature of the products people buy without, at the same time, changing people's attitudes toward safety, it may end up doing more harm than good. As injuries related to product design decrease, injuries related to product use may increase. The overall level of safety may remain unchanged; it may even decrease. But consumers will nonetheless pay higher prices for the goods they buy.

There are still other ways in which the safety regulators may unintentionally decrease the level of safety people enjoy. They may keep a product off the market that would have increased the safety and health of potential buyers, or they may stifle research and development that would otherwise lead to safer products. By banning products people want to buy, they may indirectly cause creation of black markets for those products, and the products sold illegally may be less safe than those sold legally because they are not as easily inspected and tested. To illustrate this kind of indirect effect of safety regulations, let's turn from the CPSC and the NHTSA to the oldest of safety regulators, the FDA.

──────────────────────── **Life and death under the FDA**

The thalidomide scare alerted the public to an inherent risk in pharmaceutical technology: a new drug may turn out to have dangerous side effects. These side effects may be far more harmful than any benefits that the drug promises. As we noted earlier, Congress responded to the thalidomide scare by passing a set of drug law amendments in 1962 that required more extensive testing of new drugs than had previously been required. New and tougher standards for approval of new drugs were also adopted.

The 1962 amendments had a very noticeable impact on the drug industry. In the five years prior to the 1962 changes, it took an average of about 6 months for a new drug application to be processed by the FDA; after 1962 the average delay climbed to 27.5 months. Moreover, prior to 1962 the number of new chemical entities coming on the market was 41.5 a year; after 1962 the average dropped to 16.1 a year.

Presumably, the new, stricter procedures screened out some risky drugs—a clear gain. But in reducing one kind of risk the new FDA regulations increased another kind: the risk of delaying or preventing altogether the use of beneficial new drugs.

Sam Peltzman, the student of auto safety, has also given attention to this problem. As an example, he cites a group of drugs introduced some years back to treat tuberculosis. According to his estimate, if these drugs had been delayed for two years—less than the average delay today—the result would have been forty-five thousand additional deaths. Or take the case of penicillin. Penicillin has saved tens of thousands of people from pain and death, yet the drug is known to cause serious side effects in some people. Many observers believe that penicillin, if discovered today, could not pass all of the relevant FDA tests.

This last example raises an interesting anomoly in our federal drug laws: the tough standards and testing requirements apply only to new drugs. They are not applied to drugs approved for sale before 1962. There are other anomolies as well. Once a drug has been approved for one medical purpose, the FDA cannot prevent doctors from prescribing the drug for other, nonapproved purposes. In 1978, for example, scientists discovered that the daily use of an approved drug, anturane, could more than halve the number of deaths by heart attack among former heart attack victims. The FDA has still not approved the use of anturane for this purpose, but since it has already approved the drug for another purpose, the FDA cannot stop doctors from prescribing the drug for heart attack patients.

Has the FDA actually kept useful drugs off the market? It certainly has. The FDA in 1977 finally approved a revolutionary antiulcer drug, cimetidine, but the drug was approved only after considerable delay. Peptic ulcer sufferers had been using it in Europe for several years. The FDA in 1978 finally approved sodium valproate, a drug that acts as an anticonvulsant for epileptics. But its use as an anticonvulsant was discovered twenty years earlier, and it had been available to epileptics in other countries for over a decade.

Murray Weidenbaum, a former chairman of the President's Council of Economic Advisers, furnishes some other important examples. It seems that the United States was the 30th country to approve the antiasthma drug metaporoterenol. It was the 32d country to approve the anticancer drug adriamycin, the 64th country to approve the antiallergenic drug cromolyn, and the 106th country to approve the antibacterial drug co-trimoxazole. All in all, *Medical Economics* estimates that three-quarters of the new drugs produced each year by U.S. firms go exclusively to foreign countries. Their use is barred to our own citizens.

One of the most notorious examples is a class of drugs called "beta-blockers," useful in the treatment of heart disease. A dozen or more beta-blockers, widely used in Europe, were long denied to people in this country. Professor William Wardell at the Center for the Study of Drug Development, University of Rochester, estimated that if these drugs had been available to heart patients in the U.S., ten thousand heart-related deaths per year could have been prevented.

Not all of the delay in getting drugs approved is caused by the time it takes to do all of the testing the FDA requires. In a good many cases, American companies wait for years before they do any testing at all. Why? Because testing itself is extremely costly. On the average, the FDA reviews about 120,000 pages of complex data for each new drug. And, over the last twenty years, the costs of preparing such reports have skyrocketed. In 1962, the research and development cost for a new drug was about $4 million. Today, that figure is over $50 million.

Few companies are willing to spend that much money unless the chances are good that the drug will eventually be approved and sell to a large number of customers. Take the case of sodium valproate. American drug companies judged the demand, based on the number of epileptics, to be too small to justify the high costs. So they waited until years of experience with European patients showed that the drug could probably pass the FDA tests.

Remember that it is not *always* wrong to keep useful drugs off the market during testing. The question is one of degree—of balancing one risk against another. What an economist must ask is whether the FDA has gone too far in erecting barriers to the marketing of new drugs. Once again the pioneering study was made by Sam Peltzman.

As one might imagine, Peltzman encountered serious difficulties in measuring the effects of FDA policy. Both the good effects and the harmful effects are unseen. Nonetheless, he made the Herculean effort: by using a very complex methodology, he arrived at the conclusion that the 1962 drug amendments imposed costs that far exceeded the benefits. He even attempted to translate these costs into monetary terms by assigning a monetary value to life and limb, much in the same way that courts assign such values in accident and injury cases. In monetary terms, Peltzman estimated that FDA regulations cost consumers between $250 million and $500 million a year.

Other investigators may quibble with some of Peltzman's numbers. But a growing number are agreeing with his basic conclusion: under the 1962 amendments, the FDA is simply doing more harm than good. Observers are also concerned about another related problem: each year more and more Americans are buying drugs illegally. These are drugs that the FDA says we can't have, but millions are willing to risk fines and imprisonment to buy them. What's more, such drugs often become adulterated on the black market because they escape normal inspection procedures.

Today more than ever before, doctors are telling their patients about drugs that are available in Mexico, Europe, and elsewhere, but that are banned in the United States. When the patients then buy these drugs illegally and without prescriptions, they run the risk of buying contaminated drugs. As a result, FDA policy may make things a lot worse than if no ban existed at all.

Regulation, certification, and economic efficiency

So why have regulation at all? Why not let consumers buy whatever they want to buy? Why not let producers produce and sell any product the public demands?

Economists cannot answer these questions to everyone's satisfaction. They don't even try. Instead, economists have tended to focus on the problem most easily answered by economic theory: economic efficiency. Achieving efficiency is not the same thing as minimizing accidents and injuries. If we wanted to do that we might outlaw bicycles, the nation's number one cause of accident and injury. After that we might outlaw motorcycles, and perhaps automobiles as well. These measures would certainly eliminate a lot of accidents and injuries. But the price, for most of us, would be far too high.

What, then, does economic efficiency mean in the area of safety? To explore its meaning, let's look at a very simple example.

Suppose a consumer fully understands all of the risks involved in the use of a product. In spite of this knowledge, the consumer wants to buy the product and use it. Suppose also, that in using the product, the consumer does not pose any potential harm to others. Suppose that a seller is willing to produce and sell the product. Then both buyer and seller would be better off, *from their own points of view*, if the exchange were allowed. To prevent the exchange would make both worse off than they could be. Under these circumstances disallowing the exchange would be inefficient.

Of course, in constructing our example, we just made a lot of suppositions. In the real world things may be different. When they are different, problems arise. For example, the use of some consumer products necessarily endangers other people. If we drive cars with faulty brakes we risk not only our own health and safety but that of others as well. But if we make decisions based on our own self-interest, we will take into account only personal benefits and personal costs. We will tend to ignore the additional costs and risks we create for others. Speed limit laws and laws requiring brake and headlight inspections, therefore, may be seen as attempts to keep us from imposing high costs and risks on others.

Most of our safety regulations, however, are not of this type. In most cases, the products we consume only pose a threat to the user. But for these products there is another problem that may arise: the problem of consumer information. In our hypothetical exchange we assumed that the consumer knew all of the relevant facts about the product being purchased. In the real world this is rarely true. In a complex, technological society, consumers are often not competent to evaluate all of the safety features of a product. Even if consumers have all of the technical information —scientific reports, test results, and so on—they often lack the training necessary to evaluate it. What's more, it would be very costly for consumers to become well informed about every product they use. The cost of becoming completely informed about all consumer products would be enormous: it would far exceed any possible benefit.

Consumers, then, often act out of ignorance. And because of ignorance they may think the products they buy are safer than they really are. When this happens, allowing free markets to go undisturbed might result in less safety than consumers actually want or less than they would want if they knew all of the facts.

According to some economists, then, regulation can serve a valuable function. Regulators should use their expertise to evaluate all of the technical information available and should then decide what decision a typical consumer would make if that consumer knew and appreciated all of the relevant facts. In this way, regulators help consumers get the kind of products they really want.

Other economists strongly disagree. According to them there is a better and more efficient way to deal with information problems. Instead of regulation, they claim, all we really need is *certification.* Through certification the government simply provides information to consumers—it certifies the safety features and the risks, but the ultimate choice is left to the consumers themselves.

The health hazard posed by cigarettes is an example of one problem handled through certification. Cigarettes are not outlawed, even though the Surgeon General believes that smoking is hazardous to health. Instead, manufacturers are required to post warnings on cigarette packages and in cigarette advertisements. Consumers are left free to smoke as many cigarettes as they want.

There are other current examples of certification: the CPSC has published a booklet warning homeowners of possible fire hazards associated with aluminum electrical wiring. The FDA requires posted warnings by the producers of saccharin, estrogen, oral contraceptives, and hearing aids. At the time of this writing, required warnings have also been proposed for a number of prescription drugs. In each case, consumers will be alerted to possible dangers, but they will still be able to make their own choices.

Advocates of certification say there are several reasons why certification is more efficient than regulation. First, consumers may differ radically in their attitudes toward safety. When regulators make decisions about what a typical consumer wants, they necessarily disregard the wants of millions of untypical consumers. Take the case of carcinogenic agents: under current law the FDA is required to remove a chemical agent from the market if it determines that even one person out of the entire population is likely to get cancer by using it. But judging by the number of cigarette smokers, a large number of people take a very different view toward cancer risks. What the FDA might do instead is issue a probability number. It might say that with normal consumption of product X the probability of cancer is 1 in 100,000. People could then evaluate this risk along with the price and other characteristics of the product and make their own decisions.

Second, a product which poses risks for one person may not pose any risk for another. Yet safety regulations normally impose the same standards on everyone. For example, there is some evidence that saccharin may cause bladder cancer in males. There is no evidence that it causes cancer in females. When the FDA tried to ban the sale of saccharin in 1977, however, it tried to ban sales to all consumers, male and female.

Third, the experts themselves often disagree on the safety features of consumer products. When there is disagreement, at least someone is mistaken. Regulation, however, allows no dissent. The mistakes of the regulators are imposed on all of society. And mistakes there are. One of the most dramatic was the government's attempt to protect children from flammable fabrics by forcing manufacturers to use the flame-retardant chemical, Tris. After 45 million children had been exposed, it was discovered that Tris was a dangerous, cancer-causing agent. Critics charge that if the experts themselves disagree there is no reason why consumers should have to abide by the opinion of any one of them. Instead we might let consumers do what they do with nonregulated products—rely on the expert of their choice.

Fourth, certification is essentially a method of helping consumers get the kind of products they really like. Its aim is to prevent mistakes, not to coerce. By contrast, regulation attempts to keep people from doing what they want to do. It does not try to change attitudes—only behavior. As a result, regulation often produces many of the unintended, unwanted, and perhaps unpredictable indirect effects we have examined.

Finally, proponents of certification point to the fact that many—perhaps most—safety regulations are a lot less efficient than they could be. In fact, regulators often impose regulations that they know are inefficient. Take the case of sodium nitrite, a suspected cancer-causing agent used in curing meat. In 1978, the Department of Agriculture and the FDA proposed to ban the substance. The potential cost threatened to be large: the phasing out of a 12.5 billion dollar industry and no more ham, bacon, or sausage in our diet. The potential benefits were known to be practically nil. Nitrites (or nitrates, from which they are formed) abound in natural substances. On the average, cured meats are the source of only 2 percent of the nitrites in a person's body. That's less than is contained in a normal person's saliva.

Why are regulations so often inefficient? Because many regulating decisions are the outcome of political struggles between competing interest groups. In these struggles each group is trying to achieve some goal or objective quite different from economic efficiency. Let's take a brief look at some of these struggles and see why they occur.

The politics of safety

What ultimately determines the safety standards set by government agencies? In principle these standards are determined by voters through the ballot box, through communications to their elected representatives, through lobbying efforts, and so forth. But not all citizens are equally concerned with safety regulations. Nor do they all have the same motivations. In particular, there are at least four different kinds of interests whose influence has proved to be important in the past: consumers, consumer action groups, producers, and the bureaucrats who actually set the standards. Let's look at each of these in turn.

Consumers, for their part, don't want any hidden surprises in the products they buy. They do not want to discover, after the fact, that the product they are using is less safe than they thought it was. Regulation of safety features reduces the likelihood of unforeseen risks. But why regulation rather than certification? Why not let government simply label products "safe" or "unsafe"? Wouldn't that achieve the goal of regulation without many of the undesirable side effects?

It is possible that most consumers have never thought about certification as an alternative to regulation; it is also possible that consumers sometimes make errors in their thinking about economics. But there are other reasons why fully informed consumers might prefer regulation to certification. For one thing, consumers might not want to be tempted. Shopping in the marketplace, some consumers might choose to buy less safe products for a cheaper price. Upon reflection, however, they may decide that such choices are bad ones. With regulation they would not have the opportunity to yield to the temptations of the moment. Also, consumers might want regulation not to control their own behavior but to control the behavior of their neighbors. This seems especially true in the area of drugs.

Consumer action groups, as distinct from consumers themselves, are another source of influence on safety regulation. Although these groups often claim to represent consumers in general, we treat them as a separate interest here because their goals and motivations are often quite different from those of consumers. Rather than forcing producers to supply what consumers really want, these groups often try to force producers to supply what they as "experts" believe that consumers ought to have.

A case in point is an auto safety regulation governing new cars sold in 1974. In that year auto producers were required to install an ignition system that remained inoperative as long as the seat belts were unbuckled. The regulation was actively supported by consumer groups lobbying before Congress, but consumers themselves were very annoyed. So many consumers complained to Congress that the law was repealed for the following year. The proposed saccharin ban, a lobbying goal of several "public interest" groups, is another example. After being deluged with mail from angry constituents, Congress moved quickly to block the ban.

Throughout most of the history of safety legislation, though, consumers and consumer action groups have had only a marginal influence on the content of most of our safety laws. Consumers have often communicated to Congress that "something ought to be done." But what actually *was* done was governed far more by producer interests.

This is understandable. Most of us probably have no idea what bicycle safety regulations require—even if we do know about them, we are unlikely to be thinking about bicycles when we cast our vote in the polling booth. The same holds true for most consumer products.

On the other hand, there are workers and managers who spend a good part of their lives producing bicycles or other consumer products that are subject to safety regulations. They derive all or most of their income from such activities. There are also stockholders and bondholders whose economic fortunes are closely tied to those of the regulated firms. Safety regulations are very much on the minds of these people, and for good reasons.

A safety regulation may mean the loss of a job and a substantial loss of income to those whose firms are affected. On the other hand, a safety regulation that takes a competitor's product off the market or that closes the door to foreign imports may mean more job security, more income, and a large jump in firm profits.

Take the case of the Meat Inspection Act of 1906, one of our earliest pieces of safety legislation. Indignant readers of *The Jungle* gave strong public support to the Meat Inspection Act, but it is doubtful that they appreciated its specifics. Not so the major Chicago meat-packers: they had substantial influence on the bill's provisions and actively lobbied for its passage.

The requirements of that act, and of the many subsequent acts in the years that followed, were requirements that the major packing houses were already meeting or that they could meet at minimal additional cost. The economic burden would fall upon competitors—the smaller firms that sold lower-quality products at lower prices. Moreover, the products of the largest firms could now sell at home and abroad with the U.S. government's stamp of approval. The inspection, of course, was carried out at the taxpayers' expense.

A more modern example is lawnmower safety. It appears that in 1973 most of the major producers of lawnmowers were already meeting certain minimal safety standards. But some smaller firms were not. The firms that were not meeting standards were able to sell their mowers for about five to eighteen dollars less than firms meeting standards could sell the safer mowers. The major manufacturers became worried that they might lose a lot of sales to the smaller firms, so they asked the CPSC to compel the smaller firms to meet the same safety standards the large firms had adopted.

In this case things went awry, however. The CPSC agreed in principle, but after conducting its own investigation it proposed even tougher safety standards. The new proposals would have added 24 percent to the cost of a walk-behind mower and 35 percent to the cost of a riding mower. The major firms were horrified—they concluded that the CPSC proposals would not only put the small firms out of business, but they might also drive out a lot of the large firms as well. So the majors spent about $3 million lobbying against the CPSC proposals. Modified standards were imposed in 1981.

One of the most dramatic safety battles in recent years was over the issue of air bags in automobiles. The battle pitted two giant lobbying forces: the auto industry and the insurance industry. Both sides in the debate mounted major lobbying campaigns in Congress and bought full-page advertisements in newspapers and magazines to win public support.

In this case, the insurance industry, fresh from several earlier victories in the car-safety battle, prodded Congress into requiring air bags in cars produced in the early 1980s. The case for air bags was quite controversial: if only people would buckle up, seat belts provide more protection than air bags. But a lot of people are not buckling up. The opposition of the auto producers was clearly based on economic self-interest. The car manufacturers reasoned, probably correctly, that most consumers don't want to bear the additional costs that air bags would create. As a result, the higher-priced cars would be less attractive to potential buyers.

Finally, the safety regulators themselves represent an important political interest. Consider the position of the commissioners of the FDA. We noted earlier that there are basically two kinds of mistakes they can make: they can allow a harmful drug to be sold on the market, and they can keep a useful drug off the market. The two mistakes are not equally costly to the commissioners, however.

Allowing a harmful drug to be sold on the market will undoubtedly attract public attention. As in the case of thalidomide, people will actually see the damage. It will receive media coverage. Congressional investigations will be called. Job security will be threatened.

Keeping a useful drug off the market is different. True, diseases could have been cured. Lives could have been saved. But who knows it? A few doctors. A few drug companies. Perhaps a few patients. By and large, the harm caused by this type of mistake is hidden from the public view. The penalties for making such a mistake are minor compared to the penalties for mistakes of the first type.

As a result, safety regulators often face political incentives that lead them to make too many mistakes of the second type—that lead them to keep too many useful drugs off the market. They have a political interest in adopting policies that are overly cautious, despite the fact that these policies may impose high costs on the consuming public.

An evaluation

What judgment can we make about safety regulation by the standards of efficiency, equality, and liberty?

We have gone to some length to analyze the effects of regulation by the standard of economic efficiency. The evidence suggests that many of our regulations are inefficient. Their costs are much higher than any corresponding benefits. Moreover, we could achieve greater efficiency in many areas by simply providing consumers with more information rather than attempting to regulate the products they buy. In terms of efficiency, certification beats regulation hands down.

What about our second criterion of equality? Do safety regulations affect poor consumers in a different way than they affect other consumers? At first glance it might seem that the poor have the most to gain from safety regulations. After all, they are typically less informed and less educated than are other consumers. They are also more likely to purchase cheaper, less safe products in the marketplace. A closer look at the actual impact of safety regulations, however, suggests that the poor are often harmed by regulation. And they may suffer greater burdens than other consumers.

Why? The major reason is that the demand for safety tends to rise as income rises. The more income consumers have, the more likely they are to trade some other goods and services for more safety. For example, as we noted earlier, although Ford and GM had little luck selling safety features, Mercedes has begun offering an optional safety package, including an air bag, on its high-priced cars. Conversely, the demand for safety tends to be lower when incomes are lower. At lower income levels people are more likely to trade a little safety in return for other goods and services.

Put in other terms, a poor consumer may well prefer an ordinary lawnmower to no lawnmower at all; an ordinary ladder to no ladder at all; an ordinary bicycle to no bicycle at all. When safety regulations raise the prices of the goods we buy, poor consumers are often the first to be priced out of the market. In this way safety regulations probably cause more harm to low-income consumers than to other consumers.

An illustration of this principle occurred in Philadelphia in 1974. At that time most of the older housing was painted with lead-based paint that could cause lead poisoning in children if ingested. So a federal agency disallowed the sale of any housing units unless the lead-based paint had been completely removed. The removal process was very expensive; it became practically impossible for low-income families to buy an old, moderately priced dwelling. Many of the poor families probably had no small chidren, and many were probably already living in houses or apartments painted with lead based paint. Many probably could have discovered other, less expensive ways of dealing with the hazard, but the regulations left them little choice.

Turning now to the standard of liberty, we find that a case for regulation can indeed be made if the use of a product might endanger the health and safety of someone else. But if only the immediate consumer is put at risk, it is another matter. Advocates of liberty generally hold that people "own" their bodies—they do not need to ask the permission of others before deciding what physical risks they will take. In fact, most advocates of liberty would go so far as to argue that each person has the right to commit suicide. If people have the right to commit suicide they certainly have the right to consume unsafe products if they choose.

The most dramatic recent example pitting individual liberty against safety regulation has been the case of laetrile. Many consumers, but almost no reputable medical experts, believe laetrile has remarkable powers to cure cancer. Using rhetoric that made it sound like freedom of speech or religion were at stake, legislators in several states have legalized or attempted to legalize intrastate production and use of laetrile, even though the FDA outlaws interstate commerce in the drug. Significantly, these legislative attempts have been supported by people who themselves believe the drug to be worthless but who believe in the right of others to delude themselves if they so choose.

In short, whether we look at safety regulation from the point of view of efficiency, equality, or liberty, there comes a point beyond which regulation becomes counterproductive. There is a feeling that at least some regulators have already crossed this line. Whether this feeling will give rise to a politically effective backlash, and whether that backlash itself might go too far, remains to be seen.

Questions for thought and discussion

1. One argument for safety regulation is this: "Every person's consumption of an unsafe product imposes potential costs on others. After all, if people become sick or seriously injured, society may have to take care of them."

   Do you agree? What if the person is very wealthy and can pay for his or her own medical expenses? What if the individual has adequate insurance? Should safety regulations apply only to those who are not wealthy or who are not amply insured?

2. Evaluate the following argument: "Safety regulations should apply only to the uninformed. Those consumers who are well informed should be able to purchase any product they like."

3. Do you believe a person should have the right to commit suicide? What about obligations to family or financial obligations? Does the right only apply to single people with no financial obligations?

4. One consumer believes in "safety at any price." Another consumer believes that "safety comes last" (at least up to a point). On a carefully labeled graph, show what the demand curve for safety might look like for each of these two individuals. Can you say anything about the elasticity of demand for these two individuals?

5. On a carefully labeled graph, use a demand curve to show why seat belt use is different for city driving than for highway driving. Assume that seat belt use has a price (a cost).

Selected references

Campbell, Rita R. *Food Safety Regulation: A Study in the Use and Limitations of Cost-Benefit Analysis.* Washington, D.C.: American Enterprise Institute, 1974.

Grabowski, Henry G., and John M. Vernon. *The Regulation of Pharmaceuticals: Balancing the Benefits and Risks.* Washington, D.C.: American Enterprise Institute, 1983.

Manne, Henry L., and Roger L. Miller. *Auto Safety Regulation: The Cure or the Problem.* Glen Ridge, N.J.: Thomas Horton and Daughters, 1976.

5

Consumer Fraud

Suppose an auto-repair shop confirms your suspicion that your car needs a new clutch. Actually the shop installs a used clutch and charges you for a new one. Or suppose a doctor takes out your appendix even though, unbeknownst to you, your appendix is normal. Or suppose someone sells you a house and tells you that brand-new plumbing has been installed, while in fact the pipes are old and corroded. In any of these cases you would be a victim of fraud.

Each year thousands of consumers are victimized by fraud. More still fall victim to deceptive practices that may not fall within the precise legal definition of fraud, but that are certainly fraudulent in spirit.[1] Take the case of *gypsy* automobile parts—cheap and inferior imitations of major-brand auto parts often packaged so the consumer doesn't notice the difference. Ford Motor Company, for example, makes auto parts under the brand name *Motorcraft.* Gypsy parts are sold in almost identical boxes—same coloring, same design. The only difference is that gypsy boxes have such

---

1. In law, there are precise tests for the existence of fraud; those tests exclude many deceptive practices. From an economic point of view these distinctions are largely unimportant. In this chapter we will use the word *fraud* to refer to any misleading claim or omission in a seller's promotion of a product.

names as *Motor-care* or *Motorcar* in the same type size and face as *Motor-craft*. General Motors sells parts under the name *AC-Delco*. An identical gypsy box will simply leave off the letters *AC*—or, in smaller type, the word *Replaces* will appear above *AC-Delco*.

Fraud, of course, implies consumer dissatisfaction, but consumer dissatisfaction does not necessarily imply fraud. Suppose, for example, a theater advertises a movie as "thrilling" and "exciting." A reasonable customer is expected to know that these descriptions are purely subjective; many people might think the movie is boring. Similarly, the buyer of a used car is assumed to know that future performance is somewhat less certain than for a new car; buying a used car is, in part, a gamble. Consumer dissatisfaction may also arise because a mistake is made by the buyer or seller. For example, a person might buy a coat thinking that it will be washable without carefully checking the label, which turns out to say "dry clean only." Some such mistakes are correctable; others are not. But mistake alone does not constitute fraud.

The exact distinction between fraud and nonfraud may not always be clear. It often involves such slippery notions as whether the seller *intentionally* deceived the buyer or whether the deception was unintentional. Obviously the distinction will be hard to make in some cases, but the distinction between fraud and nonfraud is still an important one, both in law and in economics. An honest seller tries to create consumer satisfaction; to the extent that buyers are happy with their purchases, sales increase. So do profits. If customers are dissatisfied, the honest seller will try to find out why and will try to make adjustments. Consumer satisfaction and the pursuit of profit go hand in hand.

Dishonest sellers, on the other hand, have different motives. They sell people products they don't want through lies and deceit. They not only *expect* consumer dissatisfaction, they expect to *profit* from it—the more deception, the more profits. Aside from the simple injustice involved, such dishonesty results in economic waste. Time, effort, and real resources are devoted to the production and sale of products that consumers do not want instead of to the production of products that they do want.

How serious is the problem of fraud? Public-opinion surveys show that consumer dissatisfaction is on the increase. Over half of all adults believe that they are getting a worse deal on consumer purchases today than they were ten years ago, and they are doing a lot more complaining. Most of these complaints do not involve fraud. But it is difficult to know exactly how much fraud is taking place. Buyers are prone to yell fraud even when there is none. And sellers, naturally, rarely admit they have defrauded anyone. Nonetheless, the evidence suggests that in some areas fraudulent practices are widespread.

Apparently one such area is automobile repair. A study conducted for the Department of Transportation in 1979 concluded that fifty-three cents of every dollar spent for auto repair work is wasted on needless work. For the nation as a whole, that comes to over $25 billion a year. As part of the study, five cars, each with a defective spark plug, were taken to different repair shops. The cost of replacing the spark plug was $13.63. But after the mechanics did other work, which they claimed was necessary, and some optional work, which they recommended, the average bill became $119.24, or $105.61 more than necessary. The abuses ranged from simple negligence to criminal fraud.

Despite the publicity given this and similar studies, consumer problems with auto-repair shops seem to be on the rise. In fact, a recent congressional survey revealed that automobile repair ranks number one on consumer complaint lists across the country. Abuses include practices such as intentionally writing repair estimates that are lower than final repair costs, installing used parts but charging consumers for new ones, and installing unnecessary replacement parts. All of these are examples of consumer fraud.

Medical surgery is another area that is highly suspect. During the 1970s, the number of operations performed rose 23 percent, while the population rose only 5 percent. There are twice as many surgeons per capita in the United States as there are in Great Britain. There are also twice the number of operations per capita in the United States. In Chapter 3, we gave reasons for thinking that some necessary operations are not done in Great Britain. On the other hand, mounting evidence suggests that many unnecessary operations are done in the United States. For example, over a quarter of all Americans have their tonsils or adenoids removed by the time they are twenty-one. But a study by Dr. Charles Blueston of Children's Hospital of Pittsburgh suggests that only 8 percent of the removals were clearly justified. An extensive study by Dr. Eugene McCarthy of Cornell University Medical College claims that, overall, two million unnecessary operations are performed each year. Appendectomies, hysterectomies, and prostate operations join tonsillectomies at the top of the suspect list.

How many of these operations involved fraud? It's not clear. Often the experts disagree on whether surgery is necessary; in many cases it is the patients themselves who push for elective surgery. But there is no doubt that the financial incentives of surgeons and hospitals play a role. One recent survey examined federal employees covered by different types of medical insurance. Those under a Blue Shield Plan— which paid surgeons on a fee-for-service basis—had twice as many operations as those enrolled in a prepaid plan where surgeons drew a flat salary regardless of whether they operated. As a presidential adviser for health issues put it, "There's an economic incentive—the more surgery you do, the more money you get."

So what should be done? Are we getting enough consumer protection? Before we answer these questions, let's take a closer look at some of the causes of fraud and some of the methods that are used to combat it.

The economic causes of fraud

A natural reaction to the problem of fraud is to regard it as a problem of bad character. After all, if people are basically honest there will be less fraud. If they are basically dishonest there will be more fraud. Although this theory is partially valid, economists usually don't approach the problem that way. Economists are more likely to ask about penalties and rewards. Where rewards are high or penalties low we expect to see a lot of fraud. Where rewards are low and penalties high we expect to see less fraud.

Looking at fraud in terms of incentives leads us to the conclusion that fraud will be most prevalent in markets where information is costly. If consumers don't know much about the product or service in question, it will be easy to find victims. Rewards will correspondingly be great. Even better, consumers may be so ignorant that they will not even realize the fraud has occurred. How many people, for example, would be able to tell whether the brake shoes a repair shop replaced were really completely worn out? If fraud is never discovered, the penalties obviously are nil.

We should point out that there is often a rational basis for ignorance on the part of consumers. Where information costs time and money to obtain, the costs of becoming informed may be greater than the benefit of escaping fraud.

Fortunately for consumers, however, honest business people often have strong economic incentives to make accurate information cheaply available. The reason is simple. In a world where information is costly, buyers typically put a lot of stock in a firm's reputation, a fact that gives firms strong incentives to protect their reputations. If a firm relies on repeat business from the same customers, deceptive practices are likely to be bad for business. Upon discovering the deception customers will cease buying and will go to competitors instead. Even if repeat sales to the same customers are infrequent, other customers will discover the fraudulent practices, and prospective sales will be lost. So most business people are quite honest, simply because, for most of them, honesty pays.

Still, some sellers may discover that the benefits of fraud are greater than the cost of a sacrificed reputation. This is especially true when consumers are not likely to discover the deception. Medical care is one example; in certain respects, auto repair is another. It is also true when the seller is relatively immune to consumer retaliation. If the seller has no fixed location, low visibility, and no stable customers, penalties may never be imposed even if the deception is discovered. Some kinds of door-to-door sales operations would fit this pattern; so would producers of gypsy auto parts.

It follows that consumer fraud, like other crimes, will sometimes pay. Moreover, the more it pays, the more of it there will be. Accordingly, if we can find ways to make fraud less profitable, we should be able to reduce the amount of fraud. Before we look at some methods to combat fraud, however, let's stop to ask a more general question. How much effort should we make to eliminate fraud?

At first glance it might seem that we should try to get rid of fraud altogether. This goal is noble but not necessarily rational. In fact, just as we can do too little to deter fraud, we can also do too much. Why? On the one hand, as we have noted, fraud involves economic waste. Real resources are used to produce and sell products that consumers do not want. On the other hand, combatting fraud also involves time, effort, and money. The attempt to eliminate all fraud would simply be too costly.

The standard of economic efficiency requires that we attempt to deter fraud until the last dollar spent on deterrence creates a dollar's worth of benefit. If we get less than a dollar's worth of benefit, then we are being wasteful in combatting fraud—we could benefit more by spending our dollars elsewhere. If we get more than a dollar's worth of benefit, then we are also being wasteful because we could be better off by spending still more to deter fraud and less on other things.

Are we making enough effort to combat fraud by this standard? Let's look first at some market responses to the problem of fraud. Then we will examine the role of government.

Combatting fraud through the market[2]

At the same time the increasing complexity of modern society makes it more difficult for a consumer to be fully informed, it also does something else. It makes information more valuable. Consumers who are willing to invest time, effort, and money to learn about the products they buy can expect a bigger payoff. Economic theory, therefore, predicts that consumers will respond to these changing conditions by investing more in information. The prediction is accurate if we are to believe a recent Louis Harris survey. That survey found that over 75 percent of adults surveyed believed that they had sharpened their buying skills over the last decade. To the degree that they actually did so, the deterrent to fraud is enhanced.

Economic theory also predicts that if the demand for information increases, more of it will be supplied. People who have technical knowledge or who specialize in obtaining such knowledge will have greater incentives to increase the supply. The supply of product information has in fact increased in three ways. First, some organizations, such as Consumers Union, have found that they can evaluate products and sell the resulting information to consumers; *Consumer Reports* magazine is the highly

---

2. Parts of this and the following section are based on Richard Posner, *Regulation of Advertising by the FTC* (Washington, D.C.: American Enterprise Institute, 1973).

successful result. Second, honest sellers find that it is in their self-interest to make more information available to consumers about their own products. Sellers of automobiles, cigarettes, and stereo equipment often publicize the results of independent studies to encourage consumers to recognize differences in product quality.

Third, honest sellers have an incentive to reveal the fraudulent claims of their competitors. The National Advertising Division of the Council of Better Business Bureaus acts as a clearinghouse for complaints by consumers and competitors. The influential newspaper *Advertising Age* regularly publicizes the council's actions, thereby putting other advertisers on notice that deceptive practices will not slip by unnoticed. In addition, the last decade has witnessed a blossoming of *comparative advertising*—advertisements used by one firm to compare its own product with a competitor's product. Instead of the traditional references to "Brand X," advertisers today are naming names. In fact, about one out of ten commercials on television today is an example of comparative advertising.

Fraud may also be deterred within the private sector through the courts. Consumers who are the victims of fraudulent practices often have a private legal remedy—they may go to court and seek compensation for the damages they have suffered. Sometimes their task is made easier by rulings that make class action suits feasible; such suits involve the pooling of a large number of small consumer claims into a single court action.

All things considered, then, the private sector responds to a higher incidence of fraud with increased resistance. These private actions probably represent the most important deterrents to consumer fraud. But are they enough? Not in every case, unfortunately.

Consider an auto repair shop in a large city. The deceptive practices of this shop may impose an enormous burden on customers collectively, but no one of them has a good incentive to fully investigate the work done on his or her car. A complete investigation would be expensive and the benefits would be small. Pressing a claim in court can be costly; court costs, in fact, may be higher than the actual damages. A class action suit is impractical unless many other similarly affected customers can be identified.

Advertising by competitors is also likely to prove impractical. If an honest repair shop exposed a dishonest one, the dishonest one would go out of business; but the honest shop could probably expect only a trickle of new customers. Most of the defrauded customers would patronize other competitors. As a consequence, honest repair shops have very weak incentives to expose dishonest ones.

Under conditions such as these, a strong argument can be made in favor of a role for government. By exposing auto-repair fraud, a government agency could create benefits well in excess of the cost of the effort for consumers as a group. In principle it could perform a service that no single customer or firm has an incentive to perform.

Is this what government is doing? Let's take a look.

======= **Combatting fraud through government**

The Federal Trade Commission (FTC) was established in 1915 as an independent federal agency. Among other duties the agency was directed to prevent "unfair methods of competition," a mandate that was later expanded to include "unfair or deceptive acts or practices." The meaning of these terms was never fully specified by Congress. Nonetheless, from its earliest days the FTC has devoted substantial resources to prosecuting consumer fraud cases.

The procedure works like this: initially, the FTC issues a complaint alleging that a particular seller has engaged in deceptive practices. If the seller wishes to challenge the complaint, an administrative hearing is held and evidence is presented. Upon a finding of guilty the FTC may order the seller to cease and desist from unlawful conduct. It may also impose fines and spell out certain requirements that the seller must follow.

How well has this procedure worked? For the first sixty years of the FTC's life, no one really tried to answer this question in a systematic way. Then Richard Posner of the University of Chicago Law School conducted a detailed study. His conclusions were profoundly disappointing.

Posner divided FTC actions into four categories. His first category consisted of cases in which no serious deception was involved. These cases did not represent wise use of FTC resources for the obvious reason that little or no harm was done in the first place.

Posner's second category consisted of cases in which serious harm was done but in which the FTC need not intervene at the taxpayers' expense because private remedies appeared to be adequate.

The third category consisted of cases of clearly criminal fraud—such as the actions of fly-by-night con artists. While action needed to be taken against such people, Posner argued that the FTC lacked the power to do so. Cease-and-desist orders would have little impact against operators who were here today and gone tomorrow; by the same token, it would be impossible to collect fines that might be imposed.

That left category four, those cases where FTC action was appropriate. These were cases of serious deception where private remedies were not effective but where the FTC's civil penalties were. Posner found that in 1963 only 11 percent of the cases handled were appropriate ones. Five years later, in 1968, the figure was down to 3 percent.

Of course, a study such as Posner's naturally requires an exercise of judgment about which cases are serious and which are not. Perhaps some economists would quarrel with some of Posner's characterizations. For example, he did not think it seriously deceptive that a toy manufacturer failed to disclose that the projectiles fired by its toy did not actually explode. (If they had actually exploded, perhaps the FTC would at least have turned the case over to the Consumer Product Safety Commission!) Nor did he think the FTC invested its resources wisely when it ordered a maker of "First Prize" bobby pins to change the brand name so the consumers wouldn't think buying the bobby pins qualified them to enter a contest. Would you feel seriously deceived by an advertisement including an athlete's endorsement of a candy bar because it did not reveal that the athlete had been paid? Posner did not count this as serious deception. Or what about a more recent FTC case challenging comic book advertisements as deceptive if, among other things, they include endorsements of the product by the same cartoon characters the comic book itself featured?

All in all, Posner's study makes us question whether the FTC has used its resources efficiently. Too much time appears to have been spent in areas where the conceivable return is small. Too little time has been spent in areas where the conceivable return is large.

The FTC has, in recent years, responded to criticisms such as those leveled by Posner. Under the aggressive leadership of Michael Pertschuk, appointed FTC chairman by President Carter, the agency began a flurry of proceedings. These were not aimed at trivial cases: the targets included such heavyweights as used car dealers, life insurance firms, funeral parlors, and health spas. The potential benefits of preventing fraud in such cases would be large.

Some economists were concerned that the remedies advocated by Pertschuk would also have heavy costs, however. A proposed standard regulating used car sales brought a particularly great outcry. If the standard raised the costs of selling a used car too much, one of the main benefits of buying a used car would be lost.

Under the Reagan administration, the FTC has been headed by an economist, James C. Miller III, formerly one of the commission's critics. Miller, like Pertschuk, does not want to waste resources on trivial cases. The agency won't file a deceptive advertising claim against a maker of Danish pastry just because someone might believe it was actually made in Denmark, says one FTC staffer. At the same time, Miller is concerned about the costs of regulations. If regulations are too burdensome, he maintains, consumers could pay more for a product in extra costs than they would gain in accurate information.

But changing the direction of a major agency like the FTC is a job like that of turning an oil tanker: it is a long time from the moment when the captain gives the order until the new course is achieved. And even aside from the problem of bureaucratic momentum, it is not clear that Congress and state legislators have the political will to back up the regulators when they get serious about the job of consumer protection. Let's see why.

The politics of consumer fraud

If government agencies at the federal, state, and local levels devoted more resources to the prevention of serious consumer fraud, consumers would surely gain. Most business firms would probably gain as well. If dishonest sellers could be removed from the market, the honest sellers would enjoy higher sales and, for a while at least, higher profits. Most of us, therefore, have an economic interest in a more vigorous war against fraud.

Unfortunately, very few consumers have a clear idea of what they want government to do or why. This inhibits the efficient working of the political marketplace. Government agencies and the legislators who create them must decide upon the specific details of policy. In doing so, they will find many concerted interests who *do* know what they want and why. In the absence of any clear and precise mandate from the general public, politicians will tend to move forward where the opposition is weak and retreat where the opposition is strong.

We saw in our analysis of product safety that "consumer protection" often becomes the captive of special interests. A product that people really want to buy may be taken off the market. Safety equipment may be required even when most customers don't want it. As a result, consumers themselves may actually be reluctant to support consumer protection legislation—they may genuinely fear, perhaps correctly, that they will be harmed by it.

A similar principle applies to honest business firms. Poorly managed consumer protection may hurt the honest as well as the dishonest, and since most firms expect consumer protection agencies to be misguided, business groups often unite in opposition. Almost all auto-repair services, good as well as bad, oppose government intrusion into their industry. Almost all doctors, honest as well as dishonest, oppose government verification of the necessity for operations.

Powerful interest groups thus emerge to oppose government attempts to combat serious fraud, and this opposition is often successful. Consider the reaction to the FTC's brief stint with aggressiveness in the late 1970s. A vast army of interests, ranging from candy makers to morticians, descended on Congress. Full page ads attacking the FTC appeared in major magazines. Dozens of bills designed to limit the FTC's powers were introduced. In some cases, the FTC's opponents appeared to have legitimate complaints. But the outcome—the first time a legislative veto had ever been imposed on a regulatory agency—left the agency much less effective in combatting fraud.

We can see, then, that the political marketplace is not completely reliable in protecting the consumer against private fraud. Small wonder that it is ineffective in protecting us against one of the biggest perpetrators of deceptive practices—government itself.

Does the government live up to its own standards?

Who is the nation's biggest advertiser? The tobacco industry? General Motors? Pepsi-Cola? None of these. It is the U.S. government. There are no official figures on government advertising expenditures, but there are some informed guesses. The trade publication *Advertising Age* estimated federal government advertising at $110 million in 1974. For the same year, the General Accounting Office (GAO) put the figure at $182 million. These figures do not include the value of time and space donated by the private sector for "public-service" advertisements. Including those costs and the salaries of some "public-affairs" officers not counted by the GAO would probably double the figure. And none of these figures includes the cost of campaign advertising, which in election years outweighs the costs of all other government advertising put together.

One of the most notoriously deceptive government advertising campaigns is the one it conducts to promote the sale of U.S. savings bonds. These are touted as a reliable way for the small investor to build a secure nest egg for future needs. But in fact, U.S. savings bonds pay significantly lower interest rates than equally secure private substitutes like certificates of deposit at savings and loan associations. In fact, the interest paid on U.S. savings bonds has, in many years, not even been sufficient to compensate for the effects of the inflation the government has generated through its fiscal and monetary policies. Far from providing a secure nest egg for the future, savings bonds may return less, in real purchasing power, than the saver puts into them to begin with.

Or consider the Social Security system, discussed at length later in this book. If a private pension fund made statements to the public anywhere nearly as misleading as those the Social Security Administration routinely makes, it would clearly have the authorities down on it in a moment.

Congress appears to put out its share of fraudulent products as well. The *Congressional Record,* for example, is required by law to be a "substantially verbatim report" of the proceedings of the Senate and the House of Representatives. But 70 percent of the *Congressional Record* now consists of remarks never uttered in either chamber. Many entries are prefaced by phrases such as "I rise" or "I speak" to give a ring of authenticity when copies of the mythical speeches are sent home to constituents.

Finally, state and local governments can also be found engaging in deception. Consider certain statements issued by the mayor of New York shortly before that city's financial crisis became public. The *New York Times* charged that if the mayor had been the officer of a private corporation, he would have been liable to prosecution for his deception. As it was, he went unprosecuted. Municipal securities experts report that the incident is by no means unique.

--- **An evaluation**

Consumer fraud finds few defenders. It should come as no surprise that all three of our standards of evaluation warrant action to deter it.

Fraud is, first of all, a source of economic inefficiency. It tricks consumers into buying goods that are worth less to them than the money they spend. Often the goods or services purchased may actually be worth less than the resources used to produce them. To the extent we are concerned with the inefficiency caused by consumer fraud, of course, we should use efficient means to combat it. Resources should be directed to those cases where the harm is greatest and the opportunities for solving the problem most promising.

There is also little reason to believe that fraud helps the poor. An occasional con artist may work his or her own way out of poverty by means of fraud, but such a person's victims are themselves likely to be poor.

Finally, fraud is a violation of individual rights and liberties. Fraud is a form of theft that, although not carried out by overt violence, has the same coercive effect as armed robbery. A fraudulent transaction has only a superficial similarity to a voluntary exchange. One-half of the exchange—the seller's promise to deliver something of value to the buyer—is never carried out.

Consumer fraud, in short, has no principled defenders. Policy debates in this area revolve around the issue of deciding the most cost-effective means of combatting the problem.

Questions for thought and discussion

1. Suppose a doctor has intentionally performed an unnecessary operation, but the patient never learns the operation was unnecessary. As a result, both patient and doctor remain happy with the exchange. Is there any economic inefficiency here? Explain.

2. The standard of economic efficiency implies that there is an *optimal* amount of effort we should make to deter fraud. It also implies that there is an *optimal* amount of effort to deter crime in general. Do you agree with this standard, or do you believe that we should make an even greater effort to combat wrongdoing? Explain.

3. Concern about fraud is more often expressed with respect to consumer sales than to purchases of firms. The assumption is that consumers are more easily deceived than business purchasers. Do you agree with the assumption? Should government spend more, less, or about the same protecting consumers as it spends protecting business firms? Why?

4. In 1977, 27 percent of all consumers complained to a government agency about that agency's poor service. But of those complaining only 37 percent were satisfied with the result. This percentage is well below the comparable percentage for private producers. Can you think of any reasons for the difference in responses?

Selected references

Posner, Richard A. *Economic Analysis of Law.* Boston: Little, Brown and Co., 1972.

_____.*Regulation of Advertising by the FTC.* Washington, D.C.: American Enterprise Institute, 1973.

Tuerck, David G., ed. *The Political Economy of Advertising.*Washington, D.C.: American Enterprise Institute, 1978.

6

Capitalism and Socialism in Garbage Collection

For centuries ideologues have debated how production ought to be organized. Should government produce all goods and services? Or should production be left to private firms? At one extreme are advocates of complete collectivism; in their view government should be the only employer, the only organizer, and the only distributor of goods and services. At the other extreme are the free-market anarchists; in their view, everything, including the provision of judges and the police, should be left to the market.

Most people probably care little about the ideological debate, but they often care a great deal about the kinds of goods and services available and the prices they have to pay for them. Surprisingly often, these "practical" concerns turn out to hinge on the "ideological" issue of how production is organized. The production of garbage-collection services is a classical case in point. What we can learn from studying the economics of garbage collection may have important implications for education, fire protection, public transportation, and many other services as well.

There is remarkable diversity in the ways production of these "public services" are organized by various cities. Some cities follow the traditional approach of providing all of these services through government.

In recent years, however, there has been a growing trend to contract out to private firms. Over the last decade, more than a half million public employee jobs have been contracted out, often with substantial savings to

69

the cities. Pelham, New York, for example, recently cut its garbage-collection bill by 25 percent by contracting with a private firm to provide the service. Other cities have made the more radical step of relying totally on the market. In 1979, Wichita, Kansas, got out of the garbage-collection business completely. Private garbage collectors in that city now compete for customers in a free market.

For years, cities have made decisions about public services without much input from economics or economists. Today, however, economists are more frequently applying the tools of their trade to problems of how to organize production. Not surprisingly, the focus of their attention has been on the question of economic efficiency.

The results of these investigations have been mixed. In some cases, theory and evidence suggest that government management of production may be necessary and desirable from an efficiency point of view. In other cases, private production may be the most efficient method. In the particular area of garbage collection, however, the private sector seems to have the upper hand.

A little later in this chapter we will look at some field studies of actual garbage-collection systems. Before doing so, however, we need a little background in the economics of incentives and monitoring.

The economics of incentives and monitoring

To give someone an *incentive* means to reward that person for behaving in one way rather than another. To *monitor* someone means to watch just how the person is behaving. Problems of monitoring and providing incentives are very important considerations in deciding how the production of services should be organized.

Monitoring and incentives are problems of social interaction. They would not exist in a Robinson Crusoe economy. Suppose Robinson wants to remove a mess of old banana peels from his hut. He doesn't have to worry about monitoring how the job is carried out—he himself, after all, is the one who must do it, and he has an incentive to do it quickly and well to leave himself more time for fishing.

Economic interactions where only two people are involved are hardly more complicated. Suppose you hire an individual worker to clean up some brush in your yard for a fixed payment of $20. Monitoring simply consists of looking to make sure the brush is gone before you hand over the money. And the worker has the same incentive Robinson Crusoe did— the quicker the job is done, the more time left for other things.

In a complex modern city, however, things may be different. Very often workers and supervisors can get by with inefficient work habits and can escape any penalty for doing so. Sanitation workers, for example, are usually paid according to the number of hours they spend on the job. Within certain boundaries, they are often able to slack off on productivity without fear of retaliation. On the other hand, if they act to raise productivity they may get no personal reward.

Suppose a work crew decides to perform a job at a more leisurely pace. Suppose they take extra-long rest breaks or fail to maintain their truck or tools properly. Why not do these things, so long as no loss of income or job results? By contrast, a worker may be especially diligent or may discover a new technique that enhances productivity. But why do so unless a reward is provided in terms of promotion or increased pay?

Here we have problems of both monitoring and incentives. If information were costless and were immediately available, we would always be able to reward and penalize workers according to how well they did their jobs. We could construct an ideal incentive system: each worker would be able to reap the full rewards of good decisions and bear the full costs of bad ones.

Unfortunately, information is not costless. This means that in order to monitor worker behavior we often need a manager. But even managers rarely monitor perfectly. For one thing, complete monitoring of worker behavior could very well cost more than the benefits. For another thing, the monitor may not be a good monitor. The monitor's decisions will also affect the efficiency of production. Ideally, the monitor should reap the benefits of good decisions and bear the cost of bad ones. But how can we assess the contribution of the monitor unless there is someone else who monitors the monitor? And who will monitor the monitor's monitor?

Monitoring workers is not the only problem that affects how production can best be organized. Monitoring and incentives concern the behavior of consumers as well. For example, if the price consumers pay for garbage removal is independent of the quantity they put out for collection, they have no incentive to reduce the volume of garbage they generate. Should one buy a trash compactor? Purchase disposable or returnable bottles? Throw away aluminum cans or sell them to reprocessing companies? If price is independent of volume, consumers will tend to make these choices based on their own convenience.

What is true of households is even more true of commercial consumers, where the options of waste disposal are typically wider. But if businesses and households are charged on the basis of the volume of garbage they generate, someone must monitor that volume.

Let's look briefly at how monitoring and incentive problems are handled in the private sector. Then we will turn to the public sector.

Monitoring and incentives in the private sector

Most private refuse companies are small and are typically owned and managed by only a few people. They are either organized as proprietorships or as corporations with very few stockholders.

Because the companies are privately owned, separate contracts are signed between the owners and each of the workers. The workers are guaranteed a fixed compensation in return for their services, but the owners have the right to hire and fire or to renegotiate salaries, depending on their assessment of worker productivity. The owners, of course, receive the difference between the firm's revenues and its expenses. If the difference is positive they realize profits; if the difference is negative they suffer financial losses.

In such a firm the owners have strong incentives to engage in efficient monitoring. They realize the full financial rewards of good managerial decisions and suffer the full financial penalties for bad ones. Through experimentation they discover how much monitoring of worker and consumer behavior pays off. Inefficient techniques are discarded in favor of efficient ones as owners strive to increase their incomes.

The owners are also spurred to efficiency by another force: *competition.* Private companies typically operate under one of two types of arrangements—either they sign contracts with individual residences and business firms or they sign a contract with a city government. In either case they run the risk of having their bids undercut by aggressive competitors.

Competition does not always work perfectly, however. Competitors have been known to collude on bids and artificially raise the prices for their services. They appear to be more successful at this when dealing with a city government than when dealing with private customers, but consumers have also been gouged on occasion. Even so, the existing competition seems to keep prices well below the cost of government-operated services. Let's see why.

Monitoring in the public sector

At first glance it may seem that a company owned by a democratic government and managed by civil servants is not altogether different from a large corporation owned and managed by private citizens. After all, each voter could be considered analogous to a shareholder. Voters are entitled to vote for political officeholders just as shareholders are entitled to vote for members of the board of directors of a corporation. Moreover, just as shareholders share in the profits and losses of corporations, so voters share in the profits and losses of government enterprises through higher or lower taxes needed to finance other government services.

True, the single voter's influence in any particular election is negligible, but the same may be said of the large corporation. For example, about three million people held shares of stock in American Telephone and Telegraph before its breakup into several parts. About half of these held fewer than fifteen shares each; no single owner had more than 1 percent of the total. Since the breakup, ownership is even more widely fragmented. Nonetheless, such huge corporations can produce efficiently. They are certainly able to compete with proprietorships and smaller firms. Can government do the same?

Sometimes, perhaps—but there is an important difference between a government-owned firm and a private firm. The difference is that in a democracy you cannot buy and sell your vote. This is not necessarily a defect of democratic society; we would probably not wish it to be otherwise. But this seemingly minor fact has a big effect on the way in which government behaves.

To see why, let's briefly consider what impetus corporate managers have to make efficient decisions when ownership of shares is widely dispersed among millions of people. Who monitors the decisions they make, and what is the effect of the monitoring activity?

The monitoring works like this: shareholders and potential shareholders, in search of personal gain, seek information about the probable future earnings of various companies. They compare their own estimates with the evaluations made by others, as those are reflected in the market price of shares of each company's stock. When they believe a stock is overvalued they sell shares; when they believe the stock is undervalued they buy shares.

The motivation for each particular trader, then, is not to penalize or reward company managers for their performance. It is instead simply to beat the market by buying and selling shares at opportune times. There are many traders doing this, and their collective efforts determine the price of a share of stock at any given time. We can be pretty certain that at any given time on any given day stock-market prices are the best available estimate of the future earnings potential of any particular company. Those prices accurately reflect all known information about the future earnings potential of every large corporation.

How can we be sure of this? Simply because if anyone had better information than other market participants, he or she would buy or sell on the basis of that information. But that very buying or selling would eventually cause the price of the stock to rise or fall until it fully reflected the new information.

If stock-market prices are the best available indicators of the current and expected future performance of large companies, stock-market prices are also the best available evaluation of the behavior of managers. But how do these prices affect the incentives any particular manager faces?

The fact is that both managers and the boards of directors who instruct those managers are very sensitive to stock-market prices. Low share prices (reflecting, say, poor management decisions) mean a company will find it hard to raise additional capital by selling new stock issues or by borrowing. Low stock prices also encourage proxy fights by disgruntled shareholders seeking a chance to profit by utilizing new management. And, of course, managers themselves lose because the value of their own stock, as well as the value of stock options they hold, depreciates as stock prices fall.

By contrast, in the political process the typical voter has very little to gain by monitoring the behavior of the civil-servant managers of public enterprises. Suppose a citizen has some special knowledge—such as a strong indication that the city Sanitation Department will run a deficit next year. There is no way that such knowledge can be immediately transformed into personal profit. In fact, the only way that such knowledge *can* be useful is if it is used to persuade a majority of voters to "throw the rascals out" and hire better managers.

But the cost of organizing a political movement to oust the sanitation bureaucracy could be enormous. And what conceivable monetary gain could accrue to the voter in return for the effort? Thirty dollars? Forty? Fifty? Whatever the figure, it represents the upper limit of the voter's financial interest in the issue. Hence, although private investors will pay thousands of dollars to professional analysts to predict the future earnings of a private corporation, who among us would pay an analyst to predict future sanitation costs?

Not only do voters have very weak incentives to monitor the behavior of government managers, the managers themselves are largely insulated from the risks faced by the private manager. Government managers have no fear of proxy fights by disgruntled stockholders seeking to gain profits by their removal. They do not have to fear takeover bids by other companies. Their ability to raise capital is not affected by stock prices. And since they do not own shares of stock in the government, they realize few of the rewards of good decisions. And, within limits, they bear none of the costs of bad decisions.

True, voters do engage in political action. They do attempt to influence the behavior of politicians by campaign contributions, lobbying efforts, and the like. But voters who decide to invest in politics often find that their returns are much higher if they direct their efforts toward some type of subsidy for their own interest groups rather than toward making the bureaucracy more efficient. Indeed, efforts at general reform typically arouse tough opposition from interest groups who are quite satisfied with the status quo.

Similarly, government managers themselves soon discover that the greatest threats to job security arise from the shifting influence of special-interest groups, not from broad-based inefficiencies. For example, the standard of efficiency dictates that managers should pay workers the lowest wages necessary to bid their services away from competing private employers. But since employees get to vote, the standard of political survival often dictates that a much higher wage should be paid.

The economic theory of business organization thus suggests that, other things being equal, government production will often be less efficient than private production. Numerous studies seem to confirm that prediction.

_____   Garbage: a look at the evidence

A number of studies of municipal garbage collection show that private carriers, on the average, outperform the municipal carriers.

One study, conducted at the Columbia University Graduate School of Business under a grant from the National Science Foundation, surveyed over two thousand cities with a combined population of 52 million. The study found that twice-a-week curbside garbage collection cost the average municipal agency 69 percent more than it cost the average private firm. What's more, municipal collection takes twice as long per household, serves fewer households per shift, and involves larger crews and higher employee absenteeism than collection by private companies.

If anything, these figures probably understate the efficiency difference between the two types of organization. In many of the cities where private collectors are used, the collectors contract directly with the city rather than with individual households. Even when cities put these contracts out for bid, they often get gouged by price-fixing agreements among private firms. In fact, the record of government purchases of goods and services from others is not much better than the record of government production of goods and services. Many notorious price-fixing cases in antitrust law involve conspiracies on bidding for government contracts.

In general, the propensity to rely on city collection rather than private collection seems to rise as city populations rise. Among cities with populations from 2,500 to 10,000, only 23 percent collect their own garbage. The proportion rises to 73 percent among cities with populations of 250,000 to 750,000. Very few of the largest cities rely on private services, although San Francisco, Portland, Boston, and Indianapolis are exceptions.

This seems to suggest that the larger the city, the easier it is for sanitation unions to secure a political foothold and the harder it is for the city to shop for less expensive alternatives. New York confirms the pattern by providing us, as it so often does, with the worst example of all.

In 1971 a city-financed study showed that private collectors could pick up garbage at $17.50 a ton compared to New York City's cost of $49. This result was hotly disputed by the sanitation workers' union, so New York City Environmental Protection Administrator Jerome Kretchner proposed a test. City and private carriers would simultaneously work in comparable areas to determine the relative efficiency of each. The test was never conducted, however—apparently the sanitation workers' union put enormous pressure on the mayor to halt it.

A private test was done five years later by Professor Emanuel Savas, who also participated in the Columbia University study. Savas compared garbage collection in two sections of Queens with collection in a similar community in Nassau County that was serviced by a private firm. The private firm charged $72 a year per household, while city collection costs were $209. Savas also compared New York City with other major cities, including San Francisco—which held costs to $40 a year per household by relying on private carriers.

The basic principle involved seems to be well understood in San Francisco, if not in New York. S. M. Tatarian, director of San Francisco's Public Works Department, says, "I shudder to think of what would happen if my department was responsible for collecting garbage. The rates would go through the roof." The reason? Because private enterprise, he explains, can do the job at a lower cost than can municipal employees, who have no incentive to do the job efficiently.

New York City also provides a vivid illustration of how wages and working conditions become political issues divorced from considerations of economic efficiency. For the last two decades the city has allowed private carriers to service business and industrial plants. Residential collection has been a city monopoly. The private companies did not hesitate to substitute two-man trucks for three-man trucks, once the cost-cutting advantages of this change were clear. For the city, however, the change was a major political problem. After years of negotiations, the city was able to purchase the new trucks only by agreeing to hefty increases in the already high salaries of sanitation workers.

An evaluation

So far we have focused almost exclusively on one aspect of the standard of efficiency: efficiency in production. We have seen that, other things being equal, government tends to be an inefficient producer of goods and services. Nonetheless, there may be some services for which government production is the only option. In other areas private production is a feasible alternative; when it is, the standards of efficiency would dictate private, as opposed to government, production. This seems to be the case in garbage collection.

Choice by the standard of equality is less clear. On the one hand, when garbage is collected by city employees the poor pay more through higher taxes—just as everyone else does. Moreover, the quality of service they receive is often inferior to the quality of service provided to higher-income groups. On the other hand, in some cities sanitation workers may themselves be drawn from the ranks of the poor. If municipal collection results in higher salaries, it may benefit some poor families while harming others. The overall effect may differ from city to city. In New York City the poor, as a group, appear clearly to be harmed by municipal, rather than private, collection. But in other cities the poor, as a group, may realize a slight benefit as a result of city collection.

Government production does not necessarily violate the standard of liberty, especially if the goods and services are sold directly to consumers. But in the case of municipal garbage collection, consumers are given little choice: they must pay taxes to finance the city service, even though better options might have been available to them. Moreover, city garbage collection often becomes a vehicle for exploitation of taxpayers by sanitation workers. This practice is inconsistent with the standard of liberty.

The policies of garbage in New York City

The vast majority of citizens would clearly benefit from some form of private, rather than governmental, garbage collection. They could have superior quality service at a lower price. But in most of our large cities the sanitation workers seem to have the upper hand, despite the fact that they are heavily outnumbered. Why?

One reason is that they are better organized. Another is that they form coalitions with other city unions. New York City provides an illustration of how these techniques work.

No one doubts that salaries, fringe benefits, and working conditions enjoyed by New York City's municipal employees are the result of raw political power. It is believed that 250,000 of the 400,000 city workers live in the city; together with relatives, their voting strength is estimated at 500,000. That's over half of the 900,000 voters who normally turn out for the Democratic Party primary, and a good chunk of the 1.7 million who vote in general elections.

This power pays off. On the average, the rate of salary increases for city employees has been twice the rate for federal employees. The biggest increases normally come in election years. Overall, city workers earn up to 25 percent more in straight salaries than do workers performing the same job in private industry. Moreover, they can typically retire after twenty years on pensions that are half of their highest salary over that time period.

In explaining a particularly lavish settlement with several city unions, an aide to former New York Mayor John Lindsay put it this way: "In the final analysis it was a political decision. The unions had the clout; they were going to get it anyway. Lindsay decided he might as well get the credit."

Questions for thought and discussion

1. What differences would you expect to find between nonprofit or publicly regulated firms on the one hand, and nonregulated, for-profit firms on the other hand, with respect to (a) aggressiveness of management, (b) incidence of stockholder proxy fights, and (c) incidence of employee discrimination on grounds of race, religion, sex, etc.?

2. In the mid 1970s, New York City faced a severe financial crisis. Expenses exceeded revenues, and the city could not borrow without a pledge to lenders to reduce expenses. Expenses were reduced, but the principal method was to lay off workers and thus reduce city services rather than to reduce salaries. Why do you think the city chose the option it did? Which option do you think the city unions preferred? Why?

3. In recent years, many economists have advocated an "educational voucher system." In its pure form, all elementary and secondary schools would be private and would compete with each other for students. Parents would select the school of their choice for their children; they would then give the school a ticket or voucher. The government would pay each school a fixed sum of money for each voucher it collected. Do you think this system would be an improvement over the present system? Why?

4. In England both telephone service and mail delivery are public monopolies. In the United States mail delivery is a public monopoly and local telephone service is a private monopoly. Many observers believe mail service is better in England than it is in the United States, while telephone service in the United States is superior to telephone service in England. Can you think of an explanation for this that is consistent with economic theory?

Selected references

Alchian, Armen, and William Allen. *Exchange and Production.* 2d ed. Belmont, Calif.: Wadsworth, 1977.

Alchian, Armen, and Harold Demsetz. "Production Information Costs and Economic Organization." *American Economic Review* 62 (1972).

Poole, Robert. *Cutting Back City Hall.* New York: Universe Books, 1980.

7

Blackouts, Brownouts, and the Cost of Electric Power

On the evening of July 13, 1977, New York City was plunged into total darkness. For the next twenty-five hours there was no electric power for most New Yorkers. People were trapped high in elevators and underground in subways. There were terrible traffic jams because there were no street lights or traffic signals. With burglar alarms out and police spread too thin, it was open season for theft and vandalism. With no electricity there was soon no water, crippling the ability to fight fires.

What followed was the nation's most infamous blackout. For two straight days the city was a scene of anarchy, looting, and arson. Over thirty-eight hundred people were arrested, but this was only a handful of the looters. Hundreds of small businesses were destroyed; many never reopened. The total losses of the victims of the rampage ran well over a billion dollars.

Why did it happen? That's not entirely clear. Political rivals blamed the mayor. The mayor blamed Consolidated Edison. Consolidated Edison blamed higher authority—the blackout, Consolidated Edison claimed, was an act of God.

Disasters like the New York blackout may have been "acts of God," beyond the control of economic policy, but the frequency and severity of lesser blackouts and brownouts have convinced a lot of people that something is fundamentally wrong with the way we are producing and

supplying electric power. Consumers are not being encouraged to conserve
at times when they ought to conserve. The result is a terrible strain on
capacity at certain times of the day and certain times of the year. A
mechanical malfunction or a bolt of lightning under these conditions can
throw an entire city into darkness.

What is more, utility companies are a lot more vulnerable to such
incidents today than they used to be. During the 1970s and 1980s,
investment in new electric generators was from one-third to one-half less
than it was in the 1960s. As a result, the extra capacity available in case of
equipment failures is falling steadily.

Blackouts are not the only problem. Producing electricity requires the
use of other energy sources, such as coal, oil, or natural gas. When people
use too much electric power they also waste other energy sources—that
means depletion of our supply of oil and gas, and it means more imported
fuel.

During the early 1980s, two sharp recessions cut industrial demand for
electric power, and the threat of brownouts and blackouts seemed to
recede for the moment. Even during this period, however, the long-term
picture continued to deteriorate. Shortages will return, the experts say,
unless some changes are made in the way the electric power industry is
regulated.

In this chapter we will look at two problems of electric power
regulation. First, we will look at the problem of how a utility with a given
generation capacity should price its power. In particular, we will examine
the case for a pricing structure that raises rates during periods of peak
demand and lowers them during off-peak periods. Second, we will raise
the question of whether current regulatory practices permit utilities to
construct enough capacity to meet demand reliably and efficiently.

The theory of peak-load pricing

We begin with the short-run problem of pricing with a given generation
capacity. In the short run, the total cost of electricity production can be
divided into two components: fixed costs and variable costs. The fixed
costs are mainly the costs of electric power generators, the cost of the
buildings that house them, and the cost of transmission lines. These are
costs that, in the short run, do not vary with the amount of electricity
produced. Variable costs include such things as labor and fuel costs. As
more electricity is produced, more fuel is needed to power the generators.
As more generating capacity is used, more manpower is needed to operate
the generators. Hence, these costs vary with the volume of electricity
produced.

The distinction between fixed costs and variable costs is not unique to
electric utilities. But there are two important differences between electric

utilities and ordinary industrial firms. First, fixed costs are very high in relation to total costs in electricity production. About 77 percent of total costs for electric utilities are fixed costs. By contrast, fixed costs are only about 46 percent of total costs for the nation's five hundred largest industrial firms. Second, electric utilities must operate most of the time with an enormous amount of excess capacity. On the average, only about 60 percent of generating capacity is being used at any one time; the remaining 40 percent is needed only to meet the very high peak demand that arises at certain times of the day and certain times of the year.

The combined effect of these two characteristics is that customers who use electricity during the peak periods cause electric companies to bear very high costs—the cost of constructing and maintaining generators that are used only during the peak period and that remain idle at other times. A very large share of your electric bill goes to pay for the utility's ability to satisfy peak demand. This problem is reinforced by the nature of variable costs.

It turns out that the variable costs of generating electricity change considerably during the day. *Base-load* electricity is the minimum amount of electricity that is needed to satisfy demand through the night. The variable costs of *base-load* electricity are lowest because it relies on very efficient generators that run twenty-four hours a day. As demand climbs, say around breakfast time, additional generators—more expensive to operate—are turned on. As demand reaches its peak around mid-afternoon, still more generators are used. These last units are the most costly of all: typically they are turbines and diesels that burn natural gas or fuel oil. And about half the fuel used is imported at very high prices.

It would seem, then, that those who use a lot of electricity during the afternoon should pay more per kilowatt hour (kwh) than those who use electricity in the middle of the night. But, often, they do not. In most places the price of electricity does not vary by time of day, nor does it vary by season of the year. All of this would change with peak-load pricing.

Peak-load pricing theory is not difficult to understand if we take one thing at a time. First, we need to ask what prices a utility should charge in the short run in order to use its existing plant and equipment efficiently. Second, we need to ask how large and what kind of capacity it should construct in the long run. The answers to these two questions, taken together, will tell us how both utilities and their customers can save a great many energy dollars.

Consider Figure 7–1, which shows the short-run situation for a typical utility. In the short run, the utility's marginal cost curve reflects such variable costs as the cost of labor and fuel. The marginal cost curve is drawn with an upward slope, reflecting the fact that each additional kilowatt hour of electricity is more expensive to produce.

We have drawn two demand curves in Figure 7–1: D_1 applies to peak-demand hours and D_2 applies to off-peak hours. To use its existing capacity efficiently, all the utility needs to do is to set its peak and off-peak

FIGURE 7–1   Daily Market for Electricity in the Short Run

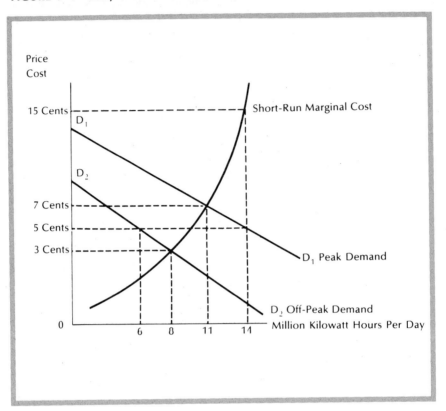

prices at the point where the marginal cost curve cuts each of the two demand curves. That gives a peak price of seven cents and an off-peak price of three cents. At these prices, demand would be eleven million kilowatt hours per day during peak periods and eight million kilowatt hours per day during off-peak periods.

Consider what would happen instead if the utility charged one uniform price—say five cents per kilowatt hour—at all times. Under these conditions, the quantity demanded during off-peak hours would fall from eight million to six million kilowatt hours, and the quantity demanded during peak hours would rise from eleven million to fourteen million kilowatt hours. Demand during the peak hours could be met by using expensive standby generators that ran only a few hours a day, at a cost of up to fifteen cents per kilowatt hour, as the figure is drawn. The alternative would be not to meet all of the peak demand. Instead, interruptible contracts with industrial users, brownouts (voltage reductions), or blackouts could be used to ration power.

Figure 7–1, then, shows how to set prices to put existing capacity to best use. Note that, in the short run, the change to peak-load pricing from uniform pricing produces two important effects: first, the total capacity required to meet peak demand is reduced; second, some use is shifted from peak periods to off-peak periods.

These two effects are very important for long-run decisions. Since peak-load pricing reduces the total capacity the utility needs, in the long run fewer generators will be needed. This means that fixed costs can be lowered. Moreover, the switch from peak use to off-peak use means that more generators of the efficient, 24-hour-a-day variety can be used. This means that in the long run, variable costs can be lower as well. All in all, long-run total costs are lower with peak-load pricing than without it.

Living with peak-load pricing

Does peak-load pricing really work? Fortunately, we do not have to rely on mere speculation. Peak-load pricing has been used in Europe for several years, and many of our own utilities are using it today.

Following the New York City blackout, the New York Public Service Commission made time-of-day pricing mandatory for large industrial and commercial users. In New York City, all customers are now charged higher rates in the summer, when air conditioners push electricity use to an annual peak. And utility companies in a majority of states have experimented with some form of peak-load pricing.

In most instances, however, the utilities have been somewhat timid about the magnitude of the rate differentials. For one thing, there is a fear of raising the wrath of consumers who have been long accustomed to traditional pricing methods. For another, there is a recognition that time-of-day pricing may cause hardships. Widening price differences, it is argued, need to come gradually in order to ease the adjustment. Still, time-of-day pricing has had an impact.

Take the case of Kohler, Wisconsin. In 1977 Wisconsin Power and Light Company put time-of-day charges into effect for its 130 large business customers. Before the change the standard charge was 1.622 cents per kwh at all times. After the change the rate rose to 2.03 cents per kwh between 8 A.M. and 10 P.M. It dropped to 1.013 cents per kwh between 10 P.M. and 8 A.M. For small users such a change may have little effect, but it made a big difference to the Kohler Company, a maker of plumbing fixtures. The company, it seems, was consuming about 60 percent of the utility's entire electrical output.

Kohler decided that the cheapest way to economize on electricity costs was to reshuffle work schedules, so it moved about 250 workers— approximately 5 percent of its work force—from the evening shift to the 10 P.M.–6:30 A.M. graveyard shift. The rescheduling came with a price tag. Kohler had to pay $25,000 in higher wages to compensate employees who were moved to the less desirable work hours. And after a new labor contract was signed in October, the extra wage bill jumped to $50,000.

But the higher wage bill was more than covered by the saving in electricity costs—in fact, Kohler estimates that it cut its annual electric bill by about $464,000.

Currently, about 2.2 million workers, 4 percent of the U.S. labor force, start their jobs later than 8 P.M. With the advent of time-of-day pricing the number is expected to rise considerably. The magnitude of the change will vary, of course, from company to company; in each case the firm will have to compare the saving on electric bills to the higher labor costs. But the greater the price differentials, the greater the incentive to shift work schedules. Kohler Company, for example, expects the daytime rates to rise relative to nighttime rates. As a result it expects to move even more workers to the graveyard shift.

There are other reactions to time-of-day pricing. Some companies use storage devices that heat or cool water during the evening for air conditioning or heat used during the day. Some install computerized controls that stagger the use of fans and motors. Many manufacturers draw more daytime power from their own generators. One way or another, most large users of electricity, such as department stores, office buildings, and manufacturers, have cut back on daytime electricity consumption in response to rate changes.

Peak-load pricing has been tried for residential users, too. Vermont has been a pioneer in this regard, with peak-load residential pricing since 1974. As a result, Vermonters have grown accustomed to doing things like loading the dishwasher at dinnertime but waiting until after the rates go down to push the button. The Central Vermont Public Service Corporation rents water heaters that have improved insulation and three times the normal holding capacity; these heaters run only at night and produce enough hot water to last all day.

Overall the savings could be substantial. Both England and France report large reductions in capital and operating expenses as a result of peak-load pricing. Forecasts have been made for the United States by the Federal Energy Administration. According to FEA projections, if the entire country switched to peak-load pricing, $60 billion could be shaved from the capital requirements of electric utilities by 1985. The agency also estimates that by 1985 the change could reduce our oil consumption by 200,000 barrels a day.

—————— Competition, monopoly, and rate suppression

Peak-load pricing, as we have seen, would promote conservation and reduce the need for electric utilities to add capacity. Even such a boost to conservation, however, would not entirely remove the need for utilities to raise capital and make investments. Some investment in new capacity will be needed in areas of the country where growth of demand is especially fast. Obsolete plants will need to be replaced with more energy-efficient generators. And investment will be needed to meet pollution control standards. This brings us to a second problem facing the electric utility industry: raising the capital needed to provide efficient and reliable service in the future.

To understand this problem, we need to look briefly at the way the electric utility industry is regulated. Over 80 percent of all electricity generated in the country is produced by privately owned utilities. But although these utilities are privately owned, they are generally not free to choose the rates they charge. Instead, rates are set by public-utility commissions—political bodies answerable directly or indirectly to the electorate. Most of the remaining electricity is produced by companies that are owned and operated by government. As a result, electricity prices are not determined by free markets—they are determined in the political arena.

This was not always so. Around the turn of the century, free competition was flourishing; in order to produce electricity, a company usually had to get a franchise from a state or local government. But these were apparently easy to obtain. In 1907, for example, over twenty-five electric companies were competing in Chicago. As time passed, however, the industry became more concentrated. Technical innovations gave rise to economies of scale. This made it possible for a single firm to service more and more customers at a lower average cost. It also provided an impetus for regulation.

At first glance it might seem that regulation primarily benefited consumers. And, true enough, there were many consumer groups pressing for regulation of electric rates. But there were important benefits sought by producers as well. In return for losing control over their rates, they gained something they cherished very much—monopoly. Although big customers could still produce their own electricity with their own generators, many other activities were prohibited.

Suppose, for example, you own a manufacturing plant and you observe that electricity rates across the county line are cheaper than those you are paying. You would like to approach the rival electric company and ask for service at the cheaper rates. Or suppose you observe that a neighboring residential user is paying higher rates than you are; you consider stringing a wire from your plant to the neighbor's home and reselling your own power to your neighbor. You could split the difference and both of you would profit. Sounds reasonable? Perhaps. But because of regulation such things are generally not allowed.

What have the total effects of regulation been? For many years economists assumed that regulation promoted economic efficiency. Two arguments seemed persuasive.

First, it was argued that competition leads to unnecessary duplication of transmission lines. After all, why have two power lines running through a neighborhood when only one will do?

Second, it was argued that under conditions of decreasing cost, one firm would capture the entire market anyway. That is because one firm can supply an entire market more cheaply than, say, two firms that are each servicing one-half of the market. But if only one firm serves the market, we do not have competition. The monopoly utility could charge prices far above marginal cost, or engage in price discrimination, or in other ways line its pockets at consumer expense.

These arguments are theoretically sound, provided that regulators set just the right price for electricity. The price should be high enough to allow a fair rate of return on capital invested in generating capacity, but not so high as to allow monopoly profits. Have regulators, in practice, managed to walk the fine line between rates that are too high and rates that are too low? A large body of economic research suggests that they have not done so.

Much of the early research on electric utility rates seemed to indicate that regulators were setting rates too high. One well known study by Harvey Averch and Leland Johnson found that in the 1960s, utilities were allowed to earn a rate of return higher than necessary to attract needed investment. As a result, Averch and Johnson argued, utilities had an incentive to build more generating capacity than was really needed. This came to be known as the AJ effect. The tendency of utilities subject to the AJ effect to overexpand may explain, in part, their lack of interest in peak-load pricing.

Since the early 1970s, things have changed. In the last fifteen years or so, regulators have tended to suppress rates below the level that allows a fair return on invested capital. This has happened partly because the slow-moving regulatory apparatus could not keep up with rising fuel costs during the 1970s. And it has happened because consumer groups advocating lower rates have achieved more influence over regulatory commissions. Whatever the reasons for this policy of rate suppression, the consequences are worrisome.

Rate suppression produces an AJ effect in reverse. Instead of investing too much in generating capacity, utilities invest too little. They keep inefficient older equipment on line longer. Meanwhile, their reserve capacity to meet emergencies and peak loads gets thinner and thinner.

In the short run, consumers benefit from rate suppression because their electric bills are lower than they otherwise would be. But in the long run, there will be problems. For one thing, consumers will pay a fuel cost penalty because utilities cannot afford to replace old plants that burn high-cost oil with new ones that burn cheaper coal. In addition, they run the risk of a return of blackouts and brownouts. All told, according to Peter Navarro, present rate suppression policies will force rates to be 11 to 33 percent higher by the turn of the century than they would be if regulators began now to permit utilities to earn a fair rate of return.

──────── Competition in the market for electric power?

If regulation has not lived up to the hopes of its supporters, perhaps it is time to take another look at the possibility of competition in supplying electric power. Although the electric power industry is less competitive now than it was in its early days, competition has not entirely disappeared. Consider, for example, the city of Lubbock, Texas. The city is served by two privately owned utilities. Each serves the entire city. Each has its own poles and its own lines. Yet citizens of Lubbock pay less than customers pay in nearby Amarillo, a city of comparable size but no competition.

Could competition work in other cities? It might. Even with only one set of transmission lines within a city, utilities could bid for the right to use those lines. The right to sell electric power would go to the lowest bidder. But the rates charged even by the lowest bidder would have to be high enough to allow a fair rate of return on invested capital. Otherwise no one would bid.

Today, with the development of extra-high-voltage transmission, it is possible to profitably transmit electricity for very long distances. For example, Los Angeles is connected to two such transmission systems— one is 850 miles long, the other, 650. The result of this new technology is that any large utility within, say, 200 miles of a city is a potential competitor for all or part of that city's market. There are 17 large utilities within 200 miles of Chicago; there are 13 in the Detroit area, 19 near Philadelphia, and 15 around St. Louis. This suggests that a great deal of competition is possible.

Competition might also work to spur peak-load pricing. Suppose a utility were charging its customers a uniform price at all times of the day. A rival firm might offer to sell "base-load" electricity—say, to a group of industrial users—for a much cheaper price. Customers would then have an incentive to use the rival firm's electricity for the base-load amount and use the original firm for the remainder. But the original firm would have to react. Since nonbase-load electricity is more expensive to produce, the original firm would have to raise its prices for daytime use. It would probably also be reluctant to give up the base-load market so easily; it could try to meet the challenge by offering to meet or undercut the rival's offer on base-load charges.

Competition would also eliminate—or reduce—unnecessary price differentials charged to different classes of users. In general, industrial users pay lower prices, partly justified on the basis of cost. Factories often maintain their own electrical distribution systems and take power at a high voltage; the costs of metering are also typically lower than for single-family dwellings. But there is some evidence that industrial users get a subsidy financed by higher prices charged to residential users. To the degree that competition can flourish, rival firms could offer residential users lower prices and eliminate such subsidies.

Another small step toward competition in electric power generation was taken in 1981. In March of that year, regulations were issued pursuant to the Public Utility Regulatory Policy Act of 1978. Under the new regulations, public utilities are required to buy surplus electricity from industrial firms which produce electricity through *cogeneration.*

In a typical cogeneration system, steam needed for heating or for a manufacturing process is also run through a turbine to produce electricity. The technique is highly efficient, since once a boiler is installed for manufacturing use, it costs little to add the turbine to get double use from the steam. In the past, the electricity-generating capacity of cogeneration went to waste if the steam needs and electric needs of a plant were not perfectly balanced. Now if there is a surplus of electricity, the local utility must buy it at the "avoided cost" rate, that is, at the marginal cost of power to the utility. Experts predict that many more industrial plants will now find cogeneration profitable.

An evaluation

From the point of view of economic efficiency, a strong argument can be made for allowing utilities to earn a fair rate of return and for some form of peak-load pricing. By charging different prices at different times of the day and different seasons of the year, utilities could encourage consumers to even out the valleys and peaks in their electricity consumption. The costs of production could be lower; electric bills could be lower as well.

The theory of competitive markets holds that when perfect competition prevails, efficient marginal cost pricing is the outcome. Thus, if the market for electricity were free and competitive, peak-load pricing would evolve naturally. When markets are regulated, the standard of efficiency implies that regulators should try to implement prices that would have prevailed if competition were present. Few believe, however, that regulatory decisions are a good substitute for genuine competition in the market. For this reason many economists believe that competition, where practicable, ought to be encouraged rather than discouraged by public-utility commissions.

The standard of equality is less clear on this issue. On the average, middle-income Americans pay about 5 to 10 percent of their incomes on utility bills. For families below the poverty line, however, the figure is from 20 to 30 percent. For some, it is as high as 50 percent. That means that a 10 percent change in the average utility bill is equal to from .5 to 1 percent of income for middle-income persons. But it is equal to from 2 to 5 percent of income for poor families.

To the degree that peak-load pricing and more competition lower electric bills, the poor will benefit more than others. On the other hand, charging every consumer the true cost of the electricity consumed may be a real hardship for some in the short run. (But remember, in the long run rate suppression leads to higher, not lower, rates for everyone.) To counter this effect, some states now provide discounts or tax credits for elderly and low-income people. A number of economists argue that this is an inefficient way to aid the poor, however. A better way, they claim, is to give more money to the poor and then charge them for the true cost of their electricity consumption along with everyone else.

Most advocates of liberty would like to see no regulation of privately owned electric utilities. As a practical matter, they believe that utility rates would be lower. But most also oppose regulation on principle: anyone, they argue, should be free to produce electricity and sell it for any price the market will bear. Municipally owned utilities are not necessarily ruled out by this standard as long as they are self-supporting. But cities should not be able to create monopolies for their own utilities, nor should they be able to tax private utilities heavily while leaving their own companies unburdened. All in all, peak-load pricing would arise in the libertarian world because free markets would produce it.

Questions for thought and discussion

1. Time-of-day pricing has been a reality in telephone service for some time, and there is no substantial opposition to it. Why do you think that there is so much more opposition to time-of-day pricing for electricity use than there is for telephone service?

2. Many cities tax electricity consumption even when there is no general sales tax on other consumer products. Can you think of any explanation for this practice? How do you think the practice affects a city's attitude toward competition in electricity production?

3. Economist Sam Peltzman found that, after adjusting for other differences, municipally owned utilities had higher costs of electricity production than did privately owned utilities. Can you offer any explanation for this result consistent with economic theory?

4. Draw a decreasing average total-cost curve on a carefully labeled graph. Now draw the associated marginal-cost curve. Can you see any problems that might result from "marginal-cost" pricing? What are they?

5. Our simple graph in Figure 7–1 assumes that the two demand curves depicted are independent of each other. Why? Is this assumption a reasonable one? Explain.

Selected references

Carron, Andrew S., and Paul W. MacAvoy. *The Decline of Service Quality in Regulated Industries.* Washington, D.C.: American Enterprise Institute, 1981.

Electric Utility Rate Reform. Washington, D.C.: American Enterprise Institute, 1977.

Navarro, Peter. *The Dimming of America.* Cambridge, Mass.: Ballinger, 1984.

8

Farm Policy: Welfare for the Rich?

There has long been an undercurrent of opposition to welfare programs in this country. Some people are simply contemptuous of the poor, while others resent giving money to those they consider lazy and idle. Perhaps it might come as a surprise to those who think that way that some of America's biggest "welfare" programs shower their benefits primarily on people who are not poor at all—and who are by no means idle. These "welfare" programs are agricultural subsidies.

No other sector of our economy has enjoyed more subsidies from government than agriculture. Since 1929 the federal government has actively pursued programs designed to raise farm incomes. At one time or another, some kind of subsidy has been given to growers of wheat, feed grains, cotton, tobacco, rice, peanuts, soybeans, dairy products, and sugar. Other government programs have fattened the pocketbooks of farmers producing lemons, cranberries, cherries, and hops.

Some of these subsidies have been included in the federal budget and have been financed by taxes. Most of the money has gone to farmers in the form of direct payments; the rest has been spent storing agricultural surpluses. The sums involved have been quite high. In 1983, for example, farm income support programs cost the government more than $28 billion. This represented almost $12,000 per farm!

But over the years many of the benefits enjoyed by farmers did not show up in the government's budget at all. They required no taxes and involved no government expenditure. These subsidies were paid to producers by consumers of agricultural products in the form of higher prices. These indirect subsidies have been estimated to add another 50 percent to the cost of promoting farmer welfare.

The details of our farm policies have changed from time to time and are still changing today. Throughout all the changes, however, certain basic elements of policy keep reappearing in different mixes and combinations. The most important of these basic elements are price supports, output restrictions, and direct subsidies. Let's look at each of these in turn.

Price supports

Figure 8–1 captures the essence of farm price supports. The supply curve in this diagram is shown to be upward sloping, reflecting the fact that at higher prices more of the product—wheat, in this case—will be produced.

There are several reasons for the upward slope of the supply curve. In the first place, not all land is equally fertile. The cost of producing wheat on very fertile land is lower because with a given amount of labor, fertilizer, and machinery, more wheat can be grown per acre than on less fertile land. Second, an acre of land of given quality will produce more wheat with better fertilizer, better cultivation, and better harvesting techniques. And third, land can often be used to produce a variety of goods. As the price of wheat rises, farmers are induced to switch from growing corn or soybeans to growing wheat instead. All this means that when the price of wheat goes up, the quantity supplied can be expected to increase.

Under a price support program, the government in effect guarantees wheat growers that they will receive a certain price for their crop. If consumers choose not to buy all of the wheat produced at this price the government stands ready to buy the remainder and store it. In Figure 8–1 the support price is clearly higher than the equilibrium free-market price. This means that a surplus develops, with quantity supplied exceeding quantity demanded.

The most obvious effect of the price support system is that income (total revenue) to farmers is higher than it would have been with free-market pricing. With price supports, income to farmers is divided into two parts: income from consumers and income from government. Consumers pay the support price multiplied by the quantity they purchase. Receipts from government are indicated by the shaded area.

The nonfarm sector suffers in two ways. First, consumers are clearly hurt by higher prices. Since the demand for most agricultural products is very inelastic, consumers will spend more on these goods than they would at free-market prices. In return they receive smaller quantities. But

**FIGURE 8–1   The Annual Market for Wheat
with Price Controls**

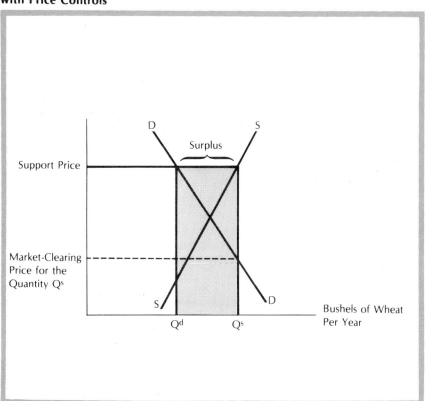

consumers are also taxpayers; that means they must pay an amount equal
to the shaded area plus the costs of storing the surplus that government
accumulates.

The amount of wheat stored under such programs has at times been
enormous. From 1977 to 1978, the annual carryover stock of wheat was
1.1 billion bushels. That figure equaled over 17 percent of all the wheat
produced in 1977. What happens to the wheat? Obviously, the government cannot sell it to domestic consumers. In order to sell the surplus, the
price of a bushel of wheat would have to fall. Buyers would hardly be
willing to pay the support price if they expected the government to turn
around and sell wheat for less the next day. For the same reason, the
wheat cannot be sold in international markets. Because part of the demand
for our wheat is an international demand, the domestic free-market price
cannot differ much from the world price.

So the government had to design other ways of getting rid of the
surplus. Some surplus wheat was given away as part of our foreign-aid
program. Some was sold at cheap prices to foreigners who otherwise
would not have purchased wheat at world prices; some was used in low-

cost school lunch programs; some deteriorated in storage. The government once even experimented with a technique that used surplus wheat in place of gravel to mix with asphalt for paving roads.

What is the effect of all this on economic efficiency? The transfer of income from consumers to producers does not in itself result in inefficiency. But there are serious indirect effects to be considered.

First, consumers would clearly like to consume more wheat and wheat products, and they are willing to pay for the additional cost of producing that wheat. At the quantity Q^d in Figure 8–1, the price they pay is clearly greater than the cost of producing one more bushel. Although they are forced to pay (through taxes) for more wheat, they are not allowed to consume it.

Second, price supports induce farmers to grow too much wheat. To see why, imagine that the government suddenly decided to sell its surplus wheat on the free market. Clearly the price would have to drop to the price we have labeled the *market-clearing price*. Roughly speaking, this is the amount consumers would be willing to pay to have the last bushel of wheat produced. But the cost of producing that bushel is equal to the support price—a price clearly greater than the extra value it creates for consumers. Economic waste results because resources are being used to produce one thing (wheat) when those resources could better be used to produce something else.

Output restrictions

If the price support system had been the only tool of farm policy in the past, surpluses would have been even greater than they were. To keep surpluses under control, however, another technique has been used: restriction of supply. There are several ways of achieving this objective, but the most interesting—and the most horrifying to nonfarmers—was to pay farmers not to produce. Thus farmers were given paychecks for retiring part of their land and for not growing wheat or other crops. Others received payments for not raising hogs. And recently dairy farmers have begun receiving subsidies in return for not milking cows. This Alice-in-Wonderland system inspired a lot of jokes, but it was really serious policy.

In all of the various forms that supply restrictions can take, the objective is to reduce the quantity produced and thus reduce the surplus. Figure 8–2 shows how such policies worked. The figure shows that without supply restrictions the quantity supplied at the support price is approximately twice the quantity demanded, leaving a large surplus. Suppose the government paid farmers to take half of their acreage out of production to erase the surplus. If it worked, this practice could save a lot of money: the farmers would not have to be paid as much not to grow wheat on a given acre as to grow wheat, since it costs less not to grow wheat than to grow it. It also costs less to store wheat that is not grown than to store wheat that is grown.

Acreage controls encounter one chronic problem, though. They do provide an incentive to take land out of crop production. But at the same time, price supports provide an incentive to pour substitute inputs (fertilizer, machinery, and so forth) into growing more wheat per acre on the land that remained in production. The result is that actual supply is not reduced in proportion to the land withdrawn. The government ends up paying farmers not to produce wheat on some acreage and, at the same time, paying the same farmers to produce extra wheat on other acres of the same farm!

In 1978, for example, the government paid farmers to take eighteen million acres of land out of wheat and corn production. This meant that growers of the two crops left about 20 percent of their land idle. Yet production of wheat and corn that year fell only 10 percent. Much the same has happened in the case of the Reagan administration's attempted production restrictions for milk. The size of the herd was reduced, but output per cow continued to rise.

Notice, by the way, that acreage restrictions introduce a new kind of inefficiency. As we have drawn Figure 8–2, the same quantity of wheat will be produced with price supports and acreage restrictions as would be produced in a free market. The difference? The wheat is produced at a much higher cost under the government program. The higher cost results because farmers are inefficiently and too intensively using other inputs instead of using more land. Economic waste results because we could have the same amount of wheat without sacrificing as much in terms of other goods and services.

Direct subsidy

As the consumer price index soared in the early 1970s, so did the prices of agricultural commodities. In spite of a brief experiment with price controls, food prices rose so high—both at home and abroad—that our surpluses vanished.

In the late 1970s, however, things took a turn for the worse. Farm incomes began falling; agricultural prices also fell relative to other prices. So Congress once again set up price supports for some crops and paid farmers not to grow others. But in the interim years a new policy had been devised that was designed especially to assist farmers without unduly encouraging consumer wrath in the supermarket.

The main ingredient of the policy is the setting of *target prices.* Farmers are assured of getting the target price, even if the market price falls below it. But unlike price supports, government does not buy surplus crops. It allows prices to clear the market and then pays the farmer the difference

FIGURE 8–2 The Annual Market for Wheat
with Price and Acreage Controls

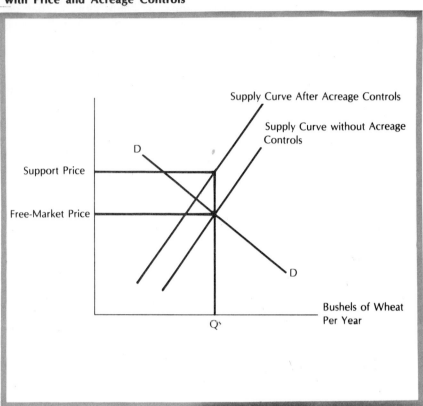

between the target price and the market-clearing price. Figure 8-3 shows
the situation where target prices are above market prices.

There is one problem. In calculating how much to produce, growers
will be guided by target prices—not by market-clearing prices. As a
consequence, they will produce until the target price equals the marginal
cost of production. As a result, the marginal cost of the last bushel
produced will be greater than the value consumers place on that bushel.

This is similar to a program of price supports because it encourages
wasteful production. It avoids another kind of waste, however: all of the
wheat produced is actually consumed instead of being placed in storage
bins.

Payment in kind

The basic elements of acreage restrictions, price supports, and target prices
can be combined in many ways. Details of federal farm programs change

FIGURE 8-3 The Annual Market for Wheat with Target Prices

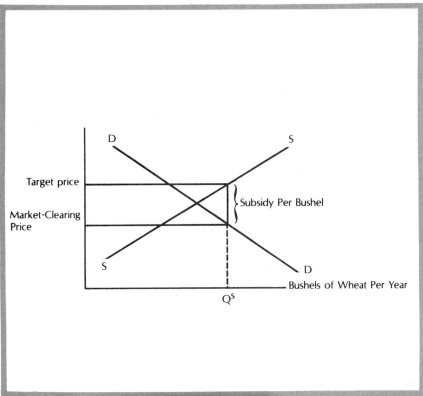

almost every year as new policy blends are tried. Consider, for example, the payment-in-kind (PIK) program instituted by the Reagan administration in 1983.

The concept of PIK was a simple one. To participate in the program, farmers would pledge to withdraw a specified acreage of corn, wheat, or cotton from production. In exchange for this pledge, the government would agree to turn over to farmers up to 95 percent of the grain or cotton that would otherwise have been grown on the land. The farmers would then be free to store the commodities they received, hoping for an increase in the price, or to sell them for whatever they would bring on the market.

PIK was intended to do four things at once. First, it was supposed to raise farm incomes. Second, it was supposed to reduce crop output by encouraging farmers to take acreage out of production. Third, it was supposed to reduce government stocks of grain, which had swelled as a result of previous years' surpluses. And fourth, it was supposed to make the federal budget look better because subsidies would be paid out in the form of grains that the government already owned instead of in the form of cash.

As is so often the case, things did not go exactly according to plan. To begin with, benefits under the PIK program were so generous that about twice the planned acreage was withdrawn from production. Then the nation was hit by a severe midsummer drought that devastated the corn crop. As a result, government stocks of grain ran short of the amount owed to farmers under the PIK program. Instead of being able to pay farmers with grain that was already in government hands, the government had to go to the open market and buy grain, which it then gave to farmers. The beneficial budgetary effects of PIK thus failed to materialize. And instead of stabilizing farm prices (long a professed goal of government programs), PIK had the effect of driving prices higher in a year when the drought would have made them high in any event. Reviewing the 1983 experience, the Reagan administration decided that PIK should not become a permanent feature of U.S. farm programs.

Why have a farm program?

The problems that all farm programs encounter raise the question of why we should have a farm program at all. Why not just let the market determine the price of wheat, corn, and cotton just as it determines the price of coal, lawnmowers, or movie tickets? The traditional defenses of farm programs point to two special problems of farming: that of price instability and that of rural poverty. Let's look at each of these in turn.

Sources of instability in farm prices are found both on the supply side and the demand side of agricultural markets. The supply curve for a crop may often shift because of factors over which farmers have little, if any, control—bad weather or crop disease may wipe out all or part of the season's crop. But rain at the right time can bring in a bumper crop. Such occurrences are inherently unpredictable.

On the demand side, studies have shown that the demand for most agricultural commodities is very inelastic. In the face of shifting supply this means that price swings will be more amplified than would be the case with elastic demand curves, as Figure 8–4 demonstrates.

Unstable prices plus inelastic demand mean unstable farm incomes. Indeed, the evidence shows that per capita net income from farming is considerably more variable than is per capita net income from nonfarm sources. Does this mean that government should try to stabilize income to farmers?

On the surface "stability" sounds desirable and "instability" sounds undesirable. But the existence of fluctuating agricultural prices does not necessarily mean that economic efficiency is improved by price supports— nor is a fluctuating income by itself a bad thing for farm families. What counts is the average income over a series of years. The typical farm family

FIGURE 8–4   Inelastic Demand Curve   Elastic Demand Curve

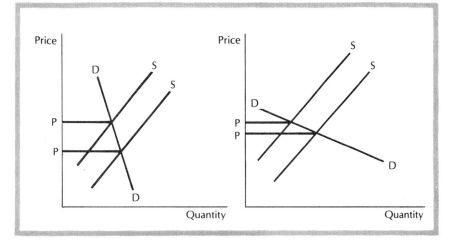

borrows and lends in order to smooth out its consumption pattern in the face of fluctuations in income. Moreover, many so-called farmers earn substantial amounts of income from nonfarm sources.

Even if stability is in some sense a "problem," there is little evidence that government payments to farmers have brought about greater stability in farm incomes. When farm prices and incomes declined during recessions, government payments also declined. When farm prices and incomes were rising during boom periods, government payments rose with them.

Finally, it should be pointed out that farmers have ways of protecting themselves from price instability. One option is to contract to sell crops in the so-called futures markets. In these markets, a farmer can make a contract with a user of grain to sell a certain quantity at an agreed price on an agreed future date. If the farmer so desires, the contract can be made before the crop is even planted, thus entirely removing uncertainty about the price. Some farmers object to selling in the futures markets because they lose the chance of a windfall profit if crop prices rise unexpectedly high. Recently, however, another kind of contract has been allowed, known as an options contract. Under such a contract, a farmer pays a user of grain to promise to buy a given quantity of grain at an agreed price on an agreed future date, but the farmer is not obligated to make the sale at that price if, in the meantime, the market price rises above the contract price.

Let's turn now from the problem of price instability to that of rural poverty. The average income of farm families is only slightly below that of nonfarm families ($25,618 compared with $27,391 in 1983). Nonetheless, many farm families are living in poverty. Census department data for 1983 showed that poverty rates outside cities were somewhat higher than those within urban areas.

Why is this so? Because of factors operating on both the supply and demand sides. Two hundred years ago, about 90 percent of the population lived on farms. As time has passed, that percentage has continued to fall. Today only 2.8 percent of our population is engaged in farming. Enormous technological advances in agriculture have meant that fewer and fewer workers are needed to produce the same amount of food.

At the same time, the growth of demand has not kept pace with the growth of supply: we are spending a declining share of our national income on agricultural goods. This is not surprising. In a poor country where hunger is a problem, we expect a larger share of income to be spent on food than in a rich country. As Adam Smith once observed, the demand for food is limited by the size of the human stomach.

Economists have a way of summarizing the effects of income changes on demand—it is called *income elasticity* of demand. Like price elasticity, income elasticity is defined in the following way:

$$\text{Income elasticity} = \frac{\text{percentage change in quantity demanded}}{\text{percentage change in income}}$$

In general, income elasticity of demand for farm products is quite high for poor countries and quite low for rich ones. For a country like Portugal, for example, income elasticity is 0.6. For the United States today it is 0.08.

As national income rises, then, the demand for food products falls relative to the demand for other goods and services. Moreover, the crops that are produced can be produced with a smaller proportion of the population. As a consequence, more and more families leave the farm.

Why do they leave? Because of low incomes. Farm incomes fall relative to nonfarm incomes; families at the margin realize they can do better by moving to the city and getting nonfarm jobs. This process has been going on for decades; and, as a consequence, there has been a persistent problem of poverty among the marginal farming families.

But although the problem is quite real, it makes little sense to cite farm poverty as justification for agricultural subsidies. Although many farm families are poor, the average farm family is far from poor. Moreover, the way the subsidies are granted insures that the wealthier the farmer, the greater the subsidy. Farm subsidies are based on farm output. Poor farm families produce perhaps as little as 1 percent of all farm output. That means that poor farmers receive about 1 percent of farm subsidies. On the other hand, about 20 percent of all farms produce about 80 percent of all farm output, and receive about 80 percent of farm subsidies.

What is true of the major subsidy programs we have looked at is even more true of some less well known subsidy programs. For example, a number of federal agencies make low-interest loans to farmers, usually wealthy ones. In 1977, the average borrower from the Federal Land Bank had a net income of $54,000 and an average net worth of over $400,000. In 1979, more than one-third of the loans made under an "economic emergency" program went to farmers with assets exceeding a half million dollars. The standard rate of interest was from 3 to 5 percent.

Subsidies to rural electric cooperatives are another example. About two thousand such organizations have been getting federal money at a 2 percent rate of interest. The result, cheap electricity, has been a bonanza for farms that are large enough to irrigate fields with generators that consume electricity voraciously.

An evaluation

We have now looked at three major types of farm subsidy programs; all three are economically inefficient because they encourage excess production. In terms of consumer demand we could be better off producing less on the farm and producing more of other goods and services. Price supports are inefficient in another way as well—part of what is produced does not go to consumers who are willing to pay for its production cost. Moreover, when acreage restrictions are added, goods are produced with inefficient production techniques.

By comparison, consider this alternative: give money to farmers, independently of what they produce, and allow free-market production and pricing. Such a policy would raise farm incomes without causing any serious distortions in the allocation of resources. Each farmer would have an incentive to produce efficiently; each would produce until the market price equaled the marginal cost of production. The value that society placed on the last bushel produced would equal the cost to society of producing it. Moreover, agricultural goods would be distributed among consumers so that bushels would always be allocated to their highest-valued use.

The farm programs we have analyzed are also inconsistent with one of the basic cornerstones of the traditional concept of human liberty: the notion that people are entitled to what they produce. It would be wrong in this view to take a person's property and give it to another unless the producer received some benefit in return or unless the producer committed some crime deserving punishment. Agricultural subsidies, in essence, are simply a way for the government to take money out of the pockets of nonfarmers and hand it over to farmers. Put another way, rather than fulfilling its role as a judge or neutral umpire, government intervenes on the part of farmers and exploits the consumers for the farmers' benefit.

Finally, farm programs tend to make the distribution of income more unequal. The money collected from consumers is collected in a way that is regressive with respect to income—for individual families, just as for entire countries, the income elasticity of demand for food tends to rise as income rises. This is reflected in the fact that poor families spend a larger share of their budget for food, and it places a burden on the consuming family that is greater because its income is lower. In contrast, the higher the farmer's income level, the more subsidy the farmer can expect to receive.

―――――――――――――――――――――――――― **The politics of farm policy**

If agricultural subsidy programs fail by all three of our evaluation criteria, then why do we have them? In general, we have them because of the political power of farm interests. Many senators and congressmen represent farming states and districts; the voters in these areas tend to be highly sensitive to issues affecting farm incomes. By contrast, these issues go largely unnoticed and largely misunderstood by voters in urban areas.

To illustrate the nature of the political problem, consider the following proposal. Suppose a bill is introduced to tax each family $100. The proceeds of the tax would go to farmers under a formula insuring that wealthy farmers get most of the proceeds. Suppose the bill is called the Bill to Aid Wealthy Farmers.

Do you think this proposal would be passed in Congress? It is highly unlikely. Each voter would be aware of her or his own burden; each would also be aware of who was ripping off whom. The public outcry would probably be enormous. Yet this is essentially what happened in 1971–72. To a lesser extent, it is still happening today.

The major difference between the Bill to Aid Wealthy Farmers and our actual farm policies is one of *information costs.* Each of us understands the meaning of $100. But how many of us understand terms like *parity price, target price,* or *payment in kind?* Unless we are studying economics for some other purpose or unless we happen to already know about agricultural policy, the cost to us of learning how we are harmed and how much we are harmed is quite high. For most people the cost of learning about farm subsidies in terms of time, energy, and money is probably greater than $100.

Even if a nonfarmer clearly understands farm subsidies, this knowledge by itself is of little value. True, the nonfarmer can use the knowledge to vote more intelligently in elections. But unless he or she can raise the awareness of other nonfarmers and organize them in effective political opposition, the value of this knowledge is very limited. Moreover, the cost of organizing opposition to the farm lobby is also quite high—surely higher than $100.

By contrast, farmers already know a great deal about farm policies. They need to have this knowledge in order to make intelligent business decisions. Moreover, farm subsidies in one form or another may account for a substantial part of their incomes. The economic incentive to any one of them to engage in political action is, therefore, quite high. Although they are clearly outnumbered by nonfarmers, they possess important advantages in the political marketplace.

The upshot is that farm interests have been extremely successful in obtaining subsidies financed by the rest of the population. The political power of the farming interests can also be observed in other areas. Throughout the 1950s and 1960s, for example, agricultural employees were exempt from the military draft. They have also been generally exempt from Social Security taxes; and until recently farm employees were systematically excluded from all minimum-wage legislation. All things considered, the record of the past would suggest that subsidies to farmers will continue to be very much a part of our future.

Questions for thought and discussion

1. From what you know of the determinants of price elasticity of demand, how can you explain the low elasticity of the demand for farm products?

2. Because of a low price elasticity of demand and a long-run rising supply curve, a policy of price supports and government purchases of the surplus quantities is a politically ideal way of subsidizing farmers. If we tried to extend a similar type of subsidy to producers of ballpoint pens, the result would be disastrous. Explain.

3. Return to our first diagram and compare the result of price supports to the result of the free-market system. Show graphically the increase in farm revenue that results from the price support system. Explain why:
   a. Consumer's contribution to increased revenue depends upon price elasticity of demand.
   b. The total increase in revenue depends only upon elasticity of supply.

Selected references

Farm Commodity Programs: An Opportunity for a Change. Washington, D.C.: American Enterprise Institute, 1973.

Heady, Earl O. *A Primer on Food, Agriculture, and Public Policy.* New York: Random House, 1967.

Houthakker, Hendrik S. *Economic Policy for the Farm Sector.* Washington, D.C.: American Enterprise Institute, 1967.

President's Council of Economic Advisers. *Economic Report of the President.* Washington, D.C.: Government Printing Office, annually. Each year's report contains a chapter on farm policy.

Schultze, Charles L. *The Distribution of Farm Subsidies: Who Gets the Benefits?* Washington, D.C.: Brookings Institution, 1971.

9

Regulation and Deregulation in the Market for Natural Gas

In 1977 it snowed in Miami for the first time in recorded history. That same winter a snowstorm almost buried Buffalo, New York. Hundreds of people were fatally trapped there and in other blizzards across the North and Northeast. It was our coldest winter in over one hundred years.

As temperatures fell, the demand for additional energy as a source of heat kept rising—but additional energy wasn't there. Interstate pipelines that delivered natural gas to most of the nation fell 20 percent short of meeting demand. As a result thousands of schools and industries closed, and over a million workers were sent home from their jobs. The natural gas shortage became a major public issue.

As usual, the shortages gave rise to demands that Congress "do something." But it was hard to get agreement on just what should be done. Everyone could see that the shortage had something to do with the way production and distribution of natural gas was regulated. But while some favored stricter regulation as the solution to the shortages, others thought gas prices should be freed from regulation altogether. After a marathon debate, Congress passed the Natural Gas Policy Act (NGPA) in 1978, a compromise law that tightened regulation in some respects and eased it in others.

In the winters following passage of the NGPA, there were few gas shortage headlines. This was partly because the country was lucky with the weather. Also, the NGPA shifted gas from producing to consuming states, and from industrial to household users, thus making shortages less visible. But the NGPA, as we will see, did not solve all the problems of natural gas policy. Instead, it has led to a new set of problems and uncertainties for this industry that supplies a quarter of our energy needs—and could potentially supply much more.

How regulation evolved

In many ways our current natural gas policy is the product of accident rather than design. The first step was taken in 1938 when Congress passed the Natural Gas Act, an act designed to give the Federal Power Commission (FPC) power to regulate prices charged by interstate pipelines. Congress was apparently concerned that the pipeline companies, which were few in number, would gouge consumers through large price hikes.

The concern did not extend to the producers of gas out in the oil fields, however. Nor did the power to regulate. At that time natural gas was largely treated as a waste byproduct of oil; accordingly, most of it was *flared* (burned as waste) in the field. Only a small portion was actually transported by pipelines to consumers for use as energy, so there seemed little reason to worry about the wellhead price that producers in the field received.

All this changed after World War II. In the early 1950s a number of gas-using states brought suit to force the FPC to regulate wellhead prices; by that time a lot more consumers were using a lot more gas, and the consumers argued that every time the wellhead price increased, the FPC had to allow the pipelines to pass along the increased cost to the final users of gas. So effective regulation (regulation that really kept prices down) meant regulating wellhead prices, too. The Supreme Court agreed—in 1954 it decided *Phillips v. Wisconsin* in favor of the users, and the current regulatory system was born.

Congress evidently did not like the Court's intervention, however; in 1956 both houses of Congress passed legislation that would have ended regulation almost as soon as it had begun. But the new law never made it onto the books. In a dramatic floor speech a senator from South Dakota revealed that an oil lobbyist had offered him a $2500 "contribution" in exchange for his vote. This scandal was too much for President Eisenhower. Rather than sign the tainted bill in an election year, he vetoed it.

Meanwhile the FPC was stuck with a job it really did not want, and one it was not at all sure how to go about doing. For the first five years, the commission tried to regulate gas producers in the same way that public-utility commissions regulate gas and electricity prices at the retail level. This meant conducting in-depth studies of the costs of production for each separate producer and setting an individual price for that producer. The attempt was disastrous—there were literally thousands of gas producers, each a little different from the next. What's more, economic conditions were constantly changing, so an enormous backlog of cases built up. The backlog was so large that in 1960 the FPC estimated that it could not finish its caseload for that year until the year 2043.

Something had to be done, so the FPC turned to a different kind of regulation. Instead of looking at each separate producer, it decided to group producers into entire regions and set prices for each region. This policy at least turned the job into something manageable, but only at the price of other problems. For instance, there is a lot of variation in the costs of production *within* a region. Gas produced from large fields is typically less costly than gas produced from small fields. Gas near the surface is less costly than gas deep underground. Gas from an already developed field is often less costly than gas in an undeveloped field. The list goes on and on.

These problems became especially evident in the early 1970s. Over the decade of the 1960s, the FPC had kept the average price of natural gas roughly constant, but the price of other fuels climbed from 10 to 25 percent over the same decade. This meant that consumers were encouraged to use more gas relative to other sources of energy, but it also meant that producers were encouraged to produce other fuels rather than gas—so people just couldn't buy all of the gas they wanted to buy. In practice that meant that most new consumers were denied any gas at all. A lot of old consumers had their gas curtailed.

Enter phase three. For lack of a better term, this phase might be called the *Exception-Making Phase*. Throughout the 1970s the FPC kept making more and more departures from phase two in order to cope with all of the new problems. It created special categories for different types of "old" gas; a category for "new" gas; a category for emergency gas; a category for imported gas—there seemed to be no limit to the number of categories that could be created.

But phase three was too little too late. The Arab oil embargo and the subsequent OPEC price increases sent other energy prices soaring. On the average the price of natural gas kept lagging behind. Consumers kept demanding more and more gas, and producers kept producing less of it. The shortages intensified and, in almost everyone's view, natural gas pricing developed into a regulatory fiasco.

Let's turn now from the history to the economics of natural gas regulation. We will begin by treating it as a simple case of maximum price control. This will give us a chance to exercise the tools of supply and demand analysis. After we have done that, we will turn to some of the complexities of regulation under the NGPA and beyond.

The supply of natural gas

How much natural gas is there in the world? No one really knows. What's more, most experts don't care. The question simply is not relevant from an economic point of view. We might just as well ask how much natural gas is in the universe. Even if we could make a good guess, our guess would have little effect on any policy decisions we are likely to make.

From an economic point of view, the relevant question is one of cost. It is not the quantity of natural gas that interests us, but the cost of producing it and using it. If a space probe discovered a massive gas field on Mars, this would be of small comfort—the cost of getting it here would be so great that it would never be used in our lifetime.

This is why geologists normally talk in terms of *reserves.* Reserves are defined as amounts of natural gas that can be profitably produced given available technology and current prices. As technology changes, or as prices change, estimated reserves also change.

For example, geologists estimate that there are some 300,000 billion cubic feet of gas—about a fifteen-year supply for the United States— trapped in tightly packed rock layers under the Colorado Rockies. But they can't figure out how to extract it for a price anyone would be willing to pay. If a technological breakthrough solves the problem, this gas would be an enormous addition to estimated reserves.

Similarly, a great deal of oil and gas sits unused at the bottom of existing wells because it is too expensive to extract. About 1 in 9 exploratory holes drilled turns up some oil and gas; but only 1 in 50 contains enough oil and gas to be produced commercially at market prices. The rest are called *dry holes.* But gas wells that were classified as dry holes years ago—when gas sold for 15 cents per thousand cubic feet—may not be "dry" today because of higher gas prices.

Every estimate of total reserves of natural gas is at best an educated guess. Moreover, because of changing technology, changing prices, and new discoveries, these estimates are constantly changing. Nonetheless, as an illustration only, we have depicted three estimates of U.S. reserves in Figure 9–1. All three were prepared by the Market Oriented Program Planning Study (MOPPS) of the Energy Research and Development Administration (ERDA). Each estimate uses different assumptions, and each shows how reserves rise with the marginal cost of production.

Although the three projections vary widely, all have one thing in common: if we are willing to spend more money getting gas out of the ground, we can have more gas. Even the most pessimistic estimate shows reserves at $3.25 per 1,000 cubic feet to be double those obtainable at $1.75.

The MOPPS curves shown in the figure are not actually supply curves for natural gas in the usual sense. To convert them to supply curves we would have to add a time dimension and consider the quantity of gas that could be produced per year at various price levels. To say that reserves would be 520 trillion cubic feet at a price of $3.25 is not to say that we could draw all that gas out in a year or two at that price.

There are several reasons why the cost of producing gas goes up the more rapidly we produce it. For one thing, only a limited quantity of

FIGURE 9–1   ERDA MOPPS STUDY

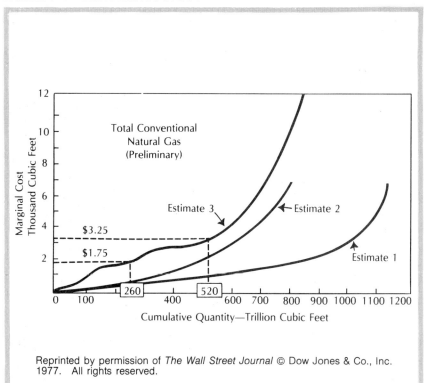

workers and equipment are available at any one time for drilling and extracting. Increasing the rate of production requires workers and materials to be bid away from competing uses, which can be done only at increased cost. Second, the amount of gas that can be recovered from any one well depends on the rate at which it is extracted. The maximum amount recoverable—about 80 percent of the total actually in the well—can be obtained only by producing at an *efficient rate*. This is usually only about a fourth to a third of the rate at which gas would naturally flow from the well. Finally, in many cases, gas pressure is needed to produce oil. For example, there are about 30 trillion cubic feet of gas under Alaska's North Slope, but to produce this gas immediately would reduce the amount of oil that could be recovered from the same source. The reduction in oil output would then have to be figured as part of the opportunity cost of producing the gas.

The supply curve for natural gas is also affected by environmental concerns. Geologists have identified areas off America's coasts as the most promising places to drill for gas and oil, but a lot of potential offshore drilling has been stymied by the fear that it would pollute oceans and beaches. The federal government has allowed exploratory drilling in only a small portion of the U.S. Outer Continental Shelf, and many coastal cities have successfully blocked attempts to lease new areas for exploration. These actions, while reflecting real concerns, nonetheless raise production and exploration costs.

In constructing a supply curve we also must be careful to distinguish production costs from distribution costs. Natural gas is plentiful in Algeria and production costs are low, but unlike oil, natural gas cannot simply be pumped into tankers and shipped to the United States. Gas requires expensive liquefication plants and special ships. By the time it arrives in the United States, Algerian gas costs double what our gas costs at domestic prices. The cost of shipping from the Middle East is even greater and, as a consequence, most of the gas in that area is flared.

Our domestic distribution costs are also high. Once a gas field is discovered, a pipeline must be constructed to connect the field with an existing pipeline. If the production capacity of the field is not large enough to pay for the cost of the pipeline it will not be built, and the gas will not be produced. Underwater pipelines now cost one million dollars a mile. As a result, less than half of the gas bill of the average residential customer represents the wellhead cost of gas.

All of this means that estimating how much gas will actually be supplied to a group of consumers at different prices is a very difficult task. In fact, estimating supply curves is probably a lot harder than estimating reserves. What studies there are, however, tend to confirm the economist's natural suspicion: the higher the price, the more gas that will be supplied.

The demand for natural gas

More than one-fourth of all energy in the United States is supplied by natural gas. If gasoline and diesel fuel used in transportation are excluded, natural gas contributes fully half of the remainder. Gas is used in heating homes, schools, and factories; it is used in a variety of manufacturing processes like melting glass and drying paint. It serves as a raw material for dozens of chemicals ranging from plastics to aspirins.

Natural gas is also used to produce other forms of energy. About 10 percent of current production is burned to generate electricity. Although natural gas itself cannot be converted into gasoline, it *is* used as an energy source in some refineries for producing gasoline along with jet fuel and heating oil. And, as we have explained, it is also used as a source of pressure in oil wells.

Almost every product we buy requires some use of natural gas. When we buy gasoline for an automobile, or a ballpoint pen, or even a bottle of aspirin, we are also paying for the natural gas needed to produce these products. So the consumer demand for aspirin and for millions of other goods ultimately determines the business demand for gas. In fact, most of the gas we consume is consumed indirectly; only one-fourth of all gas goes directly to households. The remainder is used by business firms to produce other goods and services.

Despite the complexity of it all, the demand for natural gas obeys certain fundamental principles. The first principle is that demand is sensitive to price. When the price of gas rises, consumers may react first by simply turning down their thermostats. Given a longer period to adjust they may add insulation to their homes, add wood stoves, or switch to still other energy sources. The options open to business users are often more varied than those open to homeowners. Many substitutes are available if gas is used as boiler fuel—they include electricity, coal, oil, and propane. Businesses often find it worthwhile to institute expensive but effective energy conservation measures. It is widely believed that business demand for natural gas is more elastic than household demand; but both business and household demand curves for natural gas have the normal downward-sloping shape.

A second factor affecting the demand for natural gas is the price of substitute sources of energy. As we noted earlier, the price of natural gas has been kept quite low relative to its alternatives. In fact, the average price of gas in 1981 was only about one-third of the price of equivalent energy from oil. From 1981 to 1984, as the price of oil fell, that of gas rose, partly closing the gap. Still, even in 1984 gas was being sold at a lower average price than the equivalent quantity of oil.

Availability may be as important as price. Under the current rationing system many users live in constant fear of having their supply of gas suddenly curtailed. When this happens the users will not be able to get more gas, regardless of the price they are willing to pay. The threat of such interruptions has led many companies to pay higher prices for other fuels just to make sure that energy will be there when it is needed.

Like the supply of gas, the demand for gas is also affected by environmental concerns. Gas is by far our cleanest fuel; therefore, many cities require their electric utilities to use clean-burning gas instead of coal.

Because of all of these factors, estimating a demand curve for gas can be quite complicated. And, as in the case of the supply curve, economists are uncertain about what it actually looks like. Nonetheless, for illustration only, we have shown a hypothetical market for natural gas in Figure 9–2. The diagram has a conventional upward-sloping supply curve and a downward-sloping demand curve. We have drawn them intersecting at an equilibrium price of $4.00 per thousand cubic feet (mcf). Remember, this price is only an illustration; the real equilibrium price might be higher or lower. However, the diagram does allow us to focus on some basic principles.

FIGURE 9–2   Market for Natural Gas at the Wellhead

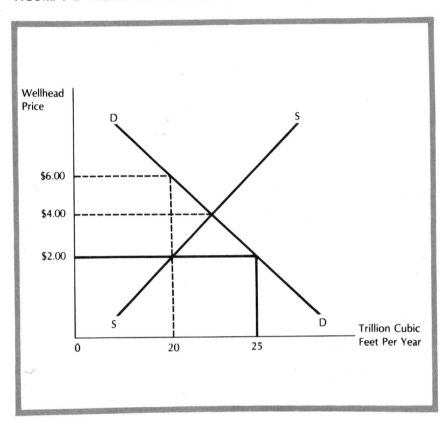

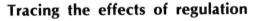

Tracing the effects of regulation

Regulatory policy can be shown in our diagram by drawing a horizontal line to represent the average price established by price controls. We have drawn this at $2.00 per thousand cubic feet. Reading from the supply curve, we see that producers are willing and able to supply 20 trillion cubic feet per year at this price. Reading from the demand curve, we see that users would be willing and able to buy 25 trillion cubic feet at the same price—if the gas were available. That leaves a gap of 5 trillion cubic feet per year between demand and supply.

The natural gas market, as shown in Figure 9–2, illustrates a point that economists agree on with a rare degree of unanimity. Placing a ceiling price (below equilibrium) on a product creates a shortage of that product. If there is no ceiling, there is no shortage. In a free market there cannot be such a thing as a persistent shortage—only a price that adjusts to changing market conditions.

Of course, even in a free market, unexpected shifts in demand might cause temporary shortages to which sellers might not, in the short run, react by changing prices. A gas company might still contract to sell gas at a certain price and then, in a period of peak demand, find its local inventories or its pipelines too small to supply the full demand. This would not happen often, however. To protect their profits and avoid alienating users, rates would be adjusted and facilities expanded to cover all but the most extraordinary contingencies.

So the most obvious effect of a price ceiling, then, is that people cannot buy all of the gas they want to buy. This means that the Federal Energy Regulatory Commission (which took over the FPC's job after 1978) has to make decisions about who gets to buy gas and who does not. In effect, FERC must do the job done by prices in other markets. In Figure 9–2, for example, only 20 trillion cubic feet per year are being supplied. So FERC has tried to limit the number of eligible buyers to insure that only this quantity will actually be demanded.

If the FERC policy is successful, eligible buyers will demand exactly 20 trillion cubic feet per year. In this case, few people will be aware that a problem exists. Unfortunately, FERC has often guessed wrong. If FERC allows too many buyers into the market, they will try to buy more than 20 trillion cubic feet. That is what happened in the winter of 1977. On the other hand, if FERC allows too few buyers into the market, the producers of gas will find that they cannot sell all of the gas they have produced.

Trying to deal with these mishaps has led FERC to adopt a seesaw policy of sometimes discouraging and later encouraging the use of gas by the same customers. In 1978, for example, industrial users and electric utilities were discouraged from using gas. The policy was so successful that by 1979 the producers of gas complained that they could not sell all of the gas they were storing. So the policy was reversed and utilities and industrial users were encouraged to use more gas. By the winter of 1981, however, there were again spot shortages, leading to closings of plants and schools in some cities.

Other, less obvious, effects of price controls have to do with efficiency. One problem is that with a price ceiling in effect, too little gas is being produced. Figure 9–2 shows that producers are producing gas until marginal production costs equal $2.00. But at the margin, consumers are willing to pay as much as $6.00. This means that, in principle, consumers would be willing to pay the additional cost of producing more gas. For the economy as a whole, the benefits of about 2.5 trillion cubic feet of extra gas are much higher than the costs of producing it.

Another problem is that gas that is produced is being used inefficiently. Suppose you are one of the lucky consumers and can buy all of the gas you want. If you are rational, you will use gas until the value of gas, at the margin, is worth about $2.00 to you. But what about those unlucky consumers—the ones who can't buy any gas at all? Why not buy more gas than you need for $2.00 and resell it to them for $2.50—or even more? Sounds reasonable? Not to the FERC.

Under current policy the resale of gas is tightly regulated. In practice this means that gas does not go to the consumers who are willing to pay the most for it. Instead it goes to the consumers whom the FERC thinks ought to have it. The result is that available gas is not applied to its highest valued uses. Some gas is being used in a way that only creates $2.00 worth of benefits; the same gas used in a different way could produce $4.00 worth of benefits or even more.

An ironic example of this type of inefficiency concerns gas produced in Texas. Texans are fond of pointing out that it is a lot less expensive to move Texas gas to Texas cities than it is to move that same gas all the way to the Northeast. Yet many Texas consumers pay higher prices for gas than do consumers in the Northeast. Why? Because the interstate pipelines which get gas from Texas at regulated prices are not allowed to sell their gas to Texas consumers. They can only sell it to favored consumers in the Northeast, who then waste much of it because they are charged such a low price.

The average-cost pricing problem

Up to this point, we have made two simplifications in our discussion of natural gas regulation. First, we have assumed a single price ceiling for natural gas from all sources. Second, we have assumed that only the wellhead price is regulated. The reality of natural gas regulation is more complex. The result is a second type of inefficiency—one resulting from average-cost pricing of gas. To understand the average-cost pricing problem, let's look at some details of regulation under the NGPA.

The NGPA imposed price controls on virtually all categories of natural gas, even previously unregulated gas sold in intrastate markets. Section 104 of the act set the price of "old" gas—gas from fields developed before 1977—at very low levels. Some old gas was priced as low as 36 cents per mcf, with its price allowed to rise only at the rate of inflation. By the end of 1982, section 104 old gas accounted for about 56 percent of the total.

Other kinds of gas were priced higher than old gas. Section 103 set prices for new gas from the most easily developed sources at a price somewhat higher than old gas. Section 102 set prices for slightly harder-to-produce gas at a level initially equal to that of section 103 gas but allowed its price to rise faster than inflation. Finally, section 107 allowed a small amount of very hard-to-produce gas, such as that from very deep wells, to be sold at an unregulated price. By 1982 some section 107 gas was selling for more than $9.00 per mcf.

These prices, ranging from less than $1 per mcf to more than $9 per mcf, are not the prices paid by consumers of natural gas, however. They are the prices paid for gas by interstate pipeline companies, and these companies are themselves subject to regulation. Again we are glossing over many complexities, but pipelines are, in effect, required to sell gas to the consumer at the average price that they pay for it, plus costs of transmission and a fair profit margin. In 1982 the average price to residential customers was about $6 per mcf—much more than the price paid for old gas, but much lower than the price of unregulated section 107 gas.

Average-cost pricing is seriously inefficient. Efficiency in production of gas requires that the least costly sources be tapped first. But the NGPA encourages pipelines to bid high for very costly deep gas and, at the same time, offers little incentive for producers of low-cost old gas to maximize their output. In fact, some old-gas wells are simply capped while elsewhere costly deep wells are drilled.

Furthermore, efficiency in use of natural gas requires that the value of gas to the customer be at least as great as the value of the resources used to produce and deliver the gas. When pipelines pay $9 or more per mcf for deep gas, add transportation costs, and then sell the gas to consumers for $6 or less, this condition clearly is not met.

Under the provisions of the NGPA, the price of most "new" gas will be deregulated in 1985. Old gas will remain under regulation as long as it lasts, however. Partial deregulation in 1985 is expected to encourage production of easier-to-find types of new gas and make more total gas available. Because old gas will still be subject to price controls, however, the average-cost pricing problem will not entirely disappear.

An evaluation

Now that we better understand the effects of natural gas policy, we can evaluate that policy according to the standards we have used before.

Judged by the standard of efficiency, the verdict is fairly clear. Economists are almost unanimous in the belief that current natural gas policy is inefficient. We have already looked at the most important reasons why. Price ceilings on natural gas cause too little gas to be produced. The marginal benefit from additional production is much higher than its marginal cost. Because of current rationing policies, gas does not always go to its highest valued use. At the same time we have been discouraging production of our own gas, we have been paying very high prices to foreigners for imported gas. We have also been using other domestic fuels that are much more expensive to produce than gas. And we have created incentives for industrial users to engage in wasteful spending to insure a steady supply of gas and other fuels.

Most economists who have examined the problem agree that the cause of efficiency would be better served by full deregulation of wellhead prices of gas. Even with full deregulation at the wellhead, many problems would still remain in the regulated pipeline industry and in the regulation of local gas distribution companies that buy from the interstate pipelines. Those problems are beyond the scope of this chapter, however.

Let's turn now to an examination of natural gas regulation from the point of view of equality. One of the chief arguments against deregulation of natural gas in the past has been the fear that it would allow producers to profit at the expense of consumers. The NGPA, however, has not kept the average price of gas from rising. Between 1978 and 1984, the real price of natural gas to the customer (that is, the price adjusted to take the effects of inflation into account) approximately doubled. A major reason was the averaging of price-controlled old gas with more costly new gas.

It should be kept in mind that even without regulation, there is a ceiling beyond which the price of natural gas cannot rise. That ceiling is imposed by the price of oil, the most easily substituted fuel. By 1985 the price of natural gas is expected to reach the energy-equivalent price of fuel oil, when differences in distribution costs are taken into account. After that point, it is unlikely that full deregulation of wellhead prices would push consumer prices up further.

Under the NGPA, regulation itself is a source of inequality. Producers whose gas falls in unregulated categories gain at the expense of those whose prices are controlled. Pipeline companies with access to a lot of regulated old gas gain at the expense of those who must pay more for new gas. And consumers in areas served by pipelines carrying old gas gain at the expense of those in regions served by less fortunate pipelines. Full deregulation of wellhead prices would iron out many of these inequalities.

Turning finally to our third standard, liberty, we find the effects of regulation clear-cut: regulation is inconsistent with the right of each person to engage in voluntary trade with others. Current policy prevents consumers and producers—and consumers and consumers—from making mutually beneficial exchanges. It infringes upon our freedom of contract. Deregulation, then, would be a step in the right directionfor people who think this standard important.

The politics of natural gas

The complicated economics of natural gas regulation have rendered the politics of deregulation equally complex. In 1978, when the NGPA was being debated, the struggle was often painted as one between producers on the one side and consumers on the other. Many consumer groups still oppose deregulation, fearing that prices would rise. As explained above, however, this aspect of the debate is fading in importance as gas prices rise toward the ceiling set by the price of fuel oil.

Much of the political action today pits one region against another, one group of pipelines against another, and one group of producers against another. Undoubtedly, full deregulation would hurt some of these groups and help others. In the struggle over self-interest, each group claims to have the best interests of consumers at heart, but these claims are often little more than window dressing.

In 1983 and 1984, as the date of partial decontrol of wellhead prices under the NGPA approached, many natural gas proposals were submitted to Congress. None of them passed. Almost no one thought that the NGPA represented the best of all possible worlds, but no coalition of interest groups emerged with enough strength to make a decisive change. Although the effects of partial decontrol are hard to predict in detail, natural gas issues will certainly continue to make news in 1985 and beyond.

Questions for thought and discussion

1. Many economists favor deregulation of the wellhead price of natural gas, but very few favor deregulation of gas pipelines. Can you think of any important differences between the production of gas and the transmission of gas that would make regulation more desirable for the pipelines than for wellhead-producers?

2. Some people have argued that deregulation of natural gas should be accompanied by a full-scale program to subsidize the utility bills of poor residential customers. Do you think this is a good idea? Explain.

3. Did partial decontrol of wellhead prices take place in 1985, as scheduled under the NGPA? If so, what were the effects?

Selected references

Broadman, Harry G., and W. David Montgomery. *Natural Gas Markets after Deregulation.* Washington, D.C.: Resources for the Future, 1984.

MacAvoy, Paul, and Robert Pindyck. *Price Controls and the Natural Gas Shortage.* Washington, D.C.: American Enterprise Institute, 1975.

Mitchell, Edward J., ed. *The Deregulation of Natural Gas.* Washington, D.C.: American Enterprise Institute, 1983.

10

Competition and Monopoly in the Market for Oil

How much oil is there in the world? As we saw in the case of natural gas, this is not an economically meaningful question. We should be asking about *reserves* instead—oil that can be extracted at existing prices with known technology. But since prices and technology change rapidly and since new discoveries are periodically made, reserves have a way of changing as we look at them.

Consider the history of reserves. In 1866 the United States Revenue Commission estimated that we had less than a dozen years' supply of oil left. In 1891 the U.S. Geological Survey assured us there was little chance of discovering oil in Texas. In 1914 the Bureau of Mines estimated total future U.S. production at 6 billion barrels—about as much as we have been producing every twenty months for many years.

The oil companies themselves have been fooled as often as has the government. In 1948 a geologist for the world's largest oil company estimated potential U.S. reserves at 110 billion to 165 billion barrels. In 1959, after we had consumed almost 30 billion of those barrels, he estimated that 391 billion barrels remained. Similar stories could be told about other natural resources such as natural gas, coal, and uranium.

If these facts and figures make you feel complacent, don't let them— that isn't why we reported them. We simply want to emphasize an important economic dimension of the issue of oil reserves: as our technology improves and as the price we are willing to pay to find and produce oil goes up, we tend to get different answers to the question of how much oil there is. Whatever oil we find in the future will have been there all along, but until technology reaches a certain stage of development and until prices reach a certain level, the oil will not be worth even looking for, let alone producing.

In keeping with this economic emphasis, then, we will focus not on the question of total reserves, but on a different set of questions. How much oil should we be producing today? Who should consume it? How hard should we be looking for more? Because the answer to each of these questions is determined in part by government policy, let's take a brief look at what our oil policy has been in the past.

A brief history of government and oil

Despite what they might say about free enterprise, major oil companies have long been firm believers in government handouts—government handouts for oil companies, that is.

Back in the 1950s great discoveries of oil were made in the Middle East. These kept world oil prices low relative to other prices, and for the first time the United States became a net importer of oil. This trend was viewed with alarm by domestic producers, who were facing ever higher drilling and exploration costs.

So the oil lobby convinced the Eisenhower administration to institute an oil import quota system. After two attempts with a voluntary approach, oil imports were subjected to mandatory quotas in 1959. The quota limited the quantity of foreign oil that was let into the U.S. market. It thus kept domestic prices higher than they would have been.

To import oil under the quota system required a license. Needless to say, the demand for import licenses was great. The government might have auctioned these licenses by selling them to the highest bidder but instead it gave them away under a formula that assured that most of the import rights went to the largest oil companies. The import licenses were, in effect, a subsidy that was estimated at nearly a million dollars a day!

Ironically, this system was defended on the grounds that a healthy domestic oil industry was essential to national defense and would assure a readily available supply of oil in case of war. Few economists have ever taken this argument seriously, however. Today our national defense posture would surely be stronger, not weaker, had we not needlessly depleted our domestic supplies so rapidly during the era of quotas. Think of it: the very same Middle East oil we were paying $40.00 a barrel for in the late 1970s could have been bought for $1.00 a barrel twenty years earlier. If this had been done, it would be the Middle East countries whose reserves were gone today—not ours!

Free import licenses were not the only thing oil producers got from the government in those days. They also got some fat tax advantages that were not available to other industries. The best known of these was the oil depletion allowance. Under normal circumstances, if a business firm buys a machine it is allowed to deduct part of the cost of that machine from its income over a series of years for tax purposes. This is a defensible practice because the machine will help generate income over those years, and we want to deduct the cost of earning income in the year in which it is realized.

Even though oil is not a man-made productive resource, the industry argued that oil under the ground is like a machine. After all, they said, eventually the oil will be depleted. They convinced Congress to allow them to deduct 27 percent of the value of oil produced each year from their income. Note that the deduction was based upon the value of the oil and had no relationship whatever to the actual expenses incurred in finding or producing that oil.

Although the depletion allowance was the best-known tax subsidy, it was by no means the largest. Better still was a provision for deducting intangible drilling costs. Ordinarily, if a company builds a building it is allowed to deduct the cost of construction only over a series of years. Later deductions are not as valuable as earlier ones, however, for the same reason that $100 today is more valuable than the right to receive $100 ten years from now.

Oil producers, by contrast, were allowed to deduct about 70 percent of drilling costs in the year in which the well was actually drilled. If the well turned out to be "dry," the total drilling cost was deductible.

Because of these and other tax advantages, the oil industry probably has cashed in on more tax subsidies than has any other industry in our country. And, needless to say, such favorable treatment encouraged more exploration and drilling than would otherwise have occurred. But this raised another problem: with all the incentives to produce oil, what happens if too much is produced? Would this not cause the price of oil to fall?

To avoid this difficulty, the industry had another trick that, once again, required the cooperation of friendly politicians. The key this time was the Texas Railroad Commission—a commission that has nothing to do with railroads and a lot to do with oil.

What the commission did was regulate the production of oil from existing Texas oil wells. Each oil well has an estimated capacity, and the commissioners decided periodically what percentage of existing capacity could be extracted each month. The commission was publicly defended as a device for conserving a valuable resource, but, fortunately for the oil producers, the dictates of conservation always seemed to coincide remarkably with their financial self-interest.

Similar commissions also exist in other oil-producing states, notably Oklahoma and Louisiana. How can we get the various commissions to coordinate their policies so that each serves the interest of all? Once again, go to Congress. Congress passed a law called the "Oil Compact," which made it easier for the states to achieve such coordination. In effect it gave its stamp of approval to a domestic oil cartel.

As time passed, though, the industry gradually lost most of those advantages. In 1969, for example, Congress lowered the depletion allowance from 27 to 22 percent. Later it further modified and limited the tax advantages both from depletion deductions and drilling cost write-offs. Import quotas were phased out, and for several years the Texas Railroad Commission allowed wells to produce at 100 percent capacity. What happened? Did the oil lobby lose its political clout? Or did it accept an apparent setback in order to cash in on another political bonanza—this one with roots in the Middle East?

A brief look at OPEC

Before 1973 very few Americans thought about oil cartels. Fewer still had ever heard of OPEC. But OPEC (the Organization of Petroleum Exporting Countries) had been formed over a decade earlier. From the beginning its purpose was to organize an effective oil monopoly and maximize the benefits to producing and exporting countries.

The original members included Abu Dhabi, Algeria, Indonesia, Iran, Iraq, Kuwait, Libya, Nigeria, Qatar, Saudi Arabia, and Venezuela. A few other countries—among them Ecuador—later joined the group. At first its efforts were largely unsuccessful. Then in 1973 came the Yom Kippur War between Israel and its Arab neighbors.

To understand why the war was so important, consider some of the necessary conditions for an effective cartel. Two are of particularly great importance: (1) The cartel members must control the bulk of the market. There must not be any substantial competition from outsiders. (2) Each member of the cartel must be willing to cut back on its own production and resist all temptations to cheat.

OPEC satisfied the first of these two requirements; over 50 percent of the world's annual crude oil consumption was produced in the Middle East alone. It did not possess the second. To see why the second condition is so difficult to achieve, let's look at a couple of graphs.

Figure 10–1 shows how the international oil market might appear from the point of view of the world as a whole. The marginal-cost curve shows that some oil can be produced fairly cheaply—for less than $.50 a barrel. In order to produce 40 billion barrels of oil, however, the marginal cost must rise to about $20.00. In our illustration, $20.00 would be the equilibrium price for oil if the oil market were perfectly competitive. On

FIGURE 10–1   The World Market for Oil

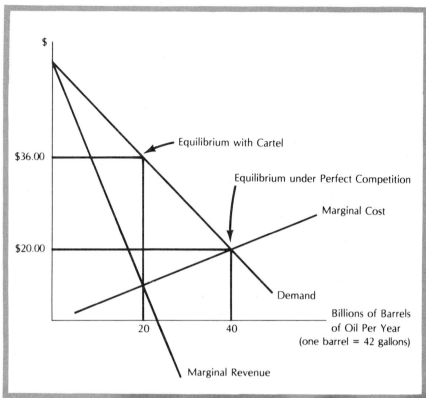

the other hand, if the producing countries organized a perfectly successful cartel, the price would rise to about $36.00. At this price, marginal cost equals marginal revenue, and profits would be maximized.

Although the numbers may not be exactly right, Figure 10–1 *does* illustrate a fundamental principle: in order to raise the price of oil, producers have to cut back their output. As the figure is drawn, they would have to cut world production back to about 20 billion barrels in order to get the price up to $36.00 per barrel. That means that each producer must limit output to less than what it profitably could produce.

To see where the temptation to cheat comes in, examine Figure 10–2, which shows the international oil market as it looks from the point of view of a single producer, such as Kuwait. Since Kuwait produces less than 3 percent of the world's oil production, the demand curve for Kuwait oil is virtually horizontal. If Kuwait was willing to cheat, it could sell all the oil it wanted at the cartel price (or at any rate, by undercutting the cartel price just a slight amount). It would make maximum profits by selling 15 billion barrels of oil—three times its permitted quota.

Of course, if Kuwait chooses such a course of action, then other cartel members will find that at a price of $36.00 they are unable to sell as much

FIGURE 10–2   The World Oil Market from Kuwait's Point of View

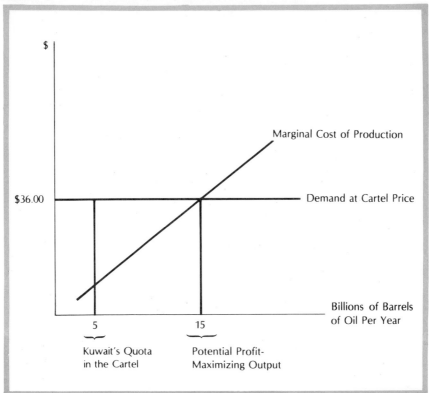

oil as before. In order to maintain a price of $36.00 for everyone else, therefore, all of the other members must make even greater sacrifices. But each in turn will say, "Why don't we do what Kuwait did—grab large profits while the others are sacrificing?" Incentives to cheat are now greater than ever. Ultimately, such cheating would cause the cartel to evaporate and prices to tumble.

In order to prevent overproduction, then, there must be great solidarity among the cartel members and a substantial initial cutback on production. Many believe that the 1973 Arab-Israeli War was crucially important in achieving these required effects. It created solidarity among the Arab countries. Also, production was cut back during the war, especially by Saudi Arabia, a country accounting for the bulk of Middle East production.

But if the 1973 war was needed to solidify OPEC, why did it not fall apart again as soon as the war was over? Many economists predicted this, but instead, prices stayed high. The answer appears to be that OPEC had help from the consuming countries—including help from the U.S. government and American oil companies.

The history of domestic and international cartels points to three things that often precipitate a collapse: (1) decreased demand for the cartel's output, (2) increased production by nonmembers, and (3) increased production of substitute products. All three forces tend to produce the same result: cartel members realize that they cannot sell their output at prevailing prices. Inventories climb, and the incentives to dump at lower prices climb with them.

So how does the current American energy policy rate in terms of these three disruptive forces? Very poorly. We already saw in Chapter 9 how current policy discourages the production of natural gas, which is the most important single substitute for imported oil. We have also been laggard in the production of coal and nuclear energy—largely for environmental reasons.

What about the other two factors? Remarkable as it may seem, the thrust of our policy was to encourage the demand for OPEC imported oil and discourage domestic production. True, there were some conservation measures that reduced some domestic demand for energy, but on balance, our national energy policies had the effect of taxing domestic production and subsidizing imports. How? Let's take a closer look.

The entitlements system

Before 1981, the oil industry was one of the most regulated industries in the country. In the two years following OPEC's rise to international prominence, Congress passed no fewer than forty-five energy bills. These laws were originally implemented by the Federal Energy Administration, which issued additional regulations and rulings. They were later administered by the Department of Energy. Energy regulations soon became nearly as complex as the nation's tax laws; even the very best oil and gas lawyers were never quite sure they fully understood the energy regulations. Indeed, if the statutes, regulations, and summaries of agency and court rulings were stacked page upon page beside a similar stack for tax laws, energy regulations would be over half the size of tax regulations in terms of sheer volume alone.

Like the tax laws, the enormous volume of energy regulations was confusing and sometimes contradictory. Naturally, the large oil companies always interpreted the rules in the way most favorable to themselves and acted accordingly, a practice that led to periodic charges that they were evading the law and overcharging consumers. The problem was that until there were hearings and appeals, no one was quite sure what the law was.

Like the regulators of natural gas, the regulators of oil created special categories of oil, depending on its source—"old" oil, "new" oil, "stripper" oil, and "imported" oil. (Of course, to the consumer, oil is just oil.) Moreover, like natural gas regulations, there were a lot of restrictions on who could buy oil from whom, who could sell oil to whom, and for what price.

Rather than attempt to summarize the energy policy of that era (a feat that would require several books of this size), we will concentrate instead on one particular aspect of that policy that was especially disturbing in view of the international scene: the practice of taxing domestic production and subsidizing imports.

It worked like this. The government set an average price that a domestic oil company can receive when it sells crude oil to a refinery. In 1981 that price was about $24.00 a barrel. In order for the refinery to purchase domestic oil at that price, it had to use purchase tickets, called *entitlements*, which cost about $6.00 a barrel. On the other hand, if an oil refinery purchased foreign oil at $36.00 a barrel, it *received* an entitlement worth about $6.00. Either way, the cost of oil to a refinery was $30.00 regardless of its source.

That meant that American consumers were consuming oil based on a cost of $30.00 a barrel for crude, while the world price was $6.00 higher. Naturally, consumers were willing to consume more petroleum products at lower prices than they were at higher ones—so the entitlement system had the net effect of increasing the demand for OPEC oil. And while foreign producers were receiving $36.00, our domestic producers were receiving much less. They were not even receiving $30.00; they were receiving only $24.00.

In short, the entitlement system encouraged imports and discouraged domestic production. As a consequence, while the world price of oil soared we continued to import more of it. In 1972, prior to the war in the Middle East, we imported about 30 percent of our oil consumption. By 1978 we were importing about 45 percent.

In addition to increasing our dependence on foreign oil, this policy was also extremely inefficient. Suppose that with the OPEC cartel it costs us $36.00 to import an additional barrel of oil. That means we must be willing to trade $36.00 worth of real goods and services for each imported barrel. Clearly, if we can produce an additional barrel of domestic oil for $35.00 or $34.00, we would be better off. We could have more oil and more other goods and services as well. But we were not doing that.

To make things worse, other countries were sometimes able to find lucrative subsidies in the midst of this regulatory fiasco. Consider the case of ship fuel. In 1980, Kuwait was selling crude oil to the U.S. for 89 cents per gallon. Because of regulations, when that oil was refined into ship fuel, it sold for 53 cents per gallon. So ships from Kuwait, filling up in U.S. ports, were paying only 53 cents for oil they sold us in unrefined form for 89 cents. Kuwait was not alone. Between 1974 and 1981, thousands of foreign ships were coming to U.S. ports to buy ship fuel. The U.S. was becoming a global filling station, subsidizing the world shipping industry.

John Kalt has estimated that the entitlements system raised U.S. oil imports by an average of two million barrels a day, roughly a 33 percent increase. All in all, the loss to the economy was more than $2.5 billion a year.[1]

---

1. Kalt's estimates are cited by George Horwich and David Leo Weimer in the source given at the end of this chapter.

———————————————————————————— **A revisionist view of OPEC**

So far we have presented the prevalent point of view of OPEC—that it is a classic cartel, whose success has been aided by Mideast politics and inept U.S. energy policy. But increasingly, a revisionist school is heard from whose members do not think OPEC is a cartel at all—or ever was.

Their reasons? A successful cartel, they argue, must have a well-developed scheme for limiting output. In general, this means that each country must be assigned a production quota, and each must agree not to produce more than its quota. Moreover, most successful cartels have some method of discouraging cheating by their members. They either punish those who cheat, or, at the very least, stand willing to pay potential cheaters not to cheat.

Yet OPEC has never had such a system of output discipline. During the early 1960s, OPEC did try various methods of assigning production quotas. But all of these attempts were abandoned long before OPEC became thought of as an effective cartel. Recent attempts to revive the quotas have not been successful.

So what about the widely publicized meetings where OPEC members set the price of oil? Those who believe that OPEC is not really a cartel argue that these meetings are more show than substance. After all, the oil ministers at these meetings do not always agree on a single price. Even when they do agree on a price, the agreements are often violated. Even Saudi Arabia, OPEC's largest producer, has undercut the prices of other OPEC members on numerous occasions.

Moreover, proponents of this view point to the war between Iran and Iraq as proof that OPEC is anything but a closely knit group of conspirators. What then is OPEC? OPEC, they argue, is precisely what it always was—an organization formed in order to gather and to assimilate technical and economic data on the market for oil.

But if OPEC is not an effective cartel, what explains the sharp rise in the price of oil during the 1970s? Those who reject the cartel theory have an answer for this question too. The important event that occurred during the early 1970s, they argue, was not that OPEC suddenly became a successful cartel. Instead, the important event was that the rights to oil in the Middle East were nationalized by the OPEC countries.

Prior to nationalization, property rights in oil in the Middle East were mainly held by the international oil companies. But these companies always realized that their property rights were very insecure. Knowing that they could not count on indefinite ownership of Middle Eastern oil, the oil companies had an incentive to produce and sell the oil as quickly as they could. In short, they pulled a lot more oil out of the oil fields than a producer with secure property rights would have.

Once the OPEC countries took over, all of this changed. Because the OPEC countries feel far more secure about their ownership of the oil fields than the oil companies did, they face different economic incentives. The countries themselves have an incentive to produce oil at a rate which will maximize their long-run wealth. This rate of production turns out to be a lower rate than the rate which would have been chosen by the oil companies.

Those who reject the cartel theory have one more argument to buttress their case. Most people, they say, regard the sharp increases in oil prices in the 1970s as "unnatural." Thus, they look for a scapegoat. But instead, the skeptics say, it was the very low price of oil in the 1950s and 1960s that was unnatural. This low price was caused by an unnaturally high rate of production by international oil companies and was reinforced by U.S. import quotas. The rise in price in the 1970s merely restored the oil market to normalcy. In fact, taking the long view, the price of oil does not seem unreasonably high today. Between 1950 and 1979, for example, food prices in the U.S. increased more in real terms than did the price of gasoline.

In short, according to the revisionist view of OPEC, each of the OPEC countries simply acts to maximize its own wealth. Each pursues its own self-interest, largely independently of the actions of other members. And the self-interest of one country is not always the same as that of the others. Today, for example, some OPEC countries, such as Algeria and Libya, are nearing the bottom of their reserves. These "price hawks" want to charge every penny they can get for their oil before it runs out—and damn the consequences. On the other hand, Saudi Arabia, with decades of reserves at current production rates, is a price "dove." Not because it is a friend of the West, but because it is afraid too high a price will boost coal conversion and exploration in non-OPEC countries, both of which threaten to ruin the market for Middle East oil in the long run.

The end of oil price controls and the windfall profits tax

Although economists disagree as to whether OPEC is or ever was a true cartel, they agree about one thing. Oil price controls and the entitlement programs were inefficient policies. After some political backing and filling, President Carter, late in his term of office, ordered a phase-out of most controls. President Reagan, soon after taking office, accelerated the phase-out. Since the spring of 1981, the prices of crude oil and refined products have been decontrolled. But all those thousands of oil and gas lawyers throughout the country were not put out of work. They have something new to keep them busy: the windfall profits tax.

The so-called windfall profits tax was part of a delicate political deal cut by pro- and antioil legislators as part of the decontrol process. In return for decontrol, the antioil forces, largely from nonproducing states, got a pound of flesh—a tax on all future oil production. In exchange for their reluctantly given decontrol votes, they got a good chunk of additional government revenue for their own committees to parcel out to their own constituents.

The theory put out for public consumption was that the tax simply took away the "windfall" profits resulting from the machinations of the OPEC cartel. But this story does not ring entirely true. There is, of course, the matter of whether OPEC was really a cartel in the first place, and whether its prices are really "abnormally" high. And more importantly, there is the fact that the so-called windfall profits tax must be paid by oil companies whether they make a profit or not. It would be more accurate to describe it as an excise tax on oil.

The exact amount of the tax that is paid depends upon the category into which the oil falls. That is where all of the old regulations come in. The tax rate paid today depends in part on how the oil being taxed was treated under the old entitlements program. For large companies, with many sources of oil, calculation of the total tax is very complex.

Basically, though, the windfall profits tax obeys the following scheme: newly discovered oil is taxed at a lower rate than oil that was discovered some time ago. As in the case of natural gas, this distinction is very hard to make. How much deeper must you drill an old well before the oil you find becomes new? Or how far away from an old well must a new one be before the most recently drilled oil counts as new oil? The answers to these questions turn out to be quite arbitrary.

Another problem with the distinction between "new" and "old" oil is the political risk it creates for the producers of oil. Once a well is drilled it is extremely tempting for politicians to view the oil coming out of the ground as old oil and proceed to tax it. The risks are real. Back in 1973, producers were told that any "new" oil could be sold at free-market prices; oil from existing fields at that time was classified as "old" and was subject to price controls. Then in 1976, price controls were placed on "new" oil. What was once "new" oil became "old" oil and only "new-new" oil got the free-market price.

The fear among producers, then, is that politicians will use the tax system in the way that price controls were used under the entitlements plan. Take the case of stripper wells, wells that produce less than ten barrels of oil each day. In 1976, owners of stripper wells were promised they could sell their oil at the world price. In response, a lot of new stripper wells came into being. But in March 1979, a "windfall profits tax" was applied to stripper wells, reducing the income from these wells by $15 per barrel.

The strategic petroleum reserve

The end of oil price controls left the U.S. far less dependent on oil imports, and especially on OPEC imports, than before. By 1981, total imports accounted for only 35 percent of total U.S. consumption, down from a peak of 45 percent in 1978. And only 15 percent of U.S. oil comes from the Persian Gulf.

A major question of oil policy for the 1980s is what more, if anything, should be done to reduce U.S. vulnerability to the interruption of foreign oil supplies. At present, the centerpiece of U.S. policy is the strategic petroleum reserve (SPR).

This is a program created by Congress after the Arab oil embargo in the early 1970s. The idea was to prevent major disruption in oil supplies in the event of another international crisis. According to the plan, the government was to buy and store oil in underground salt domes in Texas and Louisiana. The oil was to be left there and used only in case of an emergency.

The project, however, has fallen far short of its mark. According to the schedule set by President Carter, the SPR was supposed to contain 250 million barrels by the end of 1978 and 1 billion barrels by 1985. But by 1984, the reserve held only 390 million barrels. The government also appears to have been an unskillful buyer in the oil market. For a lot of the oil purchased, the Department of Energy paid as much as $3.00 more per barrel than the average price charged by OPEC countries.

Defenders of the SPR see the program as having several benefits. The primary benefit would be to cushion the initial impact of any future oil cutoff, especially in its early days when adjustment would be most painful. In addition, they see the reserve as broadening foreign policy options, as improving military flexibility, and as making a future embargo less likely.

Other observers of the oil industry question the need for the SPR. Oil, they point out, is only one of a great many substances whose supply is uncertain. Normally producers and consumers take precautions in the face of such uncertainty, and create reserves of their own. In the oil market, however, this normal process was thwarted by the entitlements program and other government controls. In the 1970s, firms that conserved and stored oil were often penalized for doing so. Under regulations then in force, the government could, and often did, take oil from those who had it and give it to those who had taken no precautions. As a consequence, there were very poor incentives for private citizens and companies to store oil.

Now that most of these regulations no longer apply, the case for a large government-created oil reserve is not as strong as it once was. Much of the job can now be done by the market. Moreover, when decisions about storing oil are made privately, the decision makers, rather than taxpayers, bear the costs of their mistakes.

Defenders of the SPR are not entirely convinced. Private reserves of oil may be less than the optimal level. First, they say, firms do not bear the full costs or receive the full benefits of their stockpiling decisions. Second, private firms must worry about the possibility that government price controls imposed in an emergency would rob them of speculative profits on reserves that they stored. The windfall profits tax imposed in the 1970s definitely creates a bad precedent in this regard.

For better or worse, the SPR does exist. This creates another problem: how should oil from it be distributed in case of an emergency? George Horwich and David Leo Weimer suggest that the government should sell options to buy oil from the reserve. The options would give a company the right to withdraw oil from the reserve at a given time (say, December 1987) and at a given price (say, 125 percent of the price prevailing at the time the option was sold). If there is a disruption, firms would begin to cash in their options; the option price (125 percent of normal, in our example) would put a limit on the short-run increase in the price of oil during the most difficult early days of the disruption. If there is no disruption, the options would expire unused. In that case, revenue from sale of the options would provide a source of income to the government that it could use, among other things, for filling or administering the SPR.

An evaluation

By the standard of efficiency, the most promising of alternative energy policies is one which encourages a free market for oil and oil products. Under the free-market solution, we would not import a barrel of oil for $36.00 unless we got $36.00 worth of benefits from it. Moreover, we would never buy a barrel of foreign oil unless our domestic producers were unable to produce an extra barrel for less than $36.00. Oil would also be consumed in an efficient way: it would tend to go to its highest valued uses, and consumers would tend to make consumption decisions based on the true opportunity cost of those decisions. In this sense a free market for oil is more efficient than the realistic alternatives.

The entitlements program was inefficient because it encouraged consumers to use too much oil and because it encouraged producers to produce too little. Eliminating the entitlements program and allowing the domestic price of oil to rise to the world price was a movement in the direction of efficiency on the consumer side of the market. Now, at least, consumers will pay the true social cost of the oil they consume. The windfall profits tax, however, continues the old policy of thwarting efficient production. The after-tax price of oil that most producers receive is much less than the value of that oil to consumers.

On the producer side of the market, then, our current policy fails the test of efficiency. So do the policies of storing huge quantities of oil in government-managed salt domes and giving massive subsidies to synfuel programs. Money collected from the windfall profits tax might be more efficiently used if it were simply given to people in the form of tax reductions.

Some have wondered whether a genuinely free market in oil can actually work. Don't the oil companies have too much monopoly power for competition to be successful? By conventional economic standards the petroleum producing and the petroleum refining industries are not highly concentrated. We usually think of a concentrated industry as one in which the largest four firms account for 50 percent or more of total industry sales. In petroleum refining, however, the largest firm accounts for less than 10 percent of the market.

Nor is there much evidence of monopoly power on the basis of profit performance. True, domestic companies watched their profits soar as the OPEC price rose. But prior to 1973, oil company earnings were modest, despite the political subsidies. The ten-year (1963–72) average return on net wealth in petroleum production and refining was only 11.7 percent, while the average of total U.S. manufacturing for the same period was 12.2 percent. It would appear that political favoritism produced only temporary gains that quickly evaporated as many firms competed to enjoy them.

The free market solution is also consistent with the standard of liberty. By this standard there should be no restrictions on the buying and selling of oil and no restrictions on the production of oil and oil products. Nor should government be able to tax "windfall" profits or subsidize "windfall" losses. The production, distribution, and use of oil should be left totally to the free choices of individuals who are participating in the free market.

What about the effects of recent policies on the distribution of income in general and on the welfare of the poor in particular? The answers to this question are very similar to the answers we gave in our analysis of natural gas policy.

On the one hand, the poor tend to share in the fortunes and misfortunes of the economy as a whole. Our national wealth is lower because of the entitlements plan. This loss of wealth affected all of us, including the poor.

Allowing the free market to work would result in unequal distribution of the benefits and burdens. Ultimately the benefits of higher oil prices flow to workers, managers, and stockholders of oil companies and owners of oil producing lands. Stockholders not only include people who own oil stocks themselves but also include indirect stockholders, such as the beneficiaries of pension funds and mutual funds that are holding oil stocks in their portfolios. Twenty-eight percent of Exxon, for example, is owned by employee pension funds. The two million owners of oil royalties are also quite diverse. The average royalty owner receives less than $600 per year, and many of these are low- and moderate-income families. On balance, however, those who derive income from oil production are probably wealthier than those who do not. So, allowing producers to sell oil in a free market probably creates more inequality of income and wealth than would be the case under alternative policies. We thus have a classic trade-off between efficiency and liberty on the one hand and equality on the other.

The politics of oil

One way of looking at our response to OPEC is to see it as a carefully constructed political compromise. Voters tend to resist large price hikes for energy and energy products in times of crisis. An increase in price is very visible; the indirect effect of price controls—more imported oil—is not as visible. So the free-market solution to the crisis of the 1970s had very little voter appeal.

The Reagan administration made a free-market response to a possible future oil crisis the official policy of the U.S. government. Doing so did not entirely solve the problem of the political popularity of the free-market approach. There remains a significant danger that a future disruption would trigger a panic reaction by Congress to reimpose price controls and some form of rationing.

Horwich and Weimer make two suggestions for avoiding this political danger. First, there should be a smooth and automatic mechanism for beginning withdrawals from the SPR during the early days of a crisis. The officials in charge of the reserve might be reluctant to release oil as a crisis developed for fear that they would be accused of "crying wolf." But such a delay might cause a sharp short-run increase in the market price of oil—just the thing that might panic Congress into imposing controls. The option scheme described above would be one way to avoid this problem.

Second, Horwich and Weimer think that standby plans should be made to allocate oil products on special terms to very poor people and to providers of emergency services. On efficiency grounds alone, it could be argued that these users should sink or swim in the marketplace along with everyone else. From a political point of view, things look different. The very poor and the emergency service providers account for only a tiny fraction of total oil consumption, but any interruption of their access to oil products would create a disproportionate political outcry. For the price of a few gallons of subsidized gasoline for city fire departments, the whole country might be saved the pain of price controls and gas lines in a future crisis.

Questions for thought and discussion

1. The major producers of chromium are the Soviet Union, South Africa, Rhodesia, Turkey, and the Philippines. The major producers of manganese, used in steel production, are the Soviet Union, Gabon, Zaire, Brazil, South Africa, and India. Do you think it is likely that the producers of chromium or manganese will form successful cartels? How do these groups of producers differ from the members of OPEC?

2. Aluminum is a very good substitute for copper. Although there is no aluminum cartel, the copper producers have a very strong international organization called CIPEC. So far CIPEC has been relatively unsuccessful in raising the earnings of its members by price increases. Can you explain why?

3. Before the Interstate Commerce Commission (ICC) was formed in 1887, major railroads experienced many unsuccessful attempts to form cartels. The major problem was rebates—secret discounts to shippers. Can you think of any reasons why railroad cartels had more difficulties than does OPEC?

Selected references

Horwich, George, and David Leo Weimer. "The Next Oil Shock—Giving the Market a Chance." *Regulation* 8 (March/April 1984): 16–24.

MacAvoy, Paul, ed. *Federal Energy Administration Regulation: Report of the Presidential Task Force.* Washington, D.C.: American Enterprise Institute, 1977.

Sunder, Shyam. *Oil Industry Profits.* Washington, D.C.: American Enterprise Institute, 1977.

11

Keep on Truckin'

The years since 1980 have been traumatic for the nation's trucking industry. After decades of cozy shelter under the protective wing of the Interstate Commerce Commission, truckers were thrust blinking into the competitive marketplace. Some couldn't stand the heat: more than 900 firms went bankrupt in 1980 and 1981 alone. But 9,000 new firms entered the industry, lured by what they saw as bright profit opportunities. The story of trucking deregulation provides a fascinating case study in the changing economic and political relationships of government and private industry.

Trucking regulation: legacy of the '30s

The story begins back in the 1930s. During the Great Depression, many Americans temporarily lost faith in the virtues of a competitive economy. Unemployment rose to intolerable levels—a quarter of the labor force was out of work in 1933. Business people complained that they could not rehire the idle workers because the prices of the goods they sold were too low to make a profit. They blamed low prices, in turn, on competition.

They thought that if competition could be controlled and prices increased, the economy could lift itself out of the Depression by its own bootstraps.[1]

The Motor Carrier Act of 1935 was a typical piece of Depression-era thinking. The Interstate Commerce Commission had been founded in the nineteenth century, ostensibly to protect farmers from the railroad monopolies. But, by the 1930s, the railroads were the ones crying out for protection. Rapidly improving trucks and roads were, for the first time, allowing motor carriers to cut into traditional railroad markets. Relatively small, high value shipments, on which railroads had traditionally made the greatest profits, were particularly vulnerable.

The larger and better-established motor carriers were worried about competition too. In many parts of the country, unemployed workers were buying second-hand trucks and giving cut-rate competition to the major carriers. Such audacious entrepreneurship was intolerable—why couldn't those drivers stay in the soup lines where they belonged? A cry of help went out to Congress and met a compassionate response.

The Motor Carrier Act, as implemented by the ICC and later refined by Congress, struck right at the heart of the competitive process. It established three legs on which trucking regulation was to rest firmly for the next forty-five years: entry restriction, minimum rate regulation, and collective ratemaking. Each played an important role.

Entry restriction was an ingenious attempt to turn trucking companies into railroads. The railroad industry, before regulation, had been sporadically troubled by competitive rate wars. But railroad competition was at least limited by the fact that once you laid the tracks, a railroad couldn't jump around and enter a new market somewhere else overnight. The trouble with trucks was they didn't require tracks—a trucker could go anywhere, compete with anyone. Acting under the authority newly granted by Congress, the ICC quickly solved that little problem by drawing the missing tracks on paper. Specifically, it granted "grandfather" rights to any motor carrier to continue to haul freight along the routes it operated in 1935— but prohibited anyone from entering a new territory without special permission. And the requirements for a new permit (formally called a "certificate of public convenience and necessity") were stiff: essentially, the new entrant had to prove that the carrier or carriers already operating the route were incapable of providing satisfactory service. And the mere fact that the established carrier's rates were high was not considered justification for letting the new entrant in.

The second leg of the regulatory restriction was minimum rate regulation. Not maximum rate regulation, like that traditionally used to keep

---

1. Today economists would see this reasoning as an example of "the fallacy of composition." True, a single firm could afford to raise its prices and take on more workers if it were able to shake off its specific competitors. It does not follow, however, that all firms could successfully do this simultaneously, or that the economy as a whole could create jobs by suppressing competition in general.

utilities and other natural monopolies from ripping off their customers. Minimum rate regulation, instead, tried to keep motor carriers from charging too little, lest in the heat of the competitive process they drive profits down to the minimum level of the textbook competitive model. Minimum rate regulation was also used, from time to time, to protect the railroads from cut-rate truck competition, but mostly it protected truckers from one another.

Finally, to round out the system, the ICC permitted motor carriers to set rates collectively. Under the aegis of the ICC, most carriers joined so-called rate bureaus, where, like one happy family, they sat down with their rivals to discuss pricing strategy. When the Justice Department challenged the rate bureaus as a gross violation of the antitrust laws, Congress passed the Reed-Bullwinkle Act in 1948 to legalize the system to which the ICC had already given administrative sanction.

The effects of regulation

Economists charged that under the system of entry restriction, minimum rate regulation, and collective ratemaking, the trucking industry operated like a classic cartel. In a study that had substantial impact on the drive to deregulate trucking, Thomas Gale Moore of Stanford's Hoover Institution estimated that regulation kept trucking rates some 10 to 20 percent higher than the competitive level. The result was to create a huge gap between revenue and average cost, as indicated in Figure 11-1.

According to Moore, trucking regulation cost the economy some $4 billion per year. This sum is represented in Figure 11-1 by the shaded rectangle. By no means did all of this sum end up in the pockets of trucking company shareholders, however.

First, according to Moore, a big chunk of that $4 billion went to members of the International Brotherhood of Teamsters. The Teamsters found regulation very useful. It would be hard to unionize an industry in which the firms had wheels, and could roll off to some other city every time they were faced with a union-organizing drive. Even if organizational efforts succeeded, it would be hard to hit unionized firms for higher than competitive wages if a nonunion competitor could roll right in and take its traffic away. But regulation kept motor carriers tied tightly to their paper tracks. They couldn't run away from the union, and at the same time, the lack of competition made it easy for them to pass high union wages along to their customers. In total, Moore estimated that Teamster members earned some $1.2 billion per year more under regulation than they would have earned in a competitive trucking industry.

Another large piece of the $4 billion excess revenue rectangle was dissipated as pure regulatory waste. Part of the waste was associated with the administrative expense of playing "Mother, may I" with the ICC every

FIGURE 11–1   Hypothetical Market for Truck Transportation Services

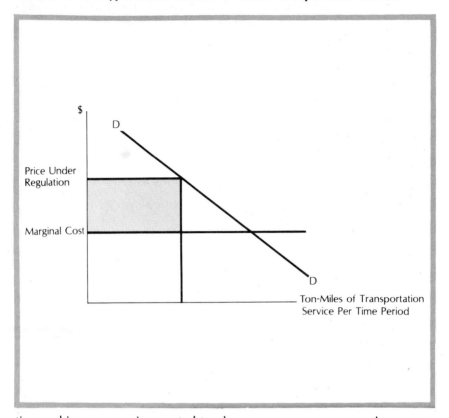

time a shipper or carrier wanted to change a rate or route or other aspect of their business relationship. But a big part of the waste was associated with the rules that forced trucks to operate as if they were trains. For example, under regulation, trucking companies often had to follow routes passing through designated "gateways," analogous to railroad junction points. A carrier having authority, say, to haul between Cincinnati and Indianapolis and between Louisville and Indianapolis could legally haul freight from Cincinnati to Louisville only if its truck actually passed through the Indianapolis gateway. That would make the trip between Cincinnati and Louisville some 217 miles—despite the fact that a perfectly good highway, just 101 miles long, connected the two cities directly!

The gateway restrictions were the most notoriously wasteful that the ICC imposed, but they were by no means the only ones. Many firms, for example, had authority to haul freight only one way along the routes they were authorized to serve. Other firms had one-way authority in the other direction, and the empty trucks of the two passed one another in the middle on the way home. Still other carriers were narrowly restricted in the type of load they could carry. In one actual case, a carrier was given permission to haul paper cups with handles, but not paper cups without handles. Trucks from two different firms thus had to back up to the loading dock to service the needs of a single paper cup factory! All in all, Moore estimated that $1.4 billion of the $4 billion of excess revenue went into this kind of pure waste.

Although regulation did not exactly provide a free lunch for the trucking industry, Moore estimated that there was a tidy sum left over after excess wages and regulatory waste was paid for. Specifically, he estimated the profits to trucking companies at $1.4 billion per year above what they could have earned in a competitive market.

Because possession of an ICC certificate of public convenience and necessity gave a firm the right to earn higher than competitive profits, those certificates became very valuable. Although the ICC was very stingy about issuing new certificates, it permitted carriers to trade certificates freely among themselves. Carriers could thus buy their way into a lucrative market by purchasing the certificate of a carrier already there—if the price was right. At public auctions and private sales, certificates brought anywhere from a few thousand to more than a million dollars, depending on the size of the market involved.

Moore's estimates of the costs of trucking regulation, and others like them, were widely accepted by economists. A few questioned them, however. Some thought Moore's estimates underestimated the degree to which the industry was able to adapt to restrictive regulations. The burdens of gateway restrictions, for example, were mitigated by the fact that firms could buy and sell ICC certificates among one another. To recall our earlier example, any firm that really wanted to haul freight from Cincinnati to Louisville on a regular basis would not use the Indianapolis gateway. Instead, it would find someone willing to sell a certificate granting direct authority. And many shippers via truck feared that although freight rates might be lower on the average without regulation, they would change frequently and unpredictably, thus making it more difficult to do business. No statistical estimates could settle the issue decisively. Instead, a social experiment would be needed—actual deregulation. But first the political climate had to be right.

The politics of deregulation

During the 1960s and 1970s, as economists became increasingly convinced of the need for regulatory reform, they also became increasingly pessimistic about the prospects for change. They saw the regulatory system as supported by an "iron triangle" of Congress, the regulatory bureaucracy, and the regulated industry itself.

The iron triangle worked like this: by law, regulatory commissioners are appointed by the president, subject to confirmation by the Senate. Presidents treat their power of appointment as a valuable bit of political capital, which they cash in by heeding recommendations of influential senators. The lawmakers, in turn, recommend the friends of powerful constituents. In the case of trucking, these constituents would be Teamster leaders or trucking firms that could supply votes or campaign funds. Commissioners would thus begin their careers with a double debt: to the helpful legislator, for providing a comfortable and well-paying job, and to the union or industry for putting their name forward.

The story of the iron triangle did not end with the appointment process, however. Once commissioners were in office, the political economy of regulation favored continued cooperation with the industry. For one thing, when a regulatory agency holds hearings on individual cases or rule changes, members of the industry are virtually the only people heard from. Of course, shippers and carriers may disagree on particular issues, or unions and employers may disagree, or large firms and small firms may disagree. But when it comes to the fundamental institutional framework that provides the pool of benefits from which all parties drink, the regulated firms, their unions, and their customers are likely to present a united front. That is always the way it was in trucking when it came to the fundamental institutions of entry control, minimum rate regulation, and collective ratemaking.

Finally, the iron triangle was reinforced by the career patterns of the commissioners themselves. The "revolving door" is a very real fact of regulatory life. Not only do many commissioners come to Washington from backgrounds in regulatory industry, but if they do their jobs well, they find a friendly reception when their terms expire. Thus a disproportionate number of ex-commissioners end up as officers of regulated firms, as partners in law firms with big regulatory caseloads, or as consultants to regulated industries.

Beginning in 1979, however, things started to go unexpectedly badly for the iron triangle in the trucking industry. President Carter appointed three commissioners with untraditionally procompetitive outlooks. One was Darius Gaskins, an economist who had played a key role in airline deregulation two years earlier. Another was Marcus Alexis, who came from the economics department at Northwestern, and later returned there beholden to no one. And a third was Tad Trantum, a Wall Street analyst who had the unusual notion (unusual for the ICC, that is) that competition was something to be taken seriously.

After Gaskins became chairman in January 1980, things began to move fast. The Carter appointees were so intent on dismantling the regulatory system, in fact, that they pressured Congress into passing legislation lest it be upstaged by administrative action. The industry was ultimately forced to acquiesce in the Motor Carrier Act of 1980 as the lesser of two evils, compared to what they feared Carter's radicals would do at the ICC.

What went wrong? For one thing, Carter, the small-business man, came to Washington with a genuine hostility toward unnecessary government regulation. But this personal commitment was not the whole story. There is no need, in Carter's case, to reject the notion, long an axiom of political science, that elected officials use their powers to maximize their chances of reelection. Instead, it appears that the president simply found a higher priority political use for his ICC appointments than appeasing the Teamsters and the trucking industry.

The more attractive alternative Carter found was to use the ICC appointments as part of an increasingly desperate effort to do something about inflation. Inflation had risen from a rate of just 4.8 percent in the election year of 1976 to over 13 percent by 1979. Fiscal and monetary policy mistakes early in Carter's term of office could not, by 1979, be corrected quickly enough to help in the next election. The program of voluntary wage and price guidelines was almost completely ineffective. But Carter's economic advisers convinced him that trucking deregulation (and deregulation of selected other industries as well) would ease inflation at least in some parts of the economy. Even if it meant the Teamsters would support the Republican nominee in 1980 (which they did), Carter thought the risk worth taking.

The effects of deregulation

As much as it had resisted deregulation, the trucking industry was not slow to adjust to the changes. There really was no choice in the matter. Each firm knew that if it did not move quickly, its competitors would. And the ICC could no longer be counted on as a shield from competitive threats.

One of the first effects of the Motor Carrier Act was a flood of applications for new operating authority. Fifteen-hundred new firms applied in 1980, then 4,600 in 1981 and 4,900 in 1982. But more important than mere changes in the numbers of applications were changes in the kind of authorities granted. There were no more applications to haul paper cups without handles—instead, firms sought and were granted broad authorities for classes of goods such as "all retail products," "food and related products," and in many cases, simply "general commodities." The geographical scope of authorities was also broadened. Instead of drawing paper railroad tracks, the ICC began handing out permits on a state-to-state basis, to and from a city to all points in the United States, and in many cases, to and from all points in the country. Furthermore, there was an increase in new entrants into the industry, as opposed to existing carriers applying for expanded authority. In the first year after the 1980 act, the proportion of new entrants rose from 7 to 13 percent of all applications.

With certificates available so easily from the ICC, the scarcity value of old certificates evaporated overnight. Within months of passage of the Motor Carrier Act, truck lines had written off as worthless certificates that had previously been valued at three-quarters of a billion dollars.

The effects of deregulation have corresponded fairly closely to the predictions that Moore and others made before 1980. By 1982, an index of trucking rates paid by large shippers had fallen to an index of 75, with the base period 1975–77 representing a level of 100. Average compensation of employees fell about 19 percent in the same period. As predicted, members of the Teamsters Union were especially hard hit. At least 100,000 members of the union lost their jobs, partly because new nonunion carriers gained market share at the expense of older unionized carriers. The rate of return on transportation investment for the largest trucking companies fell from 24 percent before deregulation to 11 percent in the year following deregulation.[2]

These numbers may overstate the long-run effects of deregulation because the period 1980–82 saw two severe recessions. It is likely that the recessions accelerated the exit of weak truckers from the industry and exaggerated the decline in rates and wages, the loss of jobs, and the drop in profitability. Nonetheless, Moore found that the recessions did not account for the entire amount of change in the industry.

Whatever the long-term impact on freight rates and profitability, it is certain that deregulation will have a lasting impact on the quality of service. Opponents of deregulation had warned that increased competition and rate cutting would lead to a decline of service quality, but the opposite seems to have happened. In one survey, 86 percent of shippers found service quality to have improved or remained unchanged, while only 14 percent experienced a decline in service quality. Forty-seven percent found service to be more prompt than before deregulation, and 73 percent found service to be more readily available.[3]

The case of CRST, an Iowa-based trucking company, illustrates the way in which firms that are innovative, cost-conscious, and responsive to customer needs have prospered under deregulation. CRST struggled to stay alive under deregulation. The ICC forced the company to spend a lot of time fighting regulations rather than running a trucking business. Once, for example, the carrier was chastised by the ICC for hauling red farm-tractor blades when its ICC authority said it could haul only industrial blades— which were identical except for being painted yellow. Like many regulated companies, CRST had to move its trucks empty many miles each year because it lacked authority to carry a different kind of freight on a return haul.

Under deregulation, CRST applied for nationwide all-commodity authority. It began to offer innovative service packages in which the needs of shippers meshed with the requirements of the carrier's own operations. For example, it was able to offer General Mills a rate 40 to 50 percent below the normal level by putting together a package that would eliminate empty

2. Thomas Gale Moore, "Rail and Truck Reform—the Record So Far," *Regulation* 7 (November/December 1983): Tables 5 and 6.
3. Ibid., Table 8.

return mileage. CRST carries cereal boxes from St. Paul to Cedar Rapids, then cereal to a South Chicago distribution center and another center at New Kingston, Pennsylvania. The truck then reloads at nearby Hershey, Pennsylvania, to carry chocolate products back to Cedar Rapids.[4]

An evaluation

What judgement can be made about truck deregulation in terms of the standards of liberty, equality, and efficiency? The answer is that it looks like a winner on all counts.

The old regime had little to recommend it on grounds of efficiency. Too many trucks were used to haul the freight, too many empty miles were run to satisfy ICC regulations, and too much fuel was burned. As suggested above, efficient truckers will continue to prosper, and at the same time, shippers will enjoy a greater range of price and service options.

The efficiency gains of deregulation will be distributed widely, as truck transportation costs are a part of virtually every good and service produced in the economy. Opponents of deregulation tried to raise the equality issue by predicting that small-town shippers would lose while only big city shippers benefited. In the survey mentioned earlier, however, only 24 percent of shippers found truckers less willing to serve out-of-the-way points, while 34 percent found them more willing to do so. On the labor front, it appears that workers operating under the fat national Teamsters contract may lose relative to those working under local contracts, and nonunion employees. If true, this will represent a move toward more equal distribution of labor income within the industry.

Finally, the cause of economic liberty has unambiguously gained. New firms can enter the industry that were barred before. Among existing carriers, those with the best entrepreneurial talent are now free to submit their ideas to the test of the marketplace.

In short, the early experience with trucking deregulation has encouraged advocates of regulatory reform in other areas of the economy.

Questions for thought and discussion

1. Some truckers contended that deregulation wouldn't work in their industry because trucks did not just move freight from point to point. Instead, they moved it within an elaborate nationwide network that required cooperation of many firms. This network, they said, could not

---

4. Based on Albert R. Karr, "Iowa Trucker Prospers after Deregulation Eases Rules on Routes," *Wall Street Journal,* 13 February 1984.

be maintained without regulation. Do you agree? Can you see any difference between this argument and the following one: The consumption of bread is not "point-to-point" (loaf to mouth) but instead is often combined with butter and strawberry jam within the network of consumption. Without regulatory coordination, how can independent bread, butter, and jam suppliers coordinate their production plans?

2. Motor carriers suffered almost $750 million in losses, at least on paper, when they had to write off the value they had previously declared for their ICC certificates. Many have insisted, in the name of fairness, that Congress partially compensate them for the losses by allowing the writeoffs as tax deductions. Do you agree that to do so would be fair? Why or why not?

3. Draw a production possibility frontier that shows *service quality* on one axis and *rate cutting* on the other. How do you think the effects of regulation can be depicted in terms of such a diagram?

Selected references

Interstate Commerce Commission, Office of Policy and Analysis. Staff Reports on Motor Carrier Regulatory Reform. Occasional series. Available directly from the ICC, Washington, D.C. 20421.

MacAvoy, Paul W., and John W. Snow, eds. *Regulation of Entry and Pricing in Truck Transportation.* Washington, D.C.: American Enterprise Institute, 1977.

Moore, Thomas Gale. "The Beneficiaries of Trucking Regulation." *Journal of Law and Economics* 21 (October 1978): 327–44.

_____. "Rail and Truck Reform—the Record So Far." *Regulation* 7 (November/December 1983): 33–41.

12

Equal Pay for Comparable Work: Women's Issue of the 80s

In 1978 a group of nurses working for the city of Denver sued the city because they were being paid less than sign painters, tree trimmers, and parking meter repairers. They claimed that their work as nurses had a worth comparable to that of the other jobs in terms of training, responsibility, and contribution to society. The only reason they were being paid less, they said, was because almost all nurses were women, whereas almost all of the painters, trimmers, and repairers were men. It looked to them like a case of illegal sex discrimination.

Nonsense, said the city. Wages for all city jobs are set by supply and demand. Sign painters are paid what they get because if they were paid less, not enough applicants would be attracted to fill the jobs. Nurses are not paid as much because plenty of people apply even at a lower wage.

In the Denver nurses' case, the law of supply and demand held up in court. The judge ruled in favor of the city. But as then-head of the Equal Employment Opportunity Commission, Eleanor Holmes Norton, predicted, the issue of equal pay for work of comparable worth was not laid to rest in Denver. Instead, it was destined to become, as Norton put it, "the women's issue of the 80s."

In 1984 the doctrine of equal pay for work of comparable worth (or CW, as we will call it) won its first major court victory. The American Federation of State, County, and Municipal Employees sued the state of

Washington, claiming very much the same sort of sex discrimination as did the Denver nurses. The key to the union's victory (aside from the luck of having a more sympathetic judge) was a consultant's study of the "worth" of various jobs, commissioned by the state itself.

Results of the study are summarized in Figure 12–1. The consultant looked at seventy-five job categories. Each of them was given a score in terms of such factors as the knowledge and skill required, the amount of problem solving involved, the responsibility of the person holding the job, and any hazards or discomforts associated with it. The scores are shown along the horizontal axis of the figure, while the salary paid for each job is shown along the vertical axis.

In an idealized world, the dots representing various jobs would all fall along an upward sloping line. Both fairness and supply and demand would dictate that people would be paid more for higher-ranked jobs. In practice, it is not surprising to find many jobs above or below the "fair pay" line because of such factors as errors in accurately scoring jobs or different degrees of unionization. The figure not only shows that many jobs do not fall right on the line, but also that almost all of the "underpaid" jobs are held predominantly by women, while almost all of the "overpaid" jobs are held predominantly by men.

The reasons for this pattern of pay are at the heart of the comparable worth controversy. In this chapter we will look at various theories that have been advanced to explain why "women's" jobs are less well paid than "men's" jobs. We will also examine the issue of whether employers should be required, as a matter of national policy, to set wages according to the CW principle. Such a policy has been endorsed by most women's rights groups and was favored in one form or another by all the major contenders for the Democratic presidential nomination in 1984. As usual, we will end the chapter with an evaluation of policy proposals and a discussion of the politics of the issue.

─────────────────── **The economics of wage determination**

According to standard economic theory, wages and salaries are set by supply and demand. The demand curve for workers of any given skill and occupation slopes downward, as shown in Figure 12–2. The supply curve of workers of any given category slopes upward.

There are two reasons for the downward slope of the demand curve. First, the demand for workers of a given type is derived from the demand for the goods or services they produce. (The demand for sign painters is derived from the demand for signs; the demand for nurses is derived from the demand for health-care services.) If workers are paid less, the product can be sold at a lower price, and people will buy more of it. Thus, lower

FIGURE 12-1 Valuing Jobs in Washington State

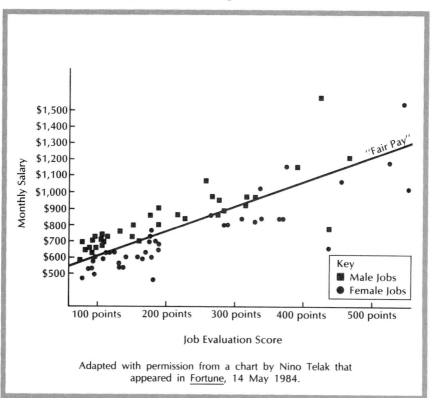

Job Evaluation Score

Adapted with permission from a chart by Nino Telak that
appeared in <u>Fortune</u>, 14 May 1984.

pay leads more workers to be hired because it affects the quantity of the product that consumers demand.

Demand curves for workers slope downward for a second reason as well. Many different inputs are used in producing any given good or service such as skilled labor, unskilled labor, machinery, energy, and materials. In many cases, inputs can be substituted for one another. Consider the case of health-care services. Nurses are a key input in the production process. Because nurses on the average are paid less than doctors, hospitals substitute nurses' services for those of doctors whenever the nurses' training permits. On the other hand, there are substitutes for nurses' services too. Still lower paid nurses' aides, orderlies, and technicians can perform many routine tasks. Electronic sensors can monitor patients' conditions and send a signal to a central nurses' station at the first sign of trouble. Such devices allow each nurse to look after more patients with no sacrifice of quality of care. The incentive that employers have to substitute less costly inputs for more costly ones whenever possible would cause the demand curve for each input to slope downward, aside from the fact that lower input costs mean lower output prices.

FIGURE 12–2 **Supply and Demand**   **Supply and Demand**
                for Nurses   **for Painters**

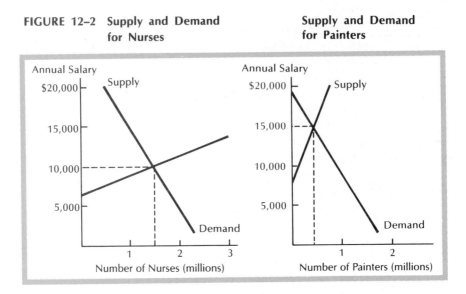

The supply curves in Figure 12–2 slope upward. This indicates that the higher the wage rate offered, the more people will be willing to work in a given occupation. One reason is that higher pay gives a greater incentive to undertake the education and training required for a job. A second reason is that a high enough level of pay will attract workers from other occupations, even if the other jobs are more interesting or offer better working conditions. Finally, the supply curve for a given job category slopes upward in part because for higher pay, people will work more hours a week or more weeks a year.

For any given job, according to standard economic theory, pay is determined by the intersection of the supply and demand curves. In Figure 12–2, the equilibrium pay for nurses is shown as $10,000 per year, and that for sign painters is shown as $14,000. Why are nurses paid less than sign painters, even though there is a much greater demand for their services? The graph makes the reason clear. Although there is a great demand for nurses, there is also a great supply. Even at the relatively low pay rate of $10,000 a year, enough people stay in the profession to fill all the jobs that are offered. The supply of sign painters is more limited, however. This is not so much because sign painters need rare skills or difficult training as it is because potential sign painters could do many other kinds of work instead. At less than $14,000 a year, some of the people currently working as sign painters would leave to become house painters, auto painters, truck drivers, or whatever else is available.

But why don't nurses also leave their jobs to become sign painters, house painters, or truck drivers when the pay drops below $14,000? Why do a million and a half people—96 percent of them women—remain nurses even at $10,000 a year? The economist's answer is that there must be something about the occupation that they like, even though the pay is low. Perhaps men and women who become nurses like to serve other people and would find painting signs unfulfilling. Perhaps they like the abundance of part-time work available in nursing, or the availability of nursing jobs in all parts of the country, or even the relative ease of entering and leaving the field once one has the training. From the point of view of supply and demand, it doesn't much matter why people want to be nurses (despite the lower pay) instead of painters or truck drivers. It is simply a fact that they do.

But isn't there another possible explanation for the low pay of nurses relative to sign painters? What about discrimination? What if employers refuse to hire women for any but low-paying jobs? Wouldn't that cut off higher-paying opportunities for women, and force them to crowd into relatively few occupations, where pay would then be driven down by oversupply?

Economists agree that if there was systematic discrimination in hiring, these would be the effects. Still, far from all of them are convinced that the low level of nurses' pay or the facts of most other CW cases, for that matter, are caused by discrimination.

The main reason for skepticism is that in the private sector, which accounts for more than 80 percent of all jobs in the U.S. economy, discrimination is unprofitable. To maximize profits, a firm must minimize the cost of producing any given level of output. If any job is paid more than the minimum needed to attract qualified applicants, the excess pay comes out of the owner's pocket.

Suppose, for example, that the going wage for painters is $7 per hour and that only men are hired as painters. Suppose too that a large pool of qualified women would be happy to lay down their steno pads and pick up a paint brush for any wage over $5 per hour. The first firm that broke with tradition and hired women painters would save $2 an hour. The saving would allow the firm to cut the price of its product a little and so give it a competitive edge in the marketplace. Other employers would have to follow suit if they did not want to see their market share eroded. As the tradition of men-only painters was abandoned, the increased supply of applicants for painting jobs would tend to drive the average level of painters' wages down. At the same time, the wider job opportunities for women would tend to force employers to pay a little more to keep their stenographers on the job.

True, the profit motive only *tends* to eliminate discrimination. Some stubborn employers may hold out against the tendency, even if it injures their profits. And in the case of employment by government (both the Denver and the Washington State cases were brought against public employers), the profit motive may not work against discrimination with the same force as in the private sector.

Still, the Washington State case and other recent CW cases do not fit the usual pattern of discrimination. Discrimination in the labor market usually takes one of two forms. Either workers doing the same job are paid different wages, or some workers are barred from applying for certain high-paid jobs. Both of these practices are outlawed by the Equal Pay Act of 1963 and the Civil Rights Act of 1964. In the Washington State case, the minority of men employed in "women's" jobs such as secretary, and the minority of women employed in "men's" jobs such as truck driver, were paid just the same as their co-workers. And the state was not accused of barring women from applying for "men's" jobs. In fact, the state had an affirmative action program that made efforts to recruit women and minority group members for jobs in which they were underrepresented.

These arguments have made many people doubt that a national CW policy is needed. But not everyone agrees. Let's look now at what the other side has to say.

─────────────────── **The case for comparable worth**

The case for CW rests on two propositions. The first is that despite the standard economic argument, supply and demand does not work to eliminate discrimination in the job market. The second is that there is a better, fairer way than supply and demand to set pay scales. Both of these propositions must hold to establish a case for CW. It would not be enough to say that supply and demand did not work perfectly unless an alternative worked better.

CW advocates often point out that institutions, as well as markets, play a role in setting wages. Although the supply and demand model implies that everyone doing the same job should get the same pay, the world doesn't work that way. One institution that gets in the way is that of seniority. Most employers pay workers more the longer they remain on the job. To a degree, this reflects the fact that more experienced workers tend to be more productive. But even in simple jobs where experience doesn't count for much, and even in a few types of jobs where young people with new ideas outperform older people with more experience, seniority tends to be reflected in higher pay. Why is this the case? Simply because both employers and workers see the seniority principle as a fair one.

Labor unions are another institution that gets in the way of supply and demand. Simple supply and demand theory cannot explain why workers in unionized steel and auto plants are paid half-again as much, or sometimes even twice as much, as people doing comparable work in nonunionized plants.

Imperfect information also interferes with the operation of supply and demand in the job market. A National Academy of Sciences report suggests that imperfect information helps explain low pay for women. Employers perceive women as less strongly attached to the job market than men. Women tend to work fewer years of their adult life than men and are more likely to leave the job market for a period in mid-career. Thus, employers may be reluctant to hire women for jobs that require extensive training, and in which frequent turnover would be expensive. Instead, they hire women mostly for lower-paying jobs in which training and job stability are less important.

Although it may be true that women on the average have a weaker attachment to the job market than men, the argument continues, these generalizations are not true of all women. Many women do want stable, long-term employment. But employers lack a good way of predicting which women applicants are which, so they lessen their risk by discriminating against women as a group.

In short, proponents of CW portray the job market as a place in which the law of supply and demand is only one among many factors influencing pay and job choice. Since the operation of supply and demand has so many exceptions, why not make still another one?

Now let's turn to the question of what is proposed in place of supply and demand to determine the relative pay of jobs. The proposed substitute is job evaluation research of the type upon which Figure 12–1 is based. Under such a system, all the jobs that each employer must fill would be analyzed in terms such as skill, hardship, and responsibility. Pay would then be set according to the rated worth of each job.

This idea is hardly new. Advocates of CW are fond of pointing out that many employers already use job evaluation in setting pay scales. A number of consulting firms specialize in making job evaluations. A national CW policy would only prod all employers to adopt a management practice that many already find profitable, they say.

——— How strong is the case for comparable worth?

Advocates of a national CW policy are right in claiming that simple supply and demand theory glosses over many details of real world job markets. But the case for CW glosses over a great many difficulties too.

First of all, it is a *non sequitur* to argue that because institutions such as labor unions and seniority systems represent departures from purely competitive markets, still more departures will make things better. A national policy forcing all employers to follow the principle of comparable worth might make no more sense than a national policy forcing all employees to join unions, or one forcing all employers to adopt some uniform type of seniority system. Unions, seniority, and CW may very well belong to a set of institutions that are useful under some circumstances, but not all.

Second, it is not clear that the National Academy of Science argument about information costs and labor market attachment is valid. The argument implies that it would be fair for employers to pay lower wages to workers (men or women) who drop in and out of the labor market whenever they feel like it. Pay scales would be unfair only if women who steadily pursued their careers earned less than men who showed equal labor market attachment.

A study by Walter Williams of George Mason University suggests, however, that men and women who are equally attached to the labor force do receive equal pay for comparable worth. Williams begins by citing data that show that women who have never married show much stronger labor market attachment than women who are married and living with their husbands. To be specific, never married women with a college education spend 88.9 percent of their working years in the labor force, while married women with the same education spend only 36.4 percent of their working years in the labor force. Similar differences in labor force attachment are seen for women with high school educations and with graduate degrees.

Williams then goes on to show that differences in earnings are more closely associated with marital status than with gender. One study showed that among men and women who have never married, women earn 99 percent as much as men, whereas among people who are married and have never been divorced, women earn only a third as much as men. Another study that Williams cites limited itself to men and women with academic careers. Never married women, it found, achieved the rank of full professor more often and earned more than never married men. Married women with academic jobs, however, earned 14 percent less than married men.

All in all, these data call into question the proposition that employers discriminate against all women simply because some married women pull down women's average degree of labor market attachment. Instead, it appears that never married men and never married women, whose degree of labor market attachment is about equal, earn about equal pay. The average pay of women, in Williams's view, is pulled down mainly by the fact that married women spend far fewer years in the labor market than married men. They earn less than married men because they accumulate less seniority and less on-the-job training.

Finally, what about the argument that job evaluation studies are as good or better a method of setting relative pay scales as is the law of supply and demand? It is true that many firms use formal job evaluation studies as an aid in setting relative pay scales. Such studies are a helpful management tool. They help a firm to keep its pay scales in line with those of other firms employing the same kinds of workers. They are also an aid to what human resource managers call "internal fairness," which simply means a pay scale under which employees can understand the reasons why some are paid more than others.

Nonetheless, even supporters of job evaluation as a tool of human resource management acknowledge certain shortcomings of the technique. First, they point out that job evaluations are to some extent subjective. No two consultants will assign the same point ratings to the same set of jobs. Second, they caution that even when job evaluations are used to set the framework for a pay system, employers must depart from the job evaluation scale when supply and demand require it. For example, one oil company assigned identical job evaluation ratings to accountants, attorneys, and petroleum engineers on such bases as complexity of the work or required education. It found, however, that it could get all the accountants and engineers it wanted for $22,000 a year, but it could not touch a petroleum engineer for less than $32,000. Why? Supply and demand.

In short, although the job evaluation technique may often be a good management tool, it is not clear that the technique would make good law. Skeptics foresee endless lawsuits about which consultant's job rankings were valid. They also foresee cases in which pay scales pegged rigidly by law to job evaluation rankings would lead to a deluge of applications for some jobs and a critical shortage of applicants for others.

An evaluation

All things considered, how would a national CW policy rate in terms of our three standards of efficiency, equality, and liberty? The question is an important one because both the courts and Congress are sure to be faced with the issue of CW policy in coming years.

Job market discrimination does hurt efficiency. Members of the groups discriminated against are barred from occupations where they could best put their skills and talents to work. Instead, they work in less productive jobs or leave the job market altogether. For a labor force of a given size, discrimination makes national product less than it otherwise would be.

It follows that policies aimed at combating discrimination arguably improve efficiency. It is not clear, however, that CW is the right sort of policy to take care of the problem. The most troublesome forms of job market discrimination, from an efficiency point of view, are those that bar certain groups from certain classes of jobs. Different pay scales for men and women doing the same work can also hurt to the extent that they discourage women from seeking jobs where such pay scales prevail. However, if men and women in a given occupation are paid the same, and if both men and women are free to move from one occupation to another, it is far from clear that further tinkering with market-determined wage scales would be helpful. At worst, some critics fear, a CW policy would lead to a situation in which some jobs were impossible to fill while others attracted long waiting lists. Such a situation would mean a less efficient job market, not a more efficient one.

Part of the case for a CW policy rests on the use of job evaluation studies by human resource managers in many private firms. A policy that is voluntarily used by profitable companies can hardly be inefficient, they say. There is a difference, however, between the voluntary use of job evaluation studies and a policy that would make such studies compulsory. Some kinds of jobs can be more accurately evaluated than others. Private managers can switch from one rating method or one consultant to another if they are not happy with the way things are going. And they are free to adjust the salary levels suggested by job evaluations if they get too many or too few applicants for a given kind of job.

Under a compulsory system, this kind of flexibility would not be present. Switching from one consultant to another, or deviating from job ratings for any reason, would become material for lawsuits and administrative appeals. In the business world, inflexibility is one of the great enemies of efficiency.

In many cases, as we have pointed out in this book, we accept policies that are inefficient if they promote fairness and equality. Is CW such a policy? At first glance, it appears to be. Pushing up the salary levels of all the people who fall below the "fairness" line in Figure 12–1 (and possibly pushing down the salaries of those above the line) would clearly promote equality—or would it?

To answer this question we must, as always, look at the indirect as well as the direct effects of a CW policy. CW would promote equality *if it had no indirect effects on the number of jobs or the choice of people to hold those jobs.* But the indirect effects of a CW policy would surely be substantial, as a little thought shows.

First, a policy of raising the relative pay of low-paid jobs held predominantly by women would reduce the number of such jobs offered by employers. Take the case of nurses. With nurses' pay higher, other things being equal, hospitals would have less incentive than before to substitute nurses' work for doctors. At the same time, they would have more incentive to substitute the work of nurses' aides and orderlies for that of nurses. They would also buy more automatic equipment to allow each nurse to handle more patients. Fewer nurses would be hired, and some already on the job might be laid off. Presumably, those who kept their jobs would tend to be those from the best nursing schools or perhaps those with the most experience. Thus a CW policy would be most helpful to those who least need the help.

A second effect of CW policy would be to attract men into occupations such as nurse and secretary that are now dominated by women. In one way, this would be welcome. Changing attitudes and equal opportunity legislation has already encouraged many women to enter careers such as law and pharmacy in which they were previously underrepresented. To generate a movement of men into traditional women's jobs would extend this process in a way that opponents of traditional gender stereotypes would approve. But a CW policy would bring men into these women's occupations at the same time that the total number of jobs in them was shrinking. Under the new, more competitive conditions, some women would prosper. These would be the women with the best educations, the strongest job skills, and the fewest distracting family commitments. The women helped most by CW, in other words, would be the kind who are already making successful inroads to occupations traditionally dominated by men.

Finally, as CW raised pay in women's occupations and attracted men into them, the characteristics of those occupations that attracted women to them in the first place would change. Sociologist Brigitte Berger cites data indicating that many American women work to help their families, which are their chief concerns. This motive steers women into work with such features as easy entry and exit, and availability of flexible hours and part-time work. But if jobs such as nurse or secretary paid more, employers would have less incentive to tailor jobs to suit the needs of such women. They would begin to insist on stronger job attachment, just as they have in occupations dominated by men. Experience and training would begin to count for more. With fewer positions open and more people of both sexes applying for the jobs, employers would be more likely to pass over women who wanted to work just to help their family.

In short, the impact of CW on equality would be mixed. The most educated and experienced women, and those most strongly attached to the labor force, would very likely be helped. They would keep their jobs and be paid more for them. Less educated and experienced women, and those who want to work to help their families, but not necessarily full-time or for their whole working-age careers, would fare less well. They would find jobs increasingly harder to get in just those occupations that traditionally have been most open to them. Increasingly, their best work opportunities would be in low-paid occupations such as sales worker, counter clerk, and assembly worker. Since these jobs have traditionally attracted men and women in about equal numbers, they would presumably not be affected by a CW policy—except to the extent that a greater supply of applicants for such jobs would depress their level of pay.

Finally, we should consider the case for a CW policy in terms of the standard of liberty. Policies that fight discrimination can be defended on the grounds that they increase personal freedom. Although there are many disputes over how far such policies should go in the direction of affirmative action and quotas, no doubt people are freer today than they were when women and minority group members were legally barred from many occupations.

It is not clear that CW would be a useful extension of this trend toward greater personal freedom, however. Women who want to move into men's occupations are already free to do so. CW would affect mainly those who have this freedom but choose not to exercise it. At the same time, a serious CW policy would constrain the freedom of employers to choose personnel practices best suited to their line of business.

The politics of comparable worth

We have seen that whether it is posed in terms of efficiency, equality, or liberty, the case for a CW policy is mixed at best. Why then does it have so much political momentum behind it? There appear to be three major reasons.

First, women's rights groups see CW as a way to reach a group of women that have not been among their main supporters. These are neither the career women struggling to break into male-dominated occupations nor nonworking women with time to devote to political causes. They are women who have jobs, but whose main interests, if Berger is correct, are their families. If women's organizations can persuade these women that there is something in the movement for them too, they will increase their political clout.

Second, a policy favored by women's rights activists tends to be perceived as one that is favorable to women in general. In the case of CW, we have seen, this proposition is doubtful. CW would help some women; it would hurt others. But political perceptions do not always allow for such ambiguities. Politicians see CW as a chance of offering women a raise—and a lot of women vote. When a CW bill comes to a vote on the Senate floor, or when a campaigning politician faces a question about CW, no one wants to create the impression of being against women.

Finally, CW policy shares a trait with many other policies: the people who are helped by it are much easier to identify than the people who would be hurt. Women who now hold jobs such as nurses and secretaries and who expect to be keeping their jobs for some time can hope for more pay as a result of CW. People who might get such jobs in the future, but will not do so if CW increases the competition for them, are not so easy to identify.

Questions for thought and discussion

1. Proponents of CW stress policies that would raise the pay of women whose jobs fall below the "fair pay" line on a chart such as that in Figure 12–1. Why not instead cut the pay of men whose jobs fall above the line? What problems would each alternative create in terms of supply and demand? Compare the two alternatives in terms of efficiency, equality, and liberty.

2. The current debate over CW policy focuses exclusively on women who work in low-paid occupations traditionally dominated by women. Why should such women get special attention from public policy compared with women in low-paying jobs not traditionally dominated by women, such as sales clerks and assembly workers? What about low-paying jobs

traditionally dominated by men, such as certain types of farm labor? Would the CW approach be applicable there too? In short, why not apply CW across the board so that pay for all jobs, not just women's jobs, would be set according to job evaluation principles rather than supply and demand?

3. Opponents of CW often say that if secretaries or nurses wanted higher pay, they should seek jobs as electricians, truck drivers, or sign painters. Some labor unions and some employers have, in fact, tried actively to recruit women for such "men's" jobs, but they have not always gotten as many women to apply as they had hoped. Why do you think more women do not apply for such relatively well paid "men's" jobs? Is it prejudice, discrimination, or stereotypes? Is it something about those jobs that most women just don't like? Discuss.

Selected references

Seligman, Daniel. " 'Pay Equity' Is a Bad Idea." *Fortune* 109 (14 May 1984): 133–40.

Treiman, Donald J., and Heidi I. Hartmann, eds. *Women, Work, and Wages: Equal Pay for Jobs of Equal Value.* Washington, D.C.: National Academy of Sciences, 1982.

Williams, Walter. *Explaining the Economic Gender Gap.* Dallas: National Center for Policy Analysis, 1983.

13

Supply and Demand Divided by the Rio Grande

Give Me Your Tired, Your Poor,
Your Huddled Masses Yearning To Be Free
—Inscription at the base of
  the Statue of Liberty

That was once our attitude—officially at least. Today things are different, especially along the two thousand mile U.S.-Mexican border that begins around Brownsville, Texas; winds up the Rio Grande River; stretches across the base of New Mexico, Arizona, and California; and extends to Tijuana, just south of San Diego.

Billions of dollars worth of illegal drugs cross this border each year. That bothers a lot of people—but what seems to bother them more than illegal drugs is illegal people. They're pouring in at a rate of a half million per year. The greatest number come from Mexico, but others come through Mexico from countries all over the world. All come for essentially the same reason: to find jobs and make money—more money than they could ever make in the countries they are leaving.

How many illegal aliens are there in this country? No one knows for sure. About one million illegal aliens are arrested each year and sent home either voluntarily or under deportation proceedings. But many of these simply return again. Estimates of the number that are living here at any one time range from three to ten million. Three to six million is a commonly mentioned range: more people than the number of Americans who are officially unemployed. Whatever the total, one thing is fairly certain: it's going to get higher.

Most of our representatives in Washington consider this phenomenon a major problem—something approaching a national crisis. President Reagan has said, "We've lost control of our own borders, and no nation can do that and survive." A lot of people outside government do not consider it a problem at all, but almost everyone agrees that the presence here of an ever-growing population of illegal immigrants will have economic, political, and social repercussions for years to come.

A brief history of U.S. immigration policy

Hard as it is to believe today, there was virtually free immigration into this country for its first hundred years. It wasn't until 1882 that the first general immigration statute was passed, a statute that established a head tax and provided for the exclusion of certain kinds of people.

Then followed the Chinese Exclusion Laws and the Gentlemen's Agreement with Japan in the first decade of this century, laws designed to decrease the inflow of Oriental labor. Even so, large-scale immigration from Europe and Asia, sometimes exceeding a million people per year, continued until the enactment and enforcement of the Quota Acts of 1921 and 1924.

The first great wave of Mexican immigration occurred between 1910 and 1914, during the Mexican Revolution; an estimated four million people streamed across the Rio Grande in those four years. Over the next fifty years, the northward flow was largely determined by economic cycles and labor-market conditions in the United States.

During World War I a labor shortage induced large numbers of Mexican workers to seek employment on farms and ranches in the Southwest; when the Great Depression hit, most of these workers were kicked back across the border. They came in even larger numbers during World War II and were aided in part by the Bracero Program—a formal agreement signed by the United States and Mexico in 1942. Under this program hundreds of thousands of Mexicans were brought into the country on a temporary basis to meet many of our labor needs, particularly the seasonal needs of agriculture.

In the late 1940s, returning servicemen again swelled the job ranks; as a result the Bracero Program formally ended in 1947, although it was continued on an informal basis. By this time, however, the number of illegal aliens was beginning to rise substantially. In the early 1950s the government initiated Operation Wetback, an unprecedented human round-up that resulted in the deportation of almost three million people in three years.

The Bracero Program was again formalized under the Eisenhower administration and lasted until 1964. In 1964 Congress, under persistent pressure from organized labor, terminated the program permanently. Today immigration quotas only allow about 400,000 people into this country each year, but millions more enter without the approval of the Immigration and Naturalization Service (INS). Let's see why.

The market for illegal labor

Right across the river from El Paso lies Ciudad Juarez. Once one of the world capitals for abortion and quick divorce, today Juarez is a portal for Mexicans seeking a dream of prosperity in the United States. Since the mid-1960s, its population has doubled, making it Mexico's third-largest city and biggest border town.

The poverty in Juarez is unspeakable by American standards. Housing is so crowded that ten or twelve people sleep in rows across the floor in a nine-by-five foot room. Outside the city garbage dump over three hundred people make their homes in shanties fashioned from cardboard, pieces of billboard, and used car parts. They scrounge for food among piles of rubbish. For those who have jobs, there is little hope of making more than two or three dollars a day.

Across the Rio Grande, things are quite different. The average wage for farm and ranch stoop labor is about $1.75 an hour; the going wage for an illegal maid is $25.00 a week. And the INS estimates that about 30 percent of the illegals working in the area make more than the minimum wage of $3.25 per hour. Small wonder that the desire to cross the river is so great.

On our side of the border, employers of every variety are more than happy to give the aliens jobs. *Texas Monthly* reports that, with only two identifiable exceptions, every major employer in El Paso is known to make a practice of hiring substantial numbers of illegal aliens. In addition, a majority of farms, ranches, and food and drink establishments in the area are run with illegal labor. In fact, it is believed that 15 percent of the residents of the entire city are there illegally.

These two cities reflect their two countries in a microcosm. Mexico has a booming population not matched by comparable economic growth. In 1940 there were approximately twenty million Mexicans, 75 percent of whom were land workers. Today, there are almost seventy million Mexicans, with the same percentage of people tied to the land. The peasants of Mexico work for wages that are depressingly low and live under conditions that are intolerable by our standards. According to one study, 17 percent of Mexico's population earns less than $75 a year.

Nor are things likely to improve. About 50 percent of the population of Mexico is under fifteen years of age. The country's population is expected to double within twenty-five years. Similar conditions apply to countries farther south—Columbia, El Salvador, Guatemala, the Dominican

Republic, Jamaica, Ecuador, and others. U.S. labor markets will become ever more attractive to the people in these countries.

In the United States today, illegal immigrants can work for restaurant owners, construction foremen, hotel managers, fabric factory supervisors, mine bosses, industrial plant managers, and countless other prospective employers. Many make up to $6.00 or $7.00 per hour. The prospect of such wages—and the added possibility of holding down two jobs by working a 16-hour day— is an irresistible lure for millions of lower-class Mexicans.

Despite the fears of many Americans, there seems to be little evidence that most Mexican illegal aliens plan to settle permanently in the United States. Most continue to maintain a pattern of "shuttle" migration, returning to Mexico after six months or less of employment in this country. It is believed that only a very small percentage stays longer than a year. The family of the illegal alien typically remains in Mexico, and, while in the United States, he sends them cash through the mail. To appreciate the magnitude of these cash flows one need only look at the Saturday afternoon *lineas de viudas* ("lines of widows") that form at post offices in the villages of the interior. Mexico alone receives more than $1 billion a year in such payments, more than from any export but oil.

Why are employers so eager to hire illegal aliens? Many employers, for obvious reasons, don't want to talk about it; those who do request anonymity. Nonetheless, scores of interviews with employers from coast to coast reveal a consistent response: illegal aliens are willing to perform jobs that American workers refuse at comparable wages, and they are exceptionally good workers.

Farmers in Idaho pay better than the minimum wage. But without some twelve to sixteen thousand illegal aliens, they believe that jobs would go begging. Says one farmer, "Without them, our production would drop 15 to 20 percent." East Coast farmers say much the same thing. After a raid by federal authorities on a Maryland farm, the employer lost the remainder of his cucumber crop. "I had to plow it under," he lamented. "I couldn't get anybody to pick it. It cost me fifteen thousand dollars."

Not only do they take jobs our own workers refuse, most employers claim they are better workers (in other words, they have a higher marginal product). This is largely because they're desperately in need of work and they're scared. A Dallas construction boss says that "they can throw up twice as much brick as any of the crews that I have." A Houston employer, who pays illegals as much as five or six dollars an hour, confides that "if I could get the rest of the men to work like they do, production would increase instantly." And in an ironic reversal of racial-cultural stereotyping, one illegal alien explained his ability to find employment this way: "I think Americans are basically lazy."

One of the most significant economic aspects of the market for illegal labor is the dramatic contrast with our own domestic labor problems. At a time when our official unemployment rate is persistently high by historic standards, many observers believe there are more illegal aliens in this country than there are unemployed citizens.

This is true even though the alien is at a disadvantage in the labor market. Many are illiterate and cannot speak English. All look for jobs in fear of detection by federal authorities; this makes it impossible for them to take advantage of the standard public and private employment agencies. Nonetheless, they find jobs, even in large cities with soaring unemployment rates.

How do they do it? Little is actually known about the mechanics of the illegal labor market, but we do know that an important link in the chain is supplied by professional people-smugglers known as *polleros* or *coyotes*. Beginning in El Paso, the smugglers pack their cargo in U-Haul trailers and truck them north to factories in Denver, St. Louis, Boston, Newark, and countless other destinations.

Coyotes will even guide their clients across the border. When security is tight the fees can be quite high. For example, after increased border security at Tijuana (which may be an even larger funnel for illegal aliens than is Juarez) smugglers were charging $250 to guide illegals across the border and transport them to Los Angeles. Clearly, this service is only available to those with money.

For wealthier clients additional services can be supplied. About three or four hundred dollars more will buy bogus back-dated documents such as rent receipts, utility bills, Social Security cards, and American work permits. The smuggling business is apparently quite profitable. Despite the risks (up to five years in prison and a $2,000 fine for each alien) it is a multimillion-dollar industry. One INS official estimates conservatively that smugglers gross around $20 million annually.

Because it is illegal, smuggling people—just like smuggling drugs—has some dangerous and unpleasant aspects. Aliens who cross the border near Tijuana have more to fear from terrifying gangs of *banditos* than they have to fear from the Border Patrol. If caught by the Border Patrol they will simply be deported; but bandit gangs, waiting in ambush on the mesa, are often poised to beat, knife, and sometimes kill them for what little money they carry. There are also reported incidents of aliens being locked in abandoned smuggling vehicles and suffocating to death. These risks seem small, however, compared to the fortunes that await the successful immigrant.

The economic consequences of illegal aliens

What are the economic consequences of illegal immigration? They are about the same as the economic consequences of legal immigration.

Economists have traditionally been sympathetic with free trade in both goods and services, a sympathy that dates back to the writings of Adam Smith. Put in simple terms, the argument goes something like this: trade between two people benefits both trading parties; each gives up something valued less for something valued more. With some qualifications the argument can be extended to whole nations of people as well. Mexico cannot sell goods (like oil) to us without eventually using our dollars to buy from us. Both countries tend to profit from the exchange.

A tariff on goods imported from Mexico not only hurts Mexico, it hurts us as well. Similarly, a tax or limitation on tourist services also tends to injure both countries. Adam Smith argued that British tariffs made England less wealthy, not more wealthy, and most modern economists agree.

Does the same argument apply to the flow of labor across international boundaries? To a great extent it does. Mexico is exporting labor services to us; in return we pay wages, which are returned to Mexico. Eventually those same dollars will be spent on goods we export to Mexico, so in essence we trade goods for labor services.

We can use a simple diagram to look at the impact on our labor markets in somewhat more detail. As workers cross the border and enter our labor markets, they expand the supply of labor available. As wages fall, two things happen. First, some of our domestic workers refuse to take jobs and are replaced by Mexican workers. Second, employers find it profitable to hire more workers and produce more goods than they did before. Figure 13–1 shows two labor-supply curves: the higher one applies if the labor supply consists only of domestic workers; the lower one applies when illegal foreign workers are included. At any wage rate the horizontal difference between these two curves indicates the additional labor hours supplied by illegal aliens. As illegal aliens enter the job market, the wage rate falls and more workers are hired, because as labor costs fall employers find it profitable to expand production. Hence, more cucumbers are produced in Maryland and more potatoes are harvested in Idaho.

In the new equilibrium, L_2 hours of labor services are utilized at a wage of W_2. Note, however, that although more workers are working after immigration than before, the number of hours worked by domestic workers has decreased by the amount L_1 less L_0. This effect leads to the charge that illegal aliens are taking jobs away from American workers.

It is very misleading, however, to visualize U.S. citizens being thrown out of their jobs because of Mexican labor. In equilibrium, all workers can be employed at the going wage; illegal aliens have no advantage over their American counterparts. In fact, as we have seen, they are at a considerable disadvantage.

Nonetheless, the impact on American workers is serious. The entry of illegal labor into American job markets makes wages, and therefore incomes, for some domestic workers lower than they would otherwise be. Even if the country as a whole can potentially gain, particular groups of

FIGURE 13-1   Market for Unskilled Labor

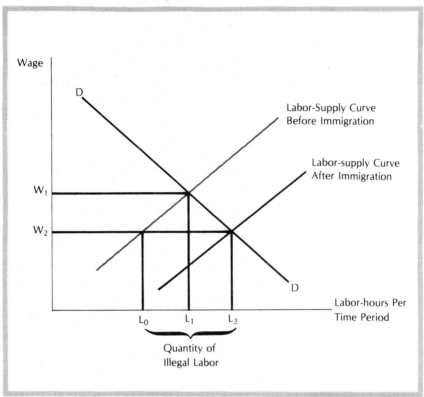

Americans will not gain. They have to choose between working at lower wages or turning to unemployment compensation and welfare assistance. Note that these options are not open to the alien worker.

Moreover, as long as we stand ready to guarantee American families a certain minimum income, the flow of illegal aliens will tend to raise the number of welfare recipients and therefore increase the cost of welfare. That by itself does not necessarily make the nation worse off—at least it doesn't if welfare consists only of taking money from some citizens and giving it to others. What *does* make the nation worse off is that these same Americans are encouraged not to work. Instead of paying them to produce, we pay them not to produce. The country as a whole winds up with fewer goods and services than it might have enjoyed.

How serious is this problem? Independent studies have shown little evidence of widescale displacement of legal resident workers by illegal aliens. That is not too surprising since disgruntled workers who lost their jobs to illegal aliens could simply report this fact to immigration authorities and watch their competitors be deported. Still, without the immigrants we would expect wages to rise as marginal businesses failed and larger concerns bid up wages for a smaller labor supply. The national unemployment rate might fall, but no one knows by how much.

Do illegal aliens place undue burdens upon our social services? No, according to a comprehensive study by Professor Julian Simon at the University of Maryland. Simon found that, compared to U.S. citizens, immigrants pay more than their share of taxes and receive less than their share of government benefits. He concluded that "immigrants, viewed in economic terms, seem an excellent bargain."

Can the tide of illegal immigration be stemmed?

Illegal immigration probably cannot be stopped, at least not for any cost we are likely to be willing to bear. Right now, entering the United States illegally the first time is a misdemeanor punishable by six months in jail and/or a $500 fine. Entering a second time carries a penalty of two years in jail and/or a $1,000 fine. But as a practical matter, most illegal aliens are simply deported.

Take the case of El Paso: authorities do not even bother with prosecution unless the illegal alien has been caught three or four times before. Even then the costs are staggering. The *El Paso Times* has estimated that the cost of holding illegal aliens in the city jail is about $4.9 to $9.2 million per year, a cost that averages out to about $45 to $65 per taxpayer.

For the country as a whole things are not much brighter. We do not have the resources to put ten million people in jail; even if we did, the cost of locating and arresting them would be enormous. The problem is a lot like the problem of marijuana—the crime is largely a "victimless" crime, where buyers and sellers are happy with the arrangement.

Moreover, as in the case of marijuana, the profits to be made from illegal immigration are enormous. Illegal aliens will typically consider the difference between their American wages and what they would receive if they remained in Mexico; even if they spend a good portion of this difference to avoid detection and deportation, they still profit from the bargain. Furthermore, the more they are willing to spend on false identity papers and covert transportation, the more it costs us to find and arrest them.

Difficult though the job of controlling illegal immigration is, Congress decided, in 1984, to try one more time. In the summer of 1984, both the House and the Senate passed the Simpson-Mazzoli bill in an effort to stem the tide.[1] Simpson-Mazzoli is an unholy compromise between conflicting interests. On the one hand, it grants amnesty to illegal immigrants who had

---

1. Although the Simpson-Mazzoli bill passed both the Senate and the House, it died in conference committee when Congress adjourned.

already been in the country a set length of time when the bill was passed. On the other hand, it introduces a controversial new tool for controlling new illegal immigration: employer sanctions.

The employer sanctions section of the Simpson-Mazzoli bill make it, for the first time, a federal crime to hire knowingly workers who are in the United States illegally. The bill provides a sliding scale of penalties, with severe punishment for repeat offenders. The wisdom of these sanctions was hotly debated before the measure narrowly passed in the House of Representatives.

One objection to the sanctions is based on doubt that they will work. Eleven states, including California and Florida, have tried employer sanctions in the past with little effect. Studies of foreign countries such as Hong Kong that use employer sanctions also show them to be an ineffective deterrent. The main weakness of sanctions is that they only require employers to ask for documentation from prospective workers. They do not, and cannot, prevent illegal immigrants from presenting bogus papers. Proposals for a tamper-proof national ID card for all citizens have been strongly resisted by civil libertarians. And besides, it is doubtful if a really tamper-proof document could be devised.

A second objection to the sanctions is based on their possible effect on legal immigrants from Mexico and elsewhere in Latin America. Many Mexican-American leaders spoke out against the Simpson-Mazzoli bill for this reason. They fear that if employers know they can be punished for hiring illegal immigrants, they may play it safe and refuse to hire anyone with a Spanish accent or a dark complexion.

However well the employer sanctions work, one thing is sure. There is little hope for cooperation from Mexico. True, it is a crime in Mexico to cross the border illegally. But Mexican authorities do little to enforce the law or to punish those who are apprehended and deported.

It's not difficult to see why: Mexico's population explosion not only depresses agricultural and industrial wages, but it also represents a potential source of future political instability. Illegal immigration serves as a safety valve for a surplus population. Between 5 and 10 percent of the population of Mexico is probably in the United States illegally. The money they send back to Mexico may approach 10 percent of that country's gross national product. It is more than the total annual tourist revenue. It not only provides a source of income for Mexican citizens, but also serves as an important source of foreign exchange with which to buy industrial products from the United States.

From Mexico's standpoint the picture is quite clear. We are capital intensive; they are labor intensive. By combining our capital with their labor both countries can produce more goods and services than they can by acting independently, and Mexico can only gain from the bargain.

There are two ways of exploiting the potential gains from trade: transport our capital to Mexico or transport Mexico's labor to the United States. Both options are currently being used. Shortly after we terminated the Bracero Program, Mexico initiated its *Maquiladora* Program, a program that allows foreign companies investing in Mexico to escape the usual prohibitions against foreign ownership and that allows them to own and control 100 percent of their investments and the land on which their plants are built. The program now covers about eighty-five foreign corporations, including such giants as RCA, AMF, and General Electric.

But the movement of people has been far more important and financially rewarding to Mexico, and, as a consequence, Mexican authorities are not eager to stop it. As Mexican President Jose Portillo once commented, "These people aren't criminals. They are ordinary people looking for jobs." And that is that.

The politics of U.S. immigration policy

The politics of immigration is complex. In part, the complexity is the result of a profound ambiguity in public feelings toward immigration in this nation of immigrants. A recent *Newsweek* poll highlighted this ambiguity. Sixty-one percent of those polled agreed with the statement that "immigrants take jobs from U.S. workers." Yet 80 percent agreed with the statements that "many immigrants work hard—often taking jobs that Americans don't want," and that "immigrants help improve our culture with their different cultures and talents." [2]

Whatever the complexities, one basic political dividing line has not changed in over a century: business is for it and organized labor is against it. Moreover, it is not hard to see why labor gained the upper hand. If the flow of immigration is suddenly increased, any particular business may realize a temporary increase in profit. If markets are competitive, however, the lower costs experienced by any one firm will also be experienced by all of its competitors. Prices will ultimately fall and, in the long run, each firm will only realize a normal rate of return on invested capital. The gains from immigration only go to business in the short run. In the long run these gains are passed along to consumers in the form of lower prices.

The impact on labor income is more permanent, however. As the flow of immigrants is increased, American workers who compete with them will receive lower wages and therefore lower income. Moreover, as long as the immigrants are here the original workers will continue to have lower incomes than they would have had without immigration. The economic impact of immigration on labor, then, is substantially greater than the impact upon business; as a consequence, organized labor has a greater incentive to mount an intensive political effort than management does.

---

2. *Newsweek*, 25 June 1984, 21.

Ironically, very few members of the AFL-CIO actually compete direct-ly with illegal aliens for jobs. The reason organized labor is so concerned with illegal aliens is because of very powerful forms of indirect competi-tion. Many products can be produced with different production tech-niques; some are capital intensive and usually require skilled workers to operate complicated machinery; but others are labor intensive and utilize large numbers of unskilled workers.

Moreover, since business managers must choose between these differ-ent production techniques, they are in effect choosing between skilled and unskilled labor. If the wage rate for unskilled labor falls relative to the wage rate for skilled labor, managers have an incentive to switch to labor-intensive techniques. The switch lowers the demand for skilled labor and hence lowers wage rates for skilled labor. Clearly, then, skilled labor has a real economic interest in policies that affect the price and availability of unskilled labor services.

Another political split in the debate over immigration reform, as we have already mentioned, pits Mexican-Americans against Anglos. Mexican-American leaders and members of Congress were almost unanimous in opposing Simpson-Mazzoli, which they saw as harmful to legal as well as illegal immigrants. Most of these leaders did welcome the bill's provisions granting amnesty to illegals who had been in the country long enough to put down roots. But some Mexican-Americans who had earned entry by following legal channels object to the idea of giving a free ride to people who broke the law to come here.

Finally, immigration has produced a split between federal interests, on the one hand, and state and local interests, on the other. As we mentioned, economists like Julian Simon believe that illegal immigrants pay more in taxes, on balance, than they collect in benefits. But the taxes they pay are largely federal social security and income taxes, while the benefits tend to be provided at the state and local level. For example, the city of Los Angeles, believed to have 10 percent of the country's illegal immigrant population, spends $100 million annually in free medical care for them, including two-thirds of its hospitals' childbirths. And Texas pays an estimat-ed $85 million a year to educate the children of illegal immigrants. As the effects of Simpson-Mazzoli become clear, it is likely that there will be renewed demands by state and local government for federal payments to cover such expenses.

An evaluation

How do we evaluate U.S. immigration policy by the standards of liberty, equality, and efficiency? That depends crucially on what significance we attach to international boundaries. Remember that these standards are ethical standards; is there any ethical significance to an international boundary?

Only the standard of liberty seems to suggest a clear answer to this question. Most libertarians believe that people have the same rights regardless of what country they live in. International boundaries have political significance but not ethical significance. That means that trade between people in different countries ought to be just as free and un-restricted as trade between people in the same country. Except perhaps for measures to protect public health, this criterion impels us to accept free immigration and emigration. This policy is a simple corollary of a policy of free international trade.

The other two standards are more flexible. We could believe in efficiency or equality within countries without accepting their application between countries. Our answers will be different depending upon what option we choose.

If, for example, we want to eliminate poverty among American citizens, we are not helped in this task by the entry of illegal aliens; their presence here tends to depress the wages of the least well off. On the other hand, if poverty in Juarez or Tijuana is just as much our concern as is poverty north of the border in El Paso or San Diego, then free immigration is clearly desirable. Since immigration will tend to lower wages in the United States and raise them in Mexico, it would have the effect of redistributing income from a wealthy country to a poor one.

Finally, the implications of efficiency are quite clear if we want international efficiency. With free immigration, mutually beneficial trade can take place between citizens of both countries. By exploiting trading opportunities both countries could produce more goods and services with the same resources. On the other hand, if we are only concerned with efficiency in the United States, and if we continue our current welfare policies, the implications are less clear. True, we could be better off by trading our own goods for Mexico's labor services, but these gains from trade come at a price. If the inflow of Mexican labor causes our own welfare rolls to swell, we suffer decreased production. We could end up paying more people not to produce when they would be willing to produce if wage rates were only higher. On balance, it's not clear in which direction the conception of efficiency points us.

Questions for thought and discussion

1. The amnesty provisions of Simpson-Mazzoli have been criticized as being unfair on the following grounds. On the one hand, people who entered the country illegally would now be granted legal alien status. On the other hand, there are people in Mexico, the Phillippines, and Hong Kong who have been waiting from five to ten years and who are

still waiting to enter this country by legal means. Do you think there was any realistic alternative that would be fair?

2. Suppose we granted citizenship to all of the illegal aliens in this country. What do you think the economic consequence would be?

3. Some observers describe El Paso as one of the most integrated cities in the United States. Many of the wealthy Irish, Jewish, Arab, and Mexican families are themselves second- and third-generation descendants of people who entered the country illegally via Mexico years ago. It is tempting to conclude from this example that illegal immigration causes no serious social problems aside from its economic effects. Do you agree?

Selected references

Hurt, Harry. "The Cactus Curtain." *Texas Monthly*, August 1977.

Simon, Julian. "Immigrants, Taxes, and Welfare in the U.S." *Population and Development Review* (March 1984).

14

Taking a Closer Look at the Minimum Wage

"Good news for low-income workers—Congress today voted to raise the federal minimum wage." Such stories have often led off TV newscasts. No doubt most viewers have agreed that the news was good; from its beginning the minimum-wage law has always been extremely popular. Despite the fact that most people are not directly affected by it, public-opinion polls have consistently shown that a large majority support it.

But in recent years, some strange things have happened. The *New York Times*, friend of the poor and traditionally an ardent supporter of a high minimum wage, reversed its position. In a startling editorial the *Times* condemned the new law as hurting the working poor more than it would help them. The *Times* was not alone; a number of Congressmen ordinarily sympathetic to organized labor also changed their minds. As a result, Congress has not raised the minimum wage since 1981.

On the surface, minimum-wage laws seem like just what low-income workers need; such laws put a floor under the wages they can be paid. Employers are required to pay at least the legal minimum, and no one is allowed to work for less. But economists have always known that minimum-wage laws have serious side effects that are very harmful to the working poor. The last poll taken of economists showed that a majority would go further than the *New York Times* did and would oppose all minimum-wage laws on principle. Let's see why.

173

Ever since the passage of the Fair Labor Standards Act of 1938, the federal minimum wage has played an important role in the labor market. In that year, employers were required to pay 25 cents an hour and 37.5 cents for overtime work in excess of 40 hours per week.

As time passed, the minimum wage was raised now and then. As Figure 14–1a shows, the minimum wage stood at $1.00 per hour in 1967. By 1981 it reached $3.35 per hour, at which level it has remained. The *nominal* level of the minimum wage—that is, its level stated in current dollars (see Figure 14–1a)—is misleading, however. It is more revealing to look at the *real* minimum wage—that is, the nominal minimum wage divided by average hourly earnings. Average hourly earnings have also risen over the years, partly because of higher labor productivity, and partly because of inflation. The real minimum wage has not always kept pace with the average. As Figure 14–1b shows, the real minimum wage reached a high of 47 percent of average earnings in 1979. Since then, it has fallen to its lowest level since 1967.

Not all workers were covered by the initial law. Important exceptions, for example, were made in agriculture, in retail trade and service industries, and for many small businesses. Over time the coverage has been greatly expanded, but some exceptions still remain. For example, businesses with sales less than $325,000 in 1981 are exempt. So are babysitters, some disabled workers, and people who care for the elderly. Employees who receive tips need be paid only 60 percent of the minimum wage. And some businesses are entitled to hire full-time students at part-time jobs that pay 85 percent of the minimum.

In some cases, workers not covered by the federal law may be covered by state laws. A number of states have minimum wages that match the federal wage; a few even exceed it. All in all it is believed that at least 93 percent of the labor force is earning the federal minimum wage or better. New legislation could push that percentage even higher.

The history of those workers earning at least the minimum wage is therefore very straightforward—as time has passed there have been more and more of them. Another history is less well known, however: the history of low-income workers out of work and seeking jobs—mainly a history of teenagers.

Back in the early 1940s, the teenage unemployment rate was relatively low, not much higher than the unemployment rate for adults. But over the years, as the number of teenagers grew in relation to the rest of the population, teenage employment problems grew too. By 1981, when the minimum wage reached $3.35, the teenage rate had climbed to 2.6 times the rate for all workers.

The problem for black teenagers has become even worse. In the early 1940s, black teenagers seemed to have few problems finding work. In fact,

FIGURE 14–1   a. Nominal Minimum Wage; b. Real Minimum Wage

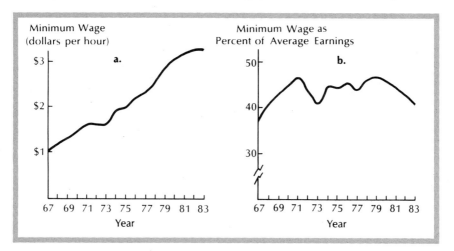

the jobless rate for black youths was less than the jobless rate for white youths. By 1949 things were different—in that year black teenagers had a jobless rate 2.8 times the national rate. And things got steadily worse. By 1971, the jobless rate for teenage blacks was 32 percent, and by 1977 the rate for black teenagers had reached the staggering figure of 40 percent.

Is there any connection between the history of teenage unemployment—black teenage unemployment in particular—and the history of the minimum wage? Economists believe there is. To see why, let's put some economic tools to work.

Tracing the economic effects of minimum wage laws

To earn the maximum possible profits, a firm must follow the proper employment policies. First, it must pay the lowest wage that will allow it to hire the number and quality of workers it needs. And second, given the wage it must pay to get those workers, it must hire an additional worker only if the value of additional production is greater than or equal to that wage. Put in economic jargon, the most the employer will be willing to pay will be a wage equal to the *value of the marginal product of labor.*

All this can be put in the form of a diagram, as in Figure 14–2, that shows a hypothetical market for unskilled labor. It assumes that employers and employees act in their own self-interest. At the equilibrium wage of $2.65 an hour, the number of labor-hours demanded is exactly equal to the number of labor-hours workers are willing to supply. In equilibrium, all

FIGURE 14–2   Market for Unskilled Labor

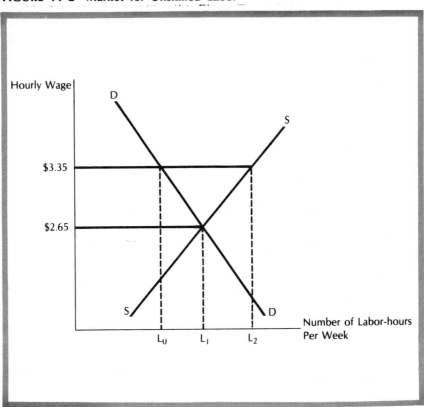

participants in the market are doing as well as they can, given the options open to them.

Suppose, though, that a minimum wage of $3.35 an hour is imposed. Workers will be willing to work more hours at the higher wage rate; some will be willing to give up some leisure hours to earn higher incomes, and others who otherwise would have stayed out of the labor force may now seek jobs. At the same time, on the demand side, the higher wage induces employers to use less labor in production. The result is unemployment. The number of labor-hours workers are willing to supply exceeds the number employers are willing to pay for. Many workers will discover that they cannot find jobs at the higher wage rate; of those who retain their jobs, many will find that they cannot work as many hours as they want to.

How can employers get by with less labor? There are several ways— one is simply to cut back on the production of goods and services. For example, in response to the boosts in the minimum wage between 1977 and 1981, many fast-food restaurants cut back on off-peak work crews. With fewer employees working at certain hours, this meant that some customers had to wait longer to be served. A few of the large restaurant chains—including Kentucky Fried Chicken, McDonald's, and Hardee's—decided to close earlier at some locations. This meant that some late-night hamburgers and chicken dinners were simply not produced.

Another way to cut back on labor usage is to have customers perform more services for themselves. Many fast-food restaurants, for example, have eliminated table service. Customers, in effect, wait on themselves. Many service stations have installed self-service gasoline pumps. Customers are given the option of pumping their own gasoline at a reduced price or getting full service at a higher price. The elimination of many delivery services is yet another example. In most cities, pizza, milk, and bread deliveries are things of the past; today buyers perform these delivery services for themselves.

A third method designed to reduce the use of labor services is automation—the use of machinery in place of people. For example, it is thought that the shift from manually operated to automatic elevators was spurred by a rising minimum wage. The introduction of labor-saving technology in the textile industry is also said to have been minimum-wage induced. Automation in the restaurant industry is yet another example. In response to the 1977–81 minimum-wage boosts, Bishop Buffets, Inc., a chain of twenty cafeterias in the Midwest, introduced overnight slow-cookers. This innovation was expected to reduce the workweek by five hours for many of Bishop's early-shift employees. The unemployment produced by a hike in the minimum wage tends to affect teenage workers more than other workers for two reasons. First, about 40 percent of the teenagers who work are working at the minimum wage. Second, at the higher minimum wage, employers are often able to attract adult workers to take the place of teenagers. Older workers are generally more productive and stay on the job longer. So by hiring them, employers can cut hiring costs and training costs. This was the response of the restaurant chain Steak n Shake to the 1977 legislation. By 1978, the chain had reduced the number of its teenage employees by one-third.

How substantial are the unemployment effects of the minimum wage overall? Economists are not entirely sure. Over the years conflicting studies have generated a continuing debate.

The Department of Labor, which usually sees eye to eye with the AFL-CIO, is required to make annual reports on the economic effects of the minimum wage, but not once in the history of the minimum wage has the department made a report showing reduced job opportunities. But economists in other branches of government and virtually all academic economists believe the effects are substantial. In recent years, studies by academic economists have without exception shown that unskilled workers, especially teenagers, are put out of work by higher minimum-wage laws.

Just how many workers lose their jobs or must work reduced hours when the minimum wage increases depends on the elasticity of demand for low-wage labor. Many economists use an elasticity of 0.5 as a good working estimate. At this elasticity, a 10 percent increase in the minimum wage would lead to a 5 percent loss in hours worked by low-wage workers.

Estimates of elasticity of demand for low-wage labor are complicated by the fact that the elasticity is greater in the long run than in the short run. It takes time to switch from manual to automatic elevators or to install slow-cookers, for example. Daniel Hamermesh has estimated that the elasticity of demand for low-wage labor may be as low as 0.3 in the short run, but as high as 0.75 to 1.0 in the long run.

Figure 14–3 shows the impact of an increase in the minimum wage rate when the long-run elasticity is higher that the short-run elasticity. In the short run, employers make decisions within the limitations of existing equipment and technology. They move up along the relatively inelastic short-run labor demand curve D-D, causing the moderate amount of short-run unemployment shown. In the long run they can redesign their operations more thoroughly to fit the higher cost of unskilled labor. As they move to the long-run demand curve D'-D', the amount of unemployment is seen to increase.

Racial discrimination: an indirect effect

In addition to the direct effect of the minimum wage on employment opportunities, there are some important indirect effects. One of the most serious of these is the indirect effect on racial discrimination.

Suppose that, with or without a minimum wage, there are some employers who have racial prejudices—and perhaps other prejudices as well. Suppose, for example, that employers tend to prefer white employees to black employees, even though whites and blacks are equally productive. In a free labor market, competition among employers would soon lead to a higher wage for white workers than for black workers; employers would then have to pay more for white workers, even though black workers are just as productive.

Under these circumstances, as we showed in Chapter 11, it would be costly to discriminate. The cost would be the difference between the wage for blacks and the wage for whites.

With a minimum-wage law in effect, however, all of this is changed; employers must pay the same wage to their low-skilled workers regardless of their race. Moreover, the minimum wage will make the supply of workers greater than the number of jobs available. Employers can then pick and choose on the basis of any standard they like—they can discriminate at zero cost!

This is the reason why Walter Williams believes that the minimum wage is largely responsible for the high unemployment among black youths. Williams points to a curious parallel between the minimum wage in the United States and in South Africa: at one point South African employers

FIGURE 14–3   Short-run and Long-run Effects

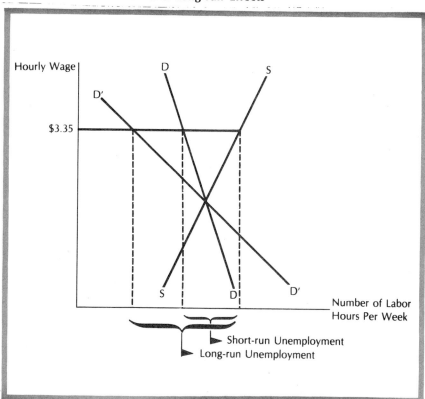

were paying black workers $.40 an hour and white workers nearly $2.00 an hour for doing the same job. But in those trades where white unions wanted to eliminate competition from black workers, they succeeded in getting special wage-equality laws passed. Faced with the choice of paying blacks and whites the same wage, employers fired the blacks.

Williams points to other laws that work against blacks in the same way the minimum wage does. The Davis Bacon Act, for example, allows the federal government to set wage floors (normally higher than the minimum wage) on federally funded construction projects. According to Williams, the act was conceived in 1931 as a device to encourage the use of union labor (mostly white) as opposed to nonunion labor; it also had the effect of forcing nonunion contractors, many of whom were black, out of business. Occupational licensing is another example; many cities restrict the number of taxicab drivers, barbers, and other professionals in ways that favor those who are already established and that work against aspiring minorities.

Can the minimum-wage law and other labor-market restrictions explain the 35 percent unemployment rate among black teenagers? Probably not all of it. For one thing, some black teenagers turn down jobs that *are* available. In many urban areas there are shortages of domestics, yard workers, janitors, and kitchen helpers. To many young blacks, these are "dead-end" or "jive" jobs. Teenagers also traditionally do not search for jobs with the same intensity as do adult workers with dependent families. In 1980, for example, the unemployment rate for married black men was 6.5 percent—1.7 times higher than the comparable rate for whites, but far less than the rate for black youths.

For these reasons the black teenage unemployment rate would probably be high even if there were no labor-market restrictions. Still, there is overwhelming evidence that the minimum-wage law takes its toll. Without it, job opportunities for young blacks and other minorities would surely be greater than they are now.

Some other indirect effects

In addition to increased racial discrimination, minimum-wage laws produce other indirect effects. Some of these hurt everyone; others benefit certain interest groups and help generate political support for the minimum wage. Let's look at a few.

1. Increased demand for competing labor services

Williams gives the following example. Suppose a fence can be produced by using one highly skilled worker or three unskilled workers. If unskilled workers are paid $12 per day, then the skilled workers can realistically demand $36 per day. Skilled workers soon find out that one way to increase their incomes is to advocate a high minimum wage in the fencing industry. At a minimum wage of $20 per day, a skilled worker could demand any wage up to $60 per day and still keep the job.

In supporting the minimum wage, the skilled workers are careful, of course, to avoid talking in terms of naked self-interest. They argue that a minimum wage "raises the standard of living," "prevents worker exploitation," "promotes worker equality," and so forth. But the real effect of the minimum wage is to price competing workers out of the market. Income is redistributed from low-skilled workers to the better-paid high-skilled workers.

In many practical situations, the competition between skilled and unskilled labor is less direct but is no less real. The automatic elevators that replaced manual operators were produced, in part, by skilled labor; so were the slow-cookers that replaced unskilled labor in many restaurants. In fact, most goods and services can be produced with different production techniques relying upon differences in employee skill levels.

Another type of competition affected by the minimum-wage law is geographical. Representatives from the New England states have long argued that the minimum wage is necessary to protect the Northern textile industry. This is not because Northern textile workers make less than the minimum wage; they typically make more. But Northern producers face intense competition from Southern textile mills where wages are generally lower. The higher wage raises production costs in the South, but not in the North. As a result it discourages the southward migration of textile production.

2. Changes in working conditions

Wages are only part of an employer's labor cost—employers also spend money to provide pleasant working conditions. They often refer to such expenditures as a *nonmonetary wage*. Faced with higher minimum wages employers have an incentive to reduce nonmonetary wages in order to offset the increase in monetary wages. For example, they might turn down the air conditioning or raise production quotas. Of course, there are limits to this type of adjustment. If perfect offsetting were possible, minimum wages would not cause unemployment or produce many of the other indirect effects we are considering. But to the extent that adjustment does occur it distorts the preferred mix of monetary to nonmonetary wages.

3. Increased vulnerability to economic changes

In free labor markets, wages in each industry tend to reflect the economic fortunes of the industry. If demand for the industry's product drops off, wages will tend to fall. With a minimum wage in force, however, this cannot happen. If employers find that they cannot reduce nonmonetary wages either, they have no other option but to lay off workers. As a result recessions tend to affect unskilled workers, particularly teenagers, more severely than workers in general. Correspondingly, during boom periods teenage employment tends to rise more dramatically than that of workers in general. The fortunes of low-income workers, therefore, tend to be very sensitive to upswings and downswings in particular industries and in the economy as a whole, partly because of the minimum wage.

A similar principle applies to changes in payroll taxes. For example, an increase in the Social Security tax (see Chapter 15) tends to lower workers' wages because it increases the employer's tax burden. If wages cannot be lowered, layoffs occur. Laws regulating working conditions, such as worker safety regulations, can have similar effects.

4. Welfare, crime, and changing lifestyles

Many economists, sociologists, and black leaders are becoming increasingly concerned about the effects of teenage unemployment on lifestyles. A view gaining wide popularity is that we should worry far more about whether teenagers have jobs than we should worry about what wage they are paid. The reason? Young people form lifelong habits in their early years that are seriously affected by the presence or absence of a job.

Most employers do not expect teenagers to be very productive—which is why they are not willing to pay very much to employ them. But in the act of getting and keeping a job teenagers soon learn the crucial importance of good work habits. They learn to report regularly for work and to do so on time. They learn that while on the job they are expected to perform certain tasks reliably, even simple ones. They learn that failure to meet these expectations results in losing the job.

For many young workers, especially in our central cities, these simple work habits do not come naturally. They are often not learned at home. Employers are aware of this, and as a result some record of employability—even at a "dead-end" job—is often essential in order to get a better job. Before employers will risk investing in employees through an on-the-job training program, they will typically want some evidence of successful past performance.

By contrast, teenagers who do not hold steady jobs often fail to learn even the most basic work habits essential to any career. Instead, they may learn a different set of habits and adopt a life-style detrimental to their long-run self-interest. The welfare syndrome and the life of crime are often very real alternatives to productive work, and the minimum-wage law may be a major factor influencing the choices that generations of young people are making.

5. Increased illegal employment

A minimum-wage law forbids mutually beneficial exchange between prospective employers and prospective employees. Unemployed workers may often be willing to work for less than the legal minimum; employers may be willing to hire them at the lower wage. Both parties could be better off. The law forbids it, but strong incentives exist to disobey the law.

The penalties for getting caught violating the minimum-wage law are not severe. In fact, for employers who are caught the first time and who are not guilty of falsifying information, paying the fine may be cheaper than paying the minimum wage. No one is quite certain how many workers are making illegal bargains with their employers. It is also difficult to separate the effects of the minimum wage from other reasons for illegal labor agreements, such as avoiding income and Social Security taxes or avoiding compliance with various regulations. Nonetheless, it appears that the volume of illegal work is on the rise.

Unfortunately for American workers most of the benefits of illegal work may accrue to foreigners. Observers believe there are anywhere from three to ten million illegal aliens in this country at any one time (see

Chapter 13). These workers often appear more attractive to employers paying less than the minimum wage than do our own citizens. Why? Illegal aliens are hiding from federal authorities—they have added incentives to protect the secrecy of illegal wage bargains.

An evaluation

Minimum-wage laws fare poorly by the standards of efficiency, equality, and liberty. Since the verdict by the standards of efficiency and liberty is more obvious, let's look at these two standards first.

To be effective, a minimum-wage law must give at least some workers higher wages than they would otherwise receive. If the law does not do this it will have no effect at all on the labor market. But if it does raise some wages, some workers will be fired, and many workers that retain their jobs will have to work fewer hours than they want to. As we saw in Figure 14–2, the number of hours worked will be reduced; this means that fewer goods and services will be produced. The economy as a whole will move inside its production-possibility frontier. Other costs will stem from some of the indirect effects of the law; increased costs of larger welfare programs and increased costs of more resources for combating crime are two examples. All of these are sources of inefficiency.

Minimum-wage laws also impinge on some fundamental liberties. By forbidding mutually beneficial exchange between prospective employers and prospective employees, such laws restrict the ability of individuals to exercise freedom of choice in the marketplace. In effect the law says this to employees: if you are able to produce something worth $3.35 an hour you may work. But if you cannot produce that much you may not work. Advocates of the standard of liberty, therefore, regard minimum-wage laws as a violation of the right of unskilled workers to produce.

What, though, about the standard of equality? True, some workers may be out of a job because of the minimum wage, but workers who retain their jobs and escape a reduction in working hours will have higher incomes. Doesn't this raise the income of poor families? At first glance this argument sounds persuasive. It is no doubt the reason why many well-meaning people have supported the minimum wage in the past, but the argument turns out to be mostly wrong.

A recent study by William R. Johnson and Edgar K. Browning takes a detailed look at the question of the distributional effects of an increase in the minimum wage. Johnson and Browning point out three reasons why an increase in the minimum wage is not an effective method of raising the incomes of low-wage households.

First, surprisingly, low-wage workers do not come predominantly from low-income households. Many low-wage workers are secondary earners in middle- and upper-income households. In fact, Johnson and Browning found that somewhat over half of all low-wage workers come from households in the top half of the national income distribution.

Second, low-income households do not get much income from low-wage jobs. Many low-income households are headed by retired people. Many others are composed of disabled persons or welfare recipients. All in all, more than 86 percent of the income of households in the lowest 10 percent of the income distribution comes from sources other than earnings from low-wage jobs.

Finally, the effects of tax and transfer programs must be taken into account. Even low-wage workers pay Social Security and other taxes on their wages. Furthermore, many welfare benefits are reduced when earnings rise. Low-wage workers thus do not get to keep all of the gains of an increase in the minimum wage even if they are lucky enough to keep their jobs.

According to Johnson and Browning, a 22 percent increase in the minimum wage rate would add just two-tenths of one percent to the income of households in the lowest 30 percent of the income distribution, after taxes, transfers, and unemployment effects are all taken into account.[1] Moreover, the small average gain of low-income households masks a very large redistributional effect among low-income families. Four low-income families out of five are actually made worse off when the minimum wage rises. These include families whose wage earners lose jobs as a result of the minimum wage increase. They also include the many low-income families who have no income from low-wage jobs to begin with, but who suffer from the increase in the cost of living that occurs when the minimum wage is raised.

To round out the picture, Johnson and Browning point out that there are redistributional effects within upper income groups too. On the average, an increase in the minimum wage hurts upper income groups. In fact, households in the upper 70 percent of the income distribution lose some $8 for every $1 gained by low-income households. But 10 percent of households in even the highest 10 percent of the income distribution gain from an increase in the minimum wage. These households include, for example, high-income households with teenage children who hold minimum wage jobs.

All in all, then, the minimum wage appears to be a very poor tool for promoting equality of income distribution.

---

1. This estimate of a 0.2 percent gain by low-income households is based on an elasticity of demand for low-income labor of 0.5. If Hamermesh's higher estimates of the long-run elasticity of demand hold, then even the lowest-income households are harmed, rather than helped, by an increase in the minimum wage.

───────────── **The politics of the minimum wage**

Tools of economic analysis help us determine which groups gain and which groups lose because of the minimum wage. This helps us identify where economic self-interest resides.

Consider organized labor, for example. Boosting the minimum wage has always had top priority for organized labor. Of course, most members of the AFL-CIO earn wages considerably above the minimum wage, but they compete directly with unskilled labor in many industries and they compete indirectly in many others. In 1977, when the latest round of minimum wage increases began, labor's goal was to place the minimum wage at 60 percent of the average wage in manufacturing. (As Figure 14-1 shows, this would have been higher than ever before in relation to the average wage.) They also pushed for an "indexing" provision that would cause the minimum wage to rise automatically as other wages rose. Both goals were turned down by Congress.

AFL-CIO head George Meany defended these proposals as "economic justice for the poor." But concern for economic justice dictates no special consideration for teenagers in Meany's view. In the face of a 17.5 percent teenage unemployment rate and a dismaying 40 percent unemployment rate for black youths, some members of Congress supported a special entry wage for youths in the 1977 bill. For the first six months on the job young workers would receive only 85 percent of the minimum. Organized labor said no.

Organized labor is often supported in its efforts by the business firms that employ skilled workers. These firms also fear competition from firms employing unskilled labor. As we noted earlier, there is often a geographical dimension to the conflict; Northern businesses often support higher minimum wages as a means of raising production costs for their Southern competitors.

Firms employing low-skilled workers, are, of course, opposed to high minimum wages; so are many interests in Southern states who see low wages as an attractive lure for firms considering relocating in warmer climes.

However, self-interest is not the whole story. Through altruism or through ignorance many people support legislation that does not personally benefit them. For example, low-paid workers tend to support higher minimum wages. Most probably expect to retain their jobs, and those who lose them may fail to see the connection between the higher minimum wage and the loss of employment opportunities.

One would think that in urban areas where unemployment rates are staggeringly high, opposition to the minimum wage would be strong indeed. In fact, it is not—most of the political representatives from these districts support a high minimum wage. They also support organized labor in most of its other objectives, even when only a small fraction of their constituents are union members. This is surprising, since most of organized labor's objectives benefit union members at the expense of nonunion workers. In the short run, businesses are affected, too; but in the long run, business firms tend to make a normal rate of return on invested capital, regardless of the labor laws. The principal distributional effect of most labor legislation is to shift income from nonunion to union workers.

Another irony is that many black leaders support higher minimum wages even though they seem to have a devastating effect on black employment. Nearly all of the black representatives in Congress support the minimum wage. They may regard this support as a necessary concession in return for labor's support of civil rights legislation, but many black economists feel the trade-off is a bad one. These economists are becoming increasingly vocal and are finding a receptive audience in large segments of the black community.

Perhaps most puzzling of all is the fact that the consuming public as a whole has been highly favorable toward minimum-wage legislation. Thirty years of polling has clearly established strong and consistent support for the principle of a minimum wage. The ratios of support to opposition range from 71 to 24 in 1947 to a low of 54 to 39 in 1965—this despite the fact that the consuming public is surely harmed. Minimum wages reduce our total output of goods and services; the prices of the goods and services that *are* produced are necessarily higher than they otherwise would be.

Why so much public support? Perhaps consumers believe that in some way they benefit, or perhaps they believe they are not affected at all and they regard support for the minimum wage as a humanitarian gesture.

In any event, given its traditional political appeal, it is very unlikely that the minimum wage will ever be abolished. As an indication, a recent attempt by the Reagan administration to revive the idea of a subminimum wage for teenagers met with no success on Capitol Hill. But there is hope. Although the minimum wage is no doubt here to stay, the pro-minimum-wage forces do not at present seem to have the power to vote an increase. The longer the nominal minimum wage stays at $3.35 an hour, the lower the real minimum wage will drift. Black teenagers, welfare mothers, and friends of the poor should rejoice.

Questions for thought and discussion

1. The following arguments have been given in favor of a minimum wage. While some valid arguments may be made, each of the following statements contains an economic fallacy. Can you identify the fallacies?

   a. "If labor costs rise, businesses will simply raise their prices and pass the cost along to the consumer. There is no reason for unemployment to occur."

    b. "Minimum wages actually create jobs rather than destroy them. Higher wages for those who remain employed will create purchasing power, which will in turn produce more jobs."

    c. "Forcing low-wage firms to pay higher wages also forces them to use labor more effectively, so that labor becomes worth the higher minimum. Studies show that after the mandated increases occur, labor productivity also rises."

2. Whether total wages paid rise or fall in response to an increase in the minimum wage depends upon the elasticity of demand for labor services. Can you show how?

3. Current law requires employers to pay time and a half for hours worked in excess of 40 per week. What effect do you think this has on the demand for labor?

4. On a carefully labeled graph, show why fluctuations in the demand for labor curve have a greater impact on employment with a minimum wage in effect than if no minimum wage exists.

Selected references

Fleisher, Belton M. *Minimum Wage Regulation in Retail Trade.* Washington, D.C.: American Enterprise Institute, 1981.

Gramlich, Edward M. "Impact of Minimum Wages on Other Wages, Employment, and Family Incomes." *Brookings Papers on Economic Activity.* Washington, D.C.: Brookings Institution, 1976.

Hamermesh, Daniel. "Subsidies for Jobs in the Private Sector." In *Creating Jobs*, edited by John Palmer. Washington, D.C.: Brookings Institution, 1978.

Johnson, William R., and Edgar K. Browning. "The Distributional and Efficiency Effects of Increasing the Minimum Wage: A Simulation." *American Economic Review* 73 (March 1983): 204–211.

Krumm, Ronald J. *The Impact of the Minimum Wage on Regional Labor Markets.* Washington, D.C.: American Enterprise Institute, 1981.

Parsons, Donald O. *Poverty and the Minimum Wage.* Washington, D.C.: American Enterprise Institute, 1980.

15

Social Security: Who Gains? Who Loses?

The Social Security system is one of our most hallowed political institutions. Any politician who suggests that Social Security is anything less than a work of genius is destined to suffer mightily at the polls. Nor is it difficult to see why. Born of the Great Depression years, Social Security has been the major source of retirement income for millions of our senior citizens. What's more, most retirees have experienced financial gain—the value of benefits received has exceeded the value of taxes paid.

Consider the case of Ida Fuller. From the time she became the first Social Security retiree in January 1941 to the time she died in January 1975, this former legal secretary drew some $21,000 in retirement benefits from the system—despite the fact that she had paid a total of only $22.54 in payroll taxes.

Not everyone covered by Social Security has done as well as Ida Fuller, of course, but most people retiring today will end up getting more out of Social Security than they would have gotten by investing their payroll taxes privately in the stock market or in corporate bonds.

If you are under 35 years of age, however, things look pretty bleak. Chances are you will be a loser, and your losses could be substantial. Consider a 30-year-old male worker making $15,000 a year and planning to retire at age 65. If current trends continue the value of taxes this worker can expect to pay over the next 35 years will exceed the value of benefits

189

he and his family can expect to receive by about $4,500. Moreover, if this worker has been working since the age of 20, he has probably *already* paid over $10,000 in Social Security taxes, and these additional taxes have no effect upon his future benefits.[1]

As a general rule, then, those who are at or nearing retirement age today will find that they have done well by Social Security. In contrast, those who are early in their careers will find the Social Security system to be a net burden—in fact, the younger they are, the larger their loss is expected to be. Let's see why.

How the system works and how it doesn't work

One of the strange things about Social Security is that the people who like it so well rarely understand how it actually works. The most common mistake is to think that Social Security works like a private insurance program or a private pension fund. One source of this mistaken view is the Social Security Administration itself.

For example, a widely circulated booklet, "Your Social Security," begins:

> The basic idea of social security is a simple one: during working years employees, their employers, and self-employed people pay social security contributions which are pooled in special trust funds. When earnings stop or are reduced because the worker retires, dies or becomes disabled, monthly cash benefits are paid to replace part of the earnings the family has lost.

The booklet goes on:

> Nine out of ten working people in the United States are now building protection for themselves and their families under the Social Security program.

The basic idea of Social Security *is* a simple one, but to understand it we must first see what is wrong with the misleading advertising we have just cited.

1. There are no trust funds

At least not in any meaningful sense. All dollars paid into the Social Security system are immediately paid out—the very day, the very hour, the

---

1. These and other estimates are contained in Martin S. Feldstein and Anthony Pellechio, "Social Security Wealth," presented at the Conference on Financing Social Security, American Enterprise Institute, October 27–28, 1977.

very minute. There are no dollars being stashed away in bank vaults for future use. In its early years, when the system ran a surplus, the extra tax dollars collected were spent on other federal programs. In more recent years, when the system has run a deficit, the extra dollars spent have come from general tax revenues. Today the system is strictly on a pay-as-you-go basis: all dollars received from Social Security taxes will be spent on Social Security benefits as they are received.

What about the mysterious "trust funds"? To see exactly how they work, let's try a simple thought experiment. Suppose you decide to set up a fund for the future purchase of a car, so you open a savings account and call it a car fund. Each month you promise to put $50 into the car fund, and each month you faithfully keep this promise. But as time passes other needs become more pressing, and you find yourself short of cash.

So what can you do? You could try to borrow money from a bank or some other lending institution, but the interest rate would be high—a lot higher than the rate earned on a savings account. Besides, getting a personal loan is always a bit of a hassle. So why not try an easier way? Why not borrow the money from the car fund? After all, if you don't trust yourself to pay your own money back, how can you ask some other lender to trust you?

So you borrow money from your car fund and you write an IOU to yourself promising to pay it back. Just to keep things honest, you even promise to pay interest to your car fund on the money borrowed. And things work out pretty well. In fact, they work out so well that you proceed to borrow all of the money in the car fund. Each month, instead of putting $50 in the fund, you simply write an IOU to the fund—a promise to pay it $50 plus interest some time in the future. Then you spend the $50 in cash on something else.

Is this one big charade? An attempt at self-delusion? Not necessarily. All of the elaborate bookkeeping may have psychological effects; it may strengthen your resolve to buy a car eventually. But don't overlook the down-to-earth realities: (1) You are operating on a pay-as-you-go standard. All of the money you earn is being spent as you earn it. (2) When the day comes to buy the car you promised yourself, you can't buy it with your own IOUs. You will have to make the sacrifices then that you are not making today.

In a similar way, the Social Security trust fund merely consists of IOUs that the government has written to itself (government bonds). All of the funds collected in the past have already been spent; the only way that benefits can be paid today—and in the future—is by collecting taxes today and in the future. The existence of the trust fund may make people feel better, but if it were abolished tomorrow the only real effect would be to relieve government accountants of some extra bookkeeping work.

This is why the statements of the Social Security Administration are so misleading. Social Security taxes paid by today's workers do not really finance their *own future* benefits, but rather *someone else's current* benefits. What nine out of ten workers are actually doing is paying taxes to finance benefits paid to people who are not working. When today's workers retire their benefits will have to be financed by taxes imposed on future generations of workers.

Failure to understand how the trust fund really works also leads to another myth: the charge that Social Security is going bankrupt. What this claim often means is that eventually the trust fund is going to "run out of money." The fund is already out of money; what it *can* run out of in the future is government IOUs. But remember—the government *has already promised to pay Social Security benefits*, IOUs or no. As we will see, whether the government will keep all of its promise may be a legitimate worry—but there is no reason to worry about the size of a fund of its own IOUs unless we seriously believe that two promises are better than one.[2]

It is instructive to compare the Social Security system with two other financial arrangements—a private pension plan on the one hand and a *Ponzi scheme* on the other. A private pension plan differs from Social Security because it is usually required to be *actuarially sound*—as premiums are paid in, the company must accumulate a fund large enough at each moment to finance all promised future benefits. In effect, by paying their premiums participants are buying a share of the fund, which in turn is invested in assets such as corporate stocks and bonds. The pension plan is not allowed to rely on future contributions to pay benefits. Even if the plan were suddenly unable to attract new participants, it would still be able to pay existing participants out of the money it had already accumulated.

A *Ponzi scheme* is similar to a private pension plan in that participants pay money now into the fund in return for a promise to get their money back, with interest, in the future. Unlike a pension plan, however, a Ponzi scheme does not set aside a fund to meet its promises. Instead it relies on recruiting new participants when its old promises come due and using their premiums to pay the initial participants. Because it does not have to tie up resources in long-term assets, a Ponzi scheme can offer its initial participants much more attractive rates of return than an actuarially sound fund— say, 20 percent return per annum. The only trouble is that in order to meet its obligations it must recruit at least 20 percent more new participants each year than it did the year before. Sooner or later the scheme is doomed to collapse, and when it does so, the last round of new participants is left holding the bag. If the organizers are as smart as the original Boston con artist who gave his name to the idea, they usually run off with the kitty just before the scheme is due to die of natural causes.

Of the two—an actuarially sound pension fund and a Ponzi scheme— the Social Security system more closely resembles the latter. There are two

---

2. It is true that Congress is committed to the goal of keeping Social Security taxes and Social Security benefits roughly equal over the long haul, so the trust fund does help us keep track of how well we are meeting this goal. But the function is merely one of bookkeeping and nothing more.

important differences, though. First, Social Security is legal and Ponzi schemes are not. And second, the Social Security system need not collapse—it can rely on the power of taxation to recruit new members to pay off old claims, whether those new members want to be recruited or not. But even this requires the consent of future voters. This brings us to our next point.

2. Social Security benefits are not guaranteed

When the Social Security Act was being debated in Congress in 1935, its framers wanted to assure the American public that their financial stake in the program would be absolutely secure. No one, it was reasoned, should feel that he was taking a chance by "investing" with the government.

"We can't ask support for a plan not at least as good as any American could buy from a private insurance company," said the report of the House Finance Subcommittee. "The very least a citizen should expect is to get his money back upon retirement."

To guarantee this, two important provisions were included in the original act. First, Congress decided that if at the retirement age of 65 a taxpayer had paid into the system without having qualified for benefits for some reason, all the taxes he or she had paid would be refunded. Second, if a fully qualified taxpayer died before reaching 65, a sum equal to the amount he or she had paid in taxes was to be given to that taxpayer's estate.

It took Congress all of four years to take back these promises. In 1939, with applications for refunds piling up, it became apparent that the financial integrity of the system was threatened. So the original act was amended and those waiting for refund checks received a form letter instead, telling how the amendment would make the system more solvent.

As time passed, the worker's assurance of benefits became even less secure. Today, workers under age 46 must pay at least ten years' worth of taxes for the right to any retirement benefits. If a male worker dies before reaching 65, his wife is entitled to collect a monthly death benefit only if she is "caring for his dependent children." If the couple's children are grown or if they never had any children, the wife is entitled only to a nominal burial fee.

Several Supreme Court rulings have further eroded the notion that workers in some sense "own" the money they pay in taxes. The court has ruled that money collected in the form of Social Security taxes need not be paid to Social Security beneficiaries. The fact that a worker has paid taxes does not necessarily obligate the government to pay that worker any benefits, and promises made by one Congress may be rescinded by a later Congress.

These rulings are regularly ignored by the public-information staff of the Social Security Administration. Instead we have been told that payroll deductions "are strictly accounted for and kept separate from the general funds in the U.S. Treasury," and that your Social Security card is "proof of your insurance policy with the government."

The crucial difference between such claims made on behalf of a government agency and similar statements made by a private insurance company is that private companies are legally obligated to abide by the terms of their contracts. The government, by and large, is under no such obligation. Whether today's youth will be able to collect retirement benefits in the future depends solely upon the willingness of future voters to shoulder increasing tax burdens. Future benefits simply are not guaranteed.

3. Benefits are largely unrelated to taxes paid

Under private insurance policies or pension plans a direct relationship exists between contributions and expected benefits. In general, the higher the premium paid, the higher the benefit the policyholder can expect to receive. Although the Social Security Administration implies that under Social Security the benefits received are related to the taxes paid, the relationship is very weak.

In practice, people who pay vastly different Social Security taxes over their working lives may receive the same benefits upon retirement. At the same time, people who pay the same amount in taxes may receive very different benefit payments. And people who continue working after the age of 65 are required to pay additional taxes, often without receiving any benefits while they continue to work.

Moreover, millions of people who pay taxes will never receive any benefits because they will not have paid taxes long enough to qualify. Many others will lose their own benefits because of their spouse's eligibility. A retired wife age 65 or over is entitled to 50 percent of her husband's benefit. A widow who is age 62 or over gets 82.5 percent of her husband's benefit. But a wife or a widow cannot receive *both* the benefit based on her earnings and the benefit she is entitled to as a wife or a widow.

In short, all sorts of considerations other than the amount paid into the program determine the amount of benefits that will be received. As a consequence, the program bears only a scant resemblance to the ordinary concept of insurance.

4. Business does not pay taxes

From its very inception the Social Security Administration has continued to propagate the idea that only part of a worker's Social Security tax is paid by the workers themselves. The remainder, it is claimed, is paid by the business firms that employ them.

Economic theory says otherwise. A business firm is nothing but a legal relationship between workers, managers, stockholders, creditors, consumers, and many others. Although governments often tax legal relationships,

relationships never bear the ultimate burden of those taxes. Only people do.

Economists generally agree that the full burden of payroll taxes ultimately falls on the workers themselves. Under current practice, a worker receiving $100 a week in wages will have $7 deducted from his or her paycheck for Social Security taxes. The employer will chip in another $7, making the total payroll tax equal to $14. To the employer the extra $7 is just another labor cost, whether the extra $7 goes to the government or to the worker.

Economists believe that in the absence of the Social Security payroll tax the worker would have received a wage of $107. In other words, the entire $7 (or 7 percent of his gross wage) is actually paid by the worker. It is likely, however, that most workers do not realize that they are paying 14 percent of their wages to finance Social Security.

It is also possible that some workers are unaware that they pay any Social Security tax at all. Along with their paychecks, workers typically also get earnings statements indicating what deductions have been made from their gross salary. Federal, state, and city income taxes are usually clearly labeled, but Social Security taxes are not—they are usually included under the heading of *FICA* (Federal Insurance Contributions Act).

For over 42 percent of all taxpayers the deduction labeled FICA is greater than the deduction for federal income tax. And, of course, the true burden of FICA taxes on the employee is twice the amount shown on the earnings statement.

The problem of future financing

Once we strip the concept of Social Security of false and improper analogies with private insurance, the idea of Social Security is a simple one. Money is transferred from workers to nonworkers. In 1981, for example, about $138 billion dollars was collected from 115 million taxpayers and paid out to 36 million recipients in the form of Social Security benefits.

The basic problem of Social Security is also simple—where to find the additional taxes to finance the increasing benefit levels Congress has promised to current and future retirees. The solutions to these problems are simple, too: future workers must bear heavier and heavier tax burdens, or future retirees must accept lower benefits, or some combination of the two.

The source of our Social Security problem dates back to the day when the program first began paying benefits to retired workers. In 1940, hundreds of thousands of people began collecting benefits after paying Social Security taxes for only 36 months. In 1950, when Congress extended coverage to 10 million self-employed individuals, many were old enough to draw benefits after paying Social Security taxes for as brief a period as 18 months. A self-employed businessperson who had paid only

$121.50 could retire on $80.00 a month in 1952. Those who are still alive—and some are—are today collecting a monthly pension of $261.80 and each has received total benefits of over $43,000 in return for $121.50 worth of taxes.

Although this example is an extreme case, as was that of Ida Fuller, it illustrates a pattern that has characterized Social Security from the beginning: higher benefit levels need higher taxes to finance them. As late as 1949, the total Social Security payroll tax was only 4 percent of the first $3,000 of income. That means that the maximum annual tax was only $60.00 per year. Since then, Congress has raised the maximum tax 25 times. Not all workers pay the maximum tax. But Social Security tax increases have been hefty for all. In 1984, some 31 percent of the federal budget went to programs for the elderly. In 1940, average monthly benefits to retired workers with no dependent children were $22. That amount rose to $118 by 1971 and to $225 by 1976. Social Security taxes amounted to a modest 2 percent of the first $3,000 of wages in 1937. Since then Congress has raised the payroll tax rate 12 times and has increased the amount of earnings subject to tax 7 times. Under the current law it will reach 14.3 percent by 1986.

What's more, if present demographic trends continue, higher and higher taxes will be needed in the future just to maintain today's benefit levels because the ratio of taxpayers to beneficiaries has been falling. In the early years there were about seven taxpayers for each beneficiary. Today the ratio is close to 3 to 1. In the next century, when today's youth reach retirement age, the ratio is expected to be 2 to 1.

In fact, in order for today's youth to retire at benefit levels currently written into law, future workers will have to pay about 20 percent of their salaries in Social Security taxes! That's in addition to the other taxes these workers will have to pay in order to finance all other government programs.

Some proposed changes

As the crisis worsened, a number of proposals that might at least partially relieve the financial strains of the Social Security system were considered. One idea was to fund part of the system with general tax revenues such as personal income taxes or corporate income taxes. Another idea was to require all workers to participate in the system. Another was to raise the retirement age. Still other proposals would alter the whole nature of Social Security—these include proposals to change Social Security into a welfare program or to make participation by workers voluntary. Let's take a brief look at each of these in turn.

1. General revenue financing

We noted earlier that Congress has been committed to the goal of keeping Social Security revenues equal to outflows over the long haul. Roughly translated this means that Social Security taxes are supposed to "finance" Social Security benefits; if we stick to this principle the payroll tax is destined to soar in the coming decades. An alternative is to allow other taxes to share more of the burden.

Two arguments are generally made in favor of this idea. First, the Social Security payroll tax is highly regressive. Workers making $3,000 a year pay 14 percent of their incomes at current prices, but because there is a ceiling on the maximum tax that can be paid, workers earning $100,000 a year pay less than 4 percent of total income in Social Security taxes. Many feel that the heavy burden on low-income workers is unfair. Income taxes, in contrast, are progressive—the higher one's income, the higher the percentage paid in taxes.

Also, many feel that it would be politically more feasible to raise income taxes than to raise Social Security taxes. If this is true, reliance on general revenues would make it easier for future politicians to pay the higher levels of benefits that have been promised to future generations.

This proposal has one major limitation, however: it would merely alter the form in which taxes are paid; it would not eliminate the total tax burden that future workers will be asked to bear. Moreover, if politicians find it easier to raise income taxes than to raise Social Security taxes they may show even less restraint in paying benefits than they have in the past, a situation that would compound the difficulties future generations will have to face.

2. Universal coverage

Currently there are about 2.8 million civilian employees of the federal government and 4 million employees of state and local governments who do not participate in the Social Security program. What's more, state and local governments employing another 8 million workers have the option of withdrawing from the system. Some have already withdrawn, and as tax rates rise the incentive will grow for others to do the same.

The reason is simple. Many government workers retire at the age of 55 on government pensions. But by working a few more years in the private sector and by paying very little in the way of Social Security taxes, these workers can qualify for Social Security benefits in addition to their government pensions. This practice is known as *double-dipping*. If participation in Social Security were made mandatory there would be no more double-dipping. Some of the system's financial problems would be relieved, at least in the short run.

3. Raising the retirement age

As things now stand, workers cannot retire until age 65 if they want to get full Social Security benefits. They can opt for retirement at age 62 with a 20 percent benefit reduction. If the retirement age were raised to age 68, 69, or 70, and if the penalty for early retirement were increased, total benefits paid could be substantially reduced.

Here again the major problem is a political one. Since 1940 the trend has been to liberalize benefits—not contract them. Raising the retirement age would be almost as difficult as lowering benefit payments in terms of the political opposition it would engender.

4. Changing the indexing scheme

As things now stand, Social Security benefits are linked to the rate of inflation. This seems only proper: if the current level of benefits is fair in terms of actual purchasing power, it should be adjusted as the purchasing power of the dollar declines. Right?

Right, but not so simple. The problem is what particular measure of inflation is fair. The inflation measure currently used is the consumer price index (CPI). This index has two major drawbacks for Social Security purposes.

First, the consumer price index gives a large weight to increases in housing costs. But the way housing costs are measured in the CPI overstates the impact of high mortgage rates, and understates the impact of the gains that accrue to homeowners when inflation pushes up the market value of their homes. The overweighting of mortgage costs is especially ironic for Social Security purposes, since more than 80 percent of elderly persons make no mortgage payments at all. So proposals have been made either to correct the measurement of housing costs in the CPI, or to link Social Security payments to an index based on the actual expenditure patterns of senior citizens.

Second, in some years the consumer price index increases more rapidly than the wages of those still employed. This is another way of saying that such inflationary shocks to the economy as oil price increases put a real burden on the population that reduces living standards. Some people argue that retired persons should bear their fair share of such burdens. One way to do this would be to say that Social Security benefits would go up each year by the amount of increase in the consumer price index, or by the amount of increase in average wages, whichever was less in that year.

5. Making Social Security a welfare program

Social Security, as we have seen, is a system that transfers income from workers to nonworkers. Many of the nonworkers are poor; many others would be poor without their Social Security checks. In this way Social Security serves some of the functions of a welfare program.

In 1981, for example, about 6 percent of those over 65 were living below the official poverty level. Without Social Security the number might be three times as high—close to 2.3 million people. Yet the majority of people receiving Social Security checks are not poor and would not be poor in the absence of Social Security. Many, in fact, are very wealthy.

Some people argue, then, that only the welfare component of Social Security serves any useful social purpose; the rest seems unnecessary. Arguing along this line leads to the conclusion that most Social Security transfers ought to be eliminated and only the welfare aspects should be preserved. Needless to say, such a radical change is unlikely to occur.

6. Allowing workers to opt out

One of the original motives behind Social Security was to force people to provide for their own retirement. If people are left free to make their own decisions about the future, some might choose to make no provision for retirement. Upon reaching old age these people would present the rest of society with an unfortunate choice: to support them in retirement or to watch them starve. Social Security, it is argued, eliminates this option.

In fact, Social Security, as we have seen, does not actually force people to provide for their own retirement. It forces them to provide for someone else's retirement. However, there is a way to accomplish the original objective and solve some long-term problems at the same time. We could insist that individuals invest in an approved retirement pension plan, much as we insist that automobile drivers carry liability insurance. The choice of which retirement program, like the choice of which liability insurance policy, could largely be left up to the individual.

Britain has taken a major step in this direction by allowing companies with approved private pension plans to opt their workers out of the government's second-tier social security scheme. (All workers are required to be in the first tier plan.) Workers who are opted out forego the right to receive second-tier social security benefits. In return they receive a reduction in their payroll tax of seven percent of taxable earnings.

The British system does not solve any short-run problems. Today's retired workers have to be paid promised benefits. And, the government has to raise the taxes to pay these benefits. But since 1978, almost half of all British workers have taken the option of opting out. That means that Britain's long-run social security obligations have been greatly reduced.

In early 1983, after these and other proposals had been debated for months, Congress passed legislation aimed at curing some of the financial problems of the Social Security system. The new law included higher Social Security taxes, a gradual rise in the retirement age from 65 to 67, a one-time reduction in cost-of-living increases for retirees, a reduction in benefits received by early retirees, some increase in coverage, and taxation of benefits of some of the wealthiest benefit recipients. Some experts believe that even these reforms are too little to make the system financially sound. Others believe they are an overcorrection. It is too soon to know their full effects.

The politics of Social Security

How did we get Social Security in the first place? Why does the program continue? Why are certain benefit formulas used rather than others? Why is the payroll tax chosen as the principal means of financing the system? As in the case of other issues examined in this book, we believe that these and countless other questions that can be asked about Social Security are best answered by considering the political pressures faced by Congress.

Some of these pressures stem from pure altruism. In the 1930s Social Security seemed like an ideal way to deal with the problem of poverty among the aged. Even today, a great many people continue to think of Social Security as a welfare scheme, and they support it for that reason. But many of the pressures put on Congress have a lot more to do with pure self-interest than with charity.

Harvard economist Martin Feldstein has estimated that of the 150 million adults of voting age in the United States about one-third—or 50 million—can expect financial loss from Social Security in its present form. The remaining 100 million can expect financial gain; the gainers, of course, are older voters who are closer to receiving benefits and thus have fewer taxpaying years left.

In terms of voting power, therefore, the gainers clearly outnumber the losers.[3] What's more, the gainers are more likely to vote. In 1980 only 52 percent of all eligible voters actually voted. But 65 percent of those 65 and over voted. Only 10.5 percent of the populaton is 65 years of age or older. But the elderly constitute 16.8 percent of all voters.

In addition, Social Security beneficiaries and those who are close to retirement tend to be very sensitive to the positions that political candidates take on Social Security questions. In the past this has not been true of younger voters. Many young voters certainly dislike paying taxes—but other taxes (such as property taxes and income taxes) and many other government programs tend to concern these voters far more than the issue of Social Security taxes.

All this helps explain why politicians have felt enormous pressure to increase benefits for older people at the expense of younger workers. Moreover, many of the particular features of the Social Security system also

---

3. If children under 18 years of age (who cannot vote) are included, the losers outnumber the gainers.

suggest that congressional action is the result of voter pressures. Social Security taxes may be regressive with respect to income because low-income workers are less aware of the true burden they have to bear in contrast to higher income groups. Social Security benefits may be regressive with respect to income because low-income retirees are more dependent upon their Social Security checks—and hence more politically sensitive to the issue—than high-income retirees. The fact that many employees have managed to escape direct participation in Social Security suggests that public employee unions are a strong lobbying force and are willing to back up their political demands by overt action on election day.

What has been true in the past may not be true in the future. Feldstein believes that if current demographic trends continue we may reach a time when over half the voters (all voters under the age of 45) can expect to lose money by participation in Social Security.[4] Since taxes will also be considerably higher than they are today, young voters may be far more sensitive to the burden of payroll taxation. At this point Social Security may undergo substantial, and perhaps radical, change.

An evaluation

Our analysis of the political pressures faced by elected officials helps us understand why this country has a Social Security program and why it has grown so fast. Nonetheless, we can still ask whether we ought to have such a program. Was it a good idea in the first place? Should it continue?

Social Security clearly violates the standard of liberty—in this case the liberty of the worker-taxpayer. Taking a percentage of people's incomes without their consent violates the Lockean principle that people are entitled to the product of their labor. The only benefit that workers receive in return is the promise that upon their retirement government will take from others and give to them. The workers' rights to dispose of their own incomes as they see fit—including the right to provide for their own retirement as they choose—are clearly violated.

The effects of Social Security on the distribution of income are less clear. Social Security taxes, we have seen, are highly regressive. Low-income workers pay a much higher percentage of their incomes to Social Security than do high-income workers. On the tax side, then, inequality is increased. Social Security benefits, on the other hand, are also regressive— the low-income retirees receive a higher percentage of preretirement wages than do high-income retirees. On the benefit side, then, inequality is reduced.

---

4. By the time this occurs most of our readers will be older than 45, when financial self-interest will dictate firm support for Social Security.

What about the degree of inequality between taxpayers and beneficiaries? Since Social Security transfers income from workers to nonworkers,
and since most of the nonworkers are retired, it would seem that such
transfers must reduce inequality of income and wealth between the two
groups. This conclusion may be false, however.

It is true that persons over age 65 have lower incomes on the average
than persons under 65—about one-half as much, in fact. But retired people
frequently have more assets. Seventy percent of the elderly own their own
homes and thus avoid the burden of housing rents or high-cost mortgages.
And every state offers some property tax relief to the elderly. Many also
derive income from unreported jobs and receive financial help from their
children. Medicare picks up a large number of medical bills.

So looking only at reported income statistics gives a misleading
picture—the aged are better off than these statistics indicate. But even after
we account for the value of wealth and other sources of assistance some
tough questions need to be answered.

Suppose we want to compare a young couple with two children to a
retired couple. What would equality mean here? Should the first family
have twice as much income as the second? That is, should we merely
perform a head count? Or should we make some allowance for the fact
that people in different circumstances may have different needs?

Another tough question has to do with the value of leisure time.
Suppose a male worker has the option to continue working at a salary of
$10,000 a year. Instead he chooses to retire. His choice reveals that he
places a higher value on retirement (leisure time) than he does on the
$10,000. So a lot of economists would argue that the worker's extra leisure
time is at least worth $10,000. Accordingly, they would argue that the
worker's real income has not been reduced at all—he has simply substituted one kind of income (leisure time) for another kind of income (money
income). If we agree with this argument, then many aged persons are much
better off than their money income and wealth would indicate.

There is yet a further difficulty. When we ask what difference Social
Security makes we have to imagine what would happen if Social Security
did not exist. That is, what would the financial position of the aged
otherwise be? To perform this mental experiment we have to recognize
that in the absence of Social Security many retirees would qualify for
welfare assistance such as food stamps. In addition, many would receive
more financial help from their children. In the days before Social Security
most of the aged relied on their children as the primary means of support.
In the modern world children might not be as charitable, but few would be
completely indifferent, either. So a great many Social Security dollars
simply replace other income transfers that would have occurred in the
absence of Social Security.

Whether Social Security creates more equality, then, probably hinges
on our answers to some tough questions: What should be done about the
value of leisure time? Should we make allowances for differences in needs?
How much income would the elderly receive without their Social Security

checks? Unfortunately, very different answers to these questions are perfectly defensible.

Many economists feel uncomfortable comparing the well-being of a 19-year-old worker with a 70-year-old retiree. The differences in circumstances are so great, they say, that such comparisons are meaningless. So they propose a different way of looking at the equality question instead. They ask, what happens to the *same generation* over time? The question is a reasonable one. But so far no one has come up with an answer.

During their working years, low-income workers pay a higher percentage of their incomes in Social Security taxes than do high-income workers. The low-income workers will also pay taxes for more years since they typically do not remain in school as long.

At the receiving end, low-income workers can expect to receive a higher percentage of their preretirement income in the form of benefits. Two factors work against them, however. For one thing, low-income workers have a shorter life expectancy, so they cannot expect to collect benefits for as many years. Second, Social Security benefits are reduced if the "retiree" continues to work at another job and receive wage income. (For every two dollars earned above a minimum level, one dollar in benefits is lost.) By contrast, people who have assets such as stocks and ' bonds are not penalized for the income they receive from these assets.

Differences in the demographics of the black and white populations of the United States further complicate the issue of the effect of the Social Security system on equality. In general, blacks do not get as good a deal from Social Security as whites do. There are two reasons for this. First, blacks have a lower life expectancy than whites. And second, the black population as a whole is younger than the white population. A black man aged 35 can expect to receive just 2 years, 8 months of Social Security checks if he retires at 65. Yet he pays exactly the same rate of Social Security taxes as his white counterpart, who can expect to receive 7 years, 6 months of benefits. A white woman aged 35 can expect to receive 44 percent more in benefits than a black woman of the same age.

The 1983 reforms of Social Security were devastating to the expectations of black participants. A study by the National Center for Policy Analysis found that a black man aged 25 lost more than 80 percent of his expected benefits as a result of the reforms, chiefly because of the scheduled increase in the retirement age. By comparison, a white man aged 25 lost just 22 percent of his expected benefits. Before the reforms, the white 25-year-old could expect to receive about four times as much in total benefits as a black of the same age. After the reforms, the white man could expect to receive fifteen times as many benefits.

Because of all of these considerations economists are uncertain about how Social Security affects inequality—whether it causes inequality for society as a whole at a certain point in time, or whether it causes inequality within a single generation over time. If Social Security does reduce inequality there is no reason to believe that it reduces it very much.

Effects on economic efficiency are more straightforward. Like any
other tax, the Social Security payroll tax distorts the work-leisure trade-off
that workers face. It discourages productive work and encourages other
nonwork activities. In 1940, when the Social Security tax was only 2
percent and income taxes were also relatively low, this distortive effect was
probably mild; today things are quite different.

Take the case of a middle-income worker making, say, $20,000 per
year. This worker would be in the 38 percent federal income tax bracket,
which means that government takes 38 cents out the next dollar he earns.
Since Social Security taxes will take another 13 cents, the combined effect
of these two taxes will take 52 cents from the worker for every additional
dollar earned.

A decade from now the disincentives to work will be even stronger. If
current inflation rates continue, the $20,000-per-year worker will have to
make $40,000 per year just to stay even with the rise in prices. Even
though such a worker's standard of living will not have improved, Social
Security taxes will have risen to 15 percent.

Economists have always known that income and payroll taxes discourage production: they tend to push society inside its production-possibility
frontier. From the point of view of efficiency this loss must be balanced by
a corresponding gain, such as an additional road or a bridge, that enhances
productivity. Unfortunately, Social Security offers few corresponding gains.
Even if workers want to make some provision for the poverty-stricken
elderly, most benefits do not go to people who are poor. In the main,
Social Security simply transfers income from one group to another. Society
as a whole has fewer goods and services as a result.

The way benefits are paid also discourages productivity. In 1981
Social Security beneficiaries under age 72 were penalized for earning more
than $5,500 per year. For each dollar earned over that amount, benefits
were reduced by 50 cents. These beneficiaries also had to pay 13.4
percent of their income in Social Security taxes. That means elderly
workers had to give up 63.4 cents for each additional dollar earned.

Some economists also believe that Social Security reduces private
savings and thereby lowers the long-term growth rate for the economy as a
whole. People who know they can count on Social Security benefits, it is
argued, will be less inclined to save for their retirement. Whereas private
savings provide a source of funds for business investment, Social Security
taxes are simply paid out to beneficiaries.

Questions for thought and discussion

1. Prior to 1940 there were virtually no government programs to systematically supplement retirement incomes for the elderly. What methods
   and institutions do you think society relied upon to deal with the

problem of retirement? Could the same methods and institutions be used today? If not, why?

2. Statistical evidence suggests that female workers are far more sensitive to payroll and income taxes than are male workers. That is, female workers are more likely to be discouraged from working by high marginal tax rates. Can you think of any reasons to explain this phenomenon? What implications do these results have for future production in this country?

3. Calculating the value Social Security has for you yourself is difficult because of two special problems. As an advanced exercise can you outline a method for making such a calculation that deals with each of them?

   a. Taxes are paid and benefits are received in different time periods, yet most people place a higher weight on a dollar today than on the promise to receive a dollar forty years from now.
   b. The benefits you can expect to receive depend upon how long you live. There is some probability that you will die this year and some probability that you will live to be ninety.

Selected references

Campbell, Colin, ed. *Financing Social Security.*Washington, D.C.: American Enterprise Institute, 1978.

Cohen, Wilbur J., and Milton Friedman. "Social Security: Universal or Selective?" Debate. Washington, D.C.: American Enterprise Institute, 1972.

Ferrara, Peter J. *Social Security: The Inherent Contradiction.* San Francisco: CATO Institute, 1980.

Goodman, John C. *Social Security in the United Kingdom: Contracting Out of the System.* Washington, D.C.: American Enterprise Institute, 1981.

National Center for Policy Analysis. *The Effect of Social Security Reforms on Black Americans.* Dallas: NCPA, 1983.

Shore, Warren. *Social Security: The Fraud in Your Future.* Riverside, New Jersey: Macmillan Publishing Company, 1975.

16

Facing the Acid Rain Problem and Other Environmental Trade-offs

Eastern New York State and northern New England are famed for their natural beauty: forests of hardwood and pine, abundant wildlife, clear mountain lakes. But today, these lakes and forests face the insidious threat of rain falling from the sky—some rain as acid as vinegar. Mountain lakes are clear because nothing lives in them—not even frogs or tadpoles.

And not just natural beauty is at stake. Acid rain eats away at buildings and machinery. It combines with other air pollutants to make a mix that irritates lungs and, some believe, causes cancer.

Acid rain is thus high on the list of action topics for American environmentalists. Yet, there is another side to the acid rain story. Acid rain is a byproduct of industrial processes that have many benefits. An important example is the burning of coal. Coal fuels the industrial Midwest. Without it, unemployment in the smokestack industries of that region would be even higher than it is now. If all coal-burning utilities had to clean up, they would have to raise their rates, at especially great cost to low-income consumers. And without coal, we would have to turn to other energy sources. These include imported oil, which makes us dependent on the vagaries of third-world politics, and nuclear power, which environmentalists hate even more than acid rain.

In short, the problem of acid rain illustrates the principle to which this chapter will be devoted: every environmental action involves trade-offs. As the environmental movement grows from infancy to maturity, it must face these trade-offs maturely. If it does not, it will face an overwhelming political backlash.

─────────────────────────────────────── **Some underlying principles**

The economic issues that must be faced by the environmental movement revolve around some of the most basic principles of economics.

The first of those principles is that we live in a world of scarcity. The aspect of global scarcity best recognized by environmentalists is that of natural resources. Mineral deposits are scarce. Agricultural land is scarce. Energy is scarce. Even the limitlessly abundant energy of the sun is scarce in an economic sense, partly because usable collection sites are scarce and partly because the equipment required to trap solar energy is itself constructed from other scarce resources.

A second aspect of scarcity does not always get explicit mention, even though it gets wide implicit recognition. That is the scarcity of *sinks*. Sinks are the opposite of sources: sources are places like mineral deposits and oil wells that we get good things out of; sinks, in the other hand, are places we put bad things into. Air, land, and water can all be used as dumping grounds. To a limited extent—varying widely according to local circumstances—sinks are self-replenishing. For example, a river may have a certain capacity to absorb organic wastes and break them down through biological processes. But when these limits are exceeded sinks can get so loaded with wastes that we don't dare put anything more in them.

The first basic principle of environmental economics, then, is that of scarcity. The second principle, really a corollary of the first, is that all economic decisions involve trade-offs. As a general rule we cannot get more of one thing without giving up something else. It is notoriously hard to find a truly free lunch, and for present purposes it is especially important to recognize that we cannot make major improvements in the quality of our environment without using up something scarce that has other valuable alternative uses.

To illustrate, let's look at one of the most highly publicized trade-offs—the one between energy and the environment. This trade-off seems to press upon us almost every time we turn around these days. Here are just a few of its hundreds of manifestations:

- One of the cheapest ways in the world to get energy is by drilling deep holes in Arabian deserts. But the energy can't be used on location, and oil tankers have an alarming tendency to wind up on the rocks.

- The only place left on the face of the earth where as much as 100 million acres of wilderness could be set aside in a single block is in

Alaska. But if we protect that wilderness we can't get out the oil and gas that may very likely lie beneath.

● We like the air in our cities to be pure and clear, so we want nonpolluting cars. But other things being equal, nonpolluting cars burn more gasoline. Of course, we can have cars that are both clean and efficient if we make them smaller and lighter, but then we are more likely to get killed if we are involved in an automobile accident. We can get around this trade-off by adding safety equipment, but that makes the cars heavier again. So we lower the speed limit, but then it takes more time to get where we are going.

● America's most abundant energy resource (excepting the sun) is coal. But coal also happens to be one of the dirtiest fuels around. We can burn coal without polluting the air if we build giant stack scrubbers or coal gassification plants, but those require vast quantities of scarce capital. And even if we scrub the stack gasses clean, burning coal puts a big strain on the capacity of our planet's atmosphere to act as a sink for carbon dioxide.

The environment and production possibilities

These and other environmental trade-offs can conveniently be illustrated diagrammatically by use of our old friend, the production-possibility frontier. Figure 16–1 shows a production-possibility frontier drawn with the horizontal axis representing *environmental quality* and the vertical axis representing *other goods and services.*

At any given time we can shift scarce resources from one use to another. If we sacrifice environmental quality to get more of other goods, we move up and to the left along the production-possibility frontier, as illustrated by arrow *A*. If we sacrifice other goods to improve the environment, we move down and to the left, following arrow *B*.

If we take a longer-term perspective we are not limited to the production-possibility frontier as it exists at a given moment in time. By creating new capital—new man-made means of production—we can push the production-possibility frontier outward. If we invest the capital in new industrial plants and equipment without attention to environmental safeguards, we may push the frontier outward in the distorted fashion indicated by arrow *C*. If we devote part of our newly formed capital to pollution control safeguards, however, it is possible over time to have more of everything and follow the path of arrow *D*.

Thinking of environmental trade-offs in terms of this production-possibility frontier helps us avoid two fallacies that one sometimes sees in debates over environmental policy. The first fallacy, advanced by some

FIGURE 16–1   Production-Possibility Frontier

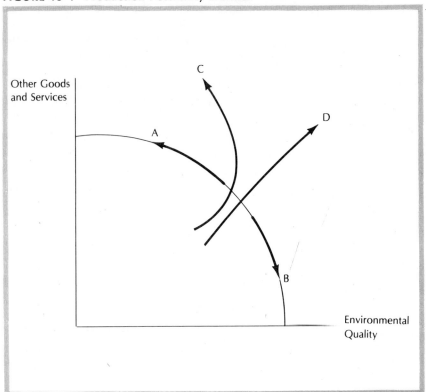

environmentalists, is that we should always choose production and consumption alternatives that maximize environmental quality. But our production-possibility frontier shows us that if we took this prescription literally,
we would have to go to the extreme lower right-hand corner of the
frontier. That would leave us with no other goods and services at all. Few
of us would really want that.

The second fallacy, advanced by some anti-environmentalists, is that
dollars spent on things like pollution control are a deadweight loss to the
economy. This misperception arises largely from the fact that the goods
and services represented by the vertical axis are easy to measure and to
add up as part of the gross national product, while environmental quality is
very hard to assign a number to. Arrow C in that figure, for example,
shows a faster growth of measured gross national product. But if we
choose to follow arrow D instead, we *do* get something in return—namely,
a more pleasant world to live in.

The production-possibility frontier is an aid to clear thinking about
environmental issues in another way as well. Notice that this production-
possibility frontier, like those we have drawn before, is not a straight line: it

is curved. The curvature indicates *that the farther we pursue any given environmental trade-off, the more severe the terms of the trade-off become.* This is a variation of the familiar law of diminishing returns.

As an example of the increasing severity of environmental trade-offs, consider the case of fluorocarbons. Fluorocarbons are common chemicals believed by some scientists to cause harmful pollution of the upper atmosphere's ozone layer. The risk is uncertain, but potentially great. To avoid the risk, environmental regulators banned the use of flourocarbons as propellants in spray cans of deodorants, paints, and other common household products. The switchover to nonfluorocarbon propellants and pump-spray deodorants didn't cost much, either in terms of investment or in terms of consumer inconvenience. But it only got rid of half the fluorocarbons.

Getting rid of the other half, if feasible at all, would involve far more costly trade-offs. The next biggest use of fluorocarbons is in refrigerators and air conditioners. In these uses there just aren't any reasonably priced, reasonably effective substitutes. It would not be impossible to eliminate the use of fluorocarbons as refrigerants—but it would certainly be much more costly than eliminating their use in hair spray. This is the sort of thing that makes our production-possibility frontier curved rather than straight.

So much for general economic principles. Keeping what we have said about scarcity and trade-offs in mind, let's turn to problems of formulating environmental policy.

--- **Environmental policy:**
Standard setting v. incentives

Referring to Figure 16-1 once more, we can characterize the short-run goal of environmental policy as that of moving the economy in the direction of arrow *B* and the long-run goal as that of moving in some such direction as arrow *D.* It is rather widely accepted that we do not want to follow a path such as *A* or *C,* which would result in further deterioration of the environment in exchange for more other goods and services. But this broad agreement on goals still leaves considerable room for controversy.

The controversy centers partly on the issue of how far to go to achieve enhanced environmental quality. This is very much a subjective judgment, one that we will discuss in the evaluation section of this chapter. For the moment, however, let's turn our attention to a somewhat different, but no less controversial, issue—that of the means employed in moving toward whatever environmental goals can be agreed upon.

The debate over the means to be used in implementing environmental policy centers on the issue of standards versus economic incentives. Under the standard-setting approach environmental regulators simply issue directives telling businesses what specific steps that they must take to control pollution. Sometimes the standards impose specific limits on the output of pollutants; sometimes they prescribe specific control technologies; sometimes they do both. In contrast, under the economic incentive approach the regulators initiate a system of rewards and penalties designed to encourage the desired environmental behavior without prescribing specific standards.

Currently, environmental policy in the United States predominantly follows the standard-setting approach. Probably the most familiar example is provided by the exhaust emission standards for automobiles; other examples include effluent standards for municipal sewage facilities, limits on sulphur dioxide emissions by coal and oil-burning electric power plants, and outright bans on certain agricultural chemicals and pesticides. Standards such as these have resulted in substantial, even dramatic, environmental improvements such as the clean-up of Oregon's Willamette River. But there is surprisingly little evidence that average environmental quality has improved on a nationwide basis. Looking toward the future, it may well be that the battles already won have been the easy ones, while the harder battles remain.

Economists are highly critical of standard setting. Among their most common criticisms are (1) that standard setting makes inefficient use of local knowledge and initiative, and (2) that standards tend to treat different cases too uniformly. Let's look at each of these in turn.

The kind of knowledge that standard setting tends to use inefficiently is localized information possessed by people on the spot. Standards have difficulty embodying such information because, by their nature, they are set centrally. The controversial regulations set recently by the Environmental Protection Agency (EPA) dealing with pollution from steel mills is a good example. The EPA initially imposed detailed standards for each part of the steel-making process, from coke ovens through finishing mills. Presumably these standards would have accomplished their objective of cleaning up the steel plants, but they were immediately attacked by people who were actually working in the steel industry. Local engineers and managers charged that there were many less expensive alternative technologies for accomplishing the same goals that the EPA had overlooked.

One approach to alleviating this kind of problem is to frame broader standards, leaving more discretion to local managers as to the means adopted in meeting those standards. Recently, Armco Steel has entered into a novel agreement with the EPA to reduce pollution control costs. Under the agreement, the EPA will police only total emissions from the plant. The choice of control method is to be left to local management.

The second problem with standards lies in the very fact that they do tend to be *standard* in the sense of treating all cases alike. Consider, for example, the case of New York's North River sewage treatment facility. It was originally designed to remove 67 percent of all organic waste from sewage dumped into the Hudson River at a construction cost of $250 million. Before construction was completed Congress passed a new law requiring a 90 percent cleanup standard for such plants; passage of the law pushed the cost up to $1 billion. The problem? Although 90 percent cleanup may be entirely appropriate for some inland rivers, such a strict standard is pointless for the Hudson, which is scoured twice daily by the ocean tides.

In order to get around these and other problems of environmental standard setting, economists widely propose an alternative strategy based on a restructuring of incentives. Instead of telling people what to do and how to do it, this strategy would aim at making it profitable for people to direct their efforts toward reaching the desired environmental goals. There are a number of alternative strategies for restructuring incentives.

One strategy begins with the idea that conflicts over pollution are, at base, conflicts over vaguely defined or ill-enforced property rights. Suppose a factory owner claims the right to use the river as a sink for disposing of wastes, while someone else wants to use it as a fishing ground. The river is public property, and in the past our legal system has not cited very precise rules governing who has access to the property and on what terms. The same kind of property rights conflicts are involved when a driver uses the air above a highway as a sink for exhaust gasses to the detriment of local residents. Today new and more exotic conflicts over environmental property rights are emerging. Should you, for example, be allowed to let the tree in your yard grow so tall that it shades my solar hot-water heater?

When property rights are ill defined or when public property is open to all on a first come, first served basis, the result is likely to be wasteful use of scarce resources and sinks. Each user tends to ignore opportunity costs imposed on others. Economists say that these become *external costs,* or *externalities,* because they are borne by people outside the organization that is making the initial decision. Thus in our earlier examples, the factory polluting the river would be said to impose an external cost on people wanting to fish, and a motorist would be said to impose an external cost on roadside residents.

Clearly defined and enforced property rights, on the other hand, can help create the incentives necessary to *internalize* such externalities. If potential air or water polluters are notified that they can be sued as public nuisances for violating the rights of other air and water users, the previously external costs are applied to decisions inside the firm. The threat of fines or damage judgments provides an incentive to invest in cost-effective clean-up technology.

If property rights are defined clearly, the threat of private lawsuits alone may be enough to provide all the incentives needed. Sometimes, however, the threat of private suits will not be effective. This is especially likely to be the case when there are a great many victims of pollution, no one of which suffers great damage from any single pollution source. To handle cases like these economists have suggested a different strategy for internalizing externalities: a pollution tax.

For example, consider sulphur dioxide pollution from coal-fired power plants, believed to be the major cause of acid rain. Proponents of pollution taxes suggest that the sulphur dioxide output of each pollution source should be monitored and a charge should be imposed—the charge could be so many cents for each pound of sulphur emitted into the air. Ideally the charge would approximate the damage done to the environment per unit of pollution. The owners of the facility would then have an incentive to install cleanup equipment, as long as the marginal cost of pollution abatement was just equal to the marginal benefit of cleaning pollution up.

Still other strategies for providing pollution abatement incentives have been discussed, but we need not look at them in detail here. They all have two features in common that, in the opinion of many economists, make them distinctly superior to the standard-setting strategy widely in use now. First, the incentives are geared to certain *goals* (such as air quality standards), leaving the choice of the most cost-effective *means* of abatement up to the particular polluter. Second, incentives can more easily be fine-tuned to avoid pollution-control overkill—to avoid forcing investment in cleanup equipment beyond the point where a dollar's investment no longer yields a dollar's benefit.

If these incentive-based strategies for pollution control are so popular with economists, though, why is so much actual legislation based on the standard-setting approach? To find out why, we must briefly examine the interaction between economic and political decision making.

━━━━━━━━━━━━━━━━━━━━━━━ **The politics of pollution control**

To the economist, environmental decision making is a matter of making delicate trade-offs and fine distinctions. Congress is also sensitive to delicate trade-offs and fine distinctions—but not in quite the same way. The difference is that rather than perceiving policy issues in terms of economic costs and benefits, Congress tends to perceive them as conflicts between opposing interest groups. The outcome may be laws that strike a delicate political balance but that make only limited economic sense.

The case of acid rain policy, still under intense debate as this is written, is a case in point. Coal-fired electric power plants, many of them in the Ohio Valley, are thought to account for 65 percent of all sulfur dioxide emissions in the United States. It is easy to see that any plan aimed at combating acid rain must somehow reduce emissions from these plants, but how?

Economists think they know at least part of the answer. There may be disagreements over how much total emissions should be reduced, but once this amount is decided, the reduction should be achieved at the least cost. In the case of electric power plants, there are two major ways to reduce emissions. One is to install stack scrubbers that remove sulfur dioxide from the waste gases caused by coal combustion. The other is to burn coal that has a low sulfur content in the first place. Both methods are expensive. A scrubber for a new plant can cost $200 million. Low-sulfur coal can cost $15 more a ton than high-sulfur coal. Economists say that each power plant should be given a pollution abatement target and then be left to choose the cheapest method.[1]

But Congress does not think that way. It does not ask how much one method or the other costs—it asks who bears the cost. The answer is very different for the two methods. Low-sulfur coal, it happens, is mined chiefly in the western states. Burning it would mean more jobs for largely nonunionized miners in the West, and fewer for largely unionized miners of high-sulfur coal in the East. Of course, eastern and midwestern legislators don't like this solution. They do like stack scrubbers, though. These would preserve mining jobs for their region and would create additional jobs to install them.

Never mind that a bill mandating scrubbers for all utilities would cost $1.6 billion per year more than the least cost approach. Never mind that this comes to $800,000 per eastern mining job saved. As this is written, the leading contender for a cure to acid rain is a bill mandating scrubbers for the fifty dirtiest power plants in the United States.

The attitude of environmental interest groups themselves does not make it any easier for Congress to strike economically intelligent trade-offs. The problem is that such groups often tend to present issues in all-or-nothing terms that deny that any trade-offs exist. The Endangered Species Act is an example. After the Supreme Court ruled that the multi-million dollar Tellico Dam in Tennessee would have to stand unused because it threatened the habitat of the three-inch snail darter, there were motions to amend the act. The most obvious suggestion was to draw a distinction between relatively important and relatively unimportant species, but environmentalists were not willing to play this game. Instead they moralized that all species great and small were equally sacred. Behind the moralizing and posturing is sometimes a hard-headed evaluation of the nuisance value of such legislation as the Endangered Species Act. The procedural delays that can be generated by environmental lawyers are often enough by themselves to intimidate the opposition.

An evaluation

How does our environmental policy look from the point of view of our standards of efficiency, equality, and liberty? In making such an evaluation we must keep two separate questions in mind. First, we need to ask whether it is good to have an environmental policy as opposed to a hands-

---

1. See Paul R. Portney, "High Price Cure for Acid Rain," *Washington Post,* 12 August 1983.

off policy. Second, we have to ask the rather different question of whether our current environmental policy is the best of all possible policies for pursuing the same objective. With these two questions in mind, let's go through our standards one by one.

As usual, we start with efficiency. Efficiency demands some sort of environmental action on the part of government, especially, at least, action to define and enforce property rights. To allow producers and consumers free access to sources and sinks without requiring any payment is an invitation to use those sources and sinks wastefully. A do-nothing policy in the environmental area is thus an inefficient policy.

Although our present environmental policies may very well be better than nothing, they are still open to severe criticism on grounds of efficiency. These criticisms are of two kinds. First, by focusing on standard setting rather than on incentives, current policies fail to encourage the people and firms they are aimed at to find the *least costly* means of achieving any given objective. Second, in at least some areas—with the endangered species policy a likely example—the trade-off between environmental quality and "other goods" has been pushed too far. Huge economic sacrifices are being made to achieve very trivial environmental gains—and sometimes no real gains will be made at all.

Overall we would be inclined to give our current environmental policy a C+ at best for efficiency, with a lot of room for improvement.

Considering the standard of liberty next, we get a similar set of answers to our questions: some environmental policy is justified, but current policies may not be the best available.

Proponents of individual liberty do not pretend that people should have unlimited freedom to pollute. They argue instead that people have a right to defend their person and property from pollution by others. What pollution really amounts to, they say, is a theft of waste disposal services. Looked at from this point of view, pollution control laws are a legitimate extension of the government's police powers.

However, these people would caution, a fine line must be drawn between using that police power to prevent one person from interfering with another's rights and using that power to interfere with a person's right to use his or her own property. Many people argue that certain zoning and land-use laws inspired by environmental concerns have, at least in some areas, over-stepped that line. And proponents of liberty would join forces with advocates of efficiency in opposition to environmental standards that not only specify the goals to be reached but that set rigid rules for how to reach those goals.

We have left the standard of equality until last because it is the standard according to which it is most difficult to defend current environmental policy—or much of any environmental policy at all. No matter how hard one tries, it is difficult to clear the environmental movement entirely of a certain degree of elitism. Take that 100-million-acre wilderness preserve in Alaska. How many poor people are ever going to get up there for a glorious week of backpacking? And if exploiting the energy reserves of that wilderness area knocked a few cents off our utility bills, who would find that relief most welcome?

The basic problem, it appears, is that when we choose to move down the production-possibility frontier away from the *other goods* and toward *environmental quality*, we all have to move together, rich and poor alike. But the rich and the poor may have radically different attitudes about how many other goods are worth sacrificing to reach any given environmental goal.

A few years ago, the NAACP put out a report on the Carter administration's energy plan that addressed this issue in no uncertain terms. "While we endorse the plan's objective of eliminating energy waste and improving utilization efficiency," the report says, "we cannot accept the notion that our people are best served by a policy based on the inevitability of energy shortage." NAACP head Mrs. Margaret Bush Wilson used even blunter language in an interview with a *Detroit News* reporter. "A limited-growth policy," she said, "tends to freeze people to whatever rung of the ladder they happen to be on. That's OK if you're a highly educated 28-year-old making $50,000 a year as a presidential adviser. It's utter disaster if you're unskilled, out of work, and living in a ghetto."

Although these comments were addressed specifically at energy policy, they could have applied equally well to land-use policy, pollution policy, or any other aspect of environmental regulation.

Questions for thought and discussion

1. A number of states now have a law that prohibits smoking in public eating places. The purpose of the law is to prevent smokers from polluting the air breathed by nonsmokers. Do you think these laws are consistent with the standard of efficiency? (Hint: Are there any externalities here? What are they?)

2. Some people have argued that environmental policy should be set entirely at the local level, not at the federal level. After all, why should the residents of San Francisco or Chicago have a voice in the pollution control policies ruling Houston or Atlanta? Do you agree? Be specific about the circumstances under which environmental policy is properly a national concern and about the evaluation criterion you are using.

3. Economist Robert Mundell once argued that, in a certain way, pollution may actually benefit the poor. Mundell observed that as the central cities became more polluted, middle- and upper-income families fled for the less polluted suburbs. As a result, housing prices in the city fell dramatically, making better housing more accessible to low-income groups. This was a bonanza for poor families, who cared a lot more

about a place to live than the quality of the air they breathed. Do you agree with Mundell that pollution actually benefits the poor? If so, is a "hands-off" policy toward pollution a good way to help the poor?

Selected references

The Clean Air Act: Proposals for Revisions. Washington, D.C.: American Enterprise Institute, 1981.

Dolan, Edwin G. *TANSTAAFL, The Economic Strategy for Environmental Crisis.* New York: Holt, Rinehart and Winston, 1971.

Mills, Edwin S. *The Economics of Environmental Quality.* New York: W. W. Norton & Company, 1978.

†